New Movements in the Study
and Teaching of History

New Movements
in the Study and Teaching
of History

Edited by MARTIN BALLARD

INDIANA UNIVERSITY PRESS
BLOOMINGTON & LONDON

Second printing 1971
Published 1970 by Indiana University Press

Copyright © 1970 Martin Ballard, Peter Bamford,
C. C. Bayne-Jardine, Marcus Cunliffe, C. D. Darlington,
Robert Douch, G. R. Elton, Sheila Ferguson, R. N. Hallam,
Charles L. Hannam, Derek Heater, Dwight W. Hoover,
William M. Lamont, W. H. McNeill, Peter Mathias,
Arnold Toynbee, D. C. Watt, E. A. Wrigley

Library of Congress catalog card number: 77-126205
ISBN: 253-34020-9

Printed in Great Britain

Contents

Introduction

MARTIN BALLARD

Change and the Curriculum

An educated man must have a certain minimum of general knowledge. Even if he knows very little about science and cannot add or subtract, he must have heard of Mendel and Kepler. Even if he is tone deaf he must know something about Debussy and Verdi; even if he is a pure sociologist he must be aware of Circe and the Minotaur, of Kant and Montaigne, of Titus Oates and Tiberius Gracchus.[1]

The history teacher will start reading this statement of Robert Conquest's in 'Black Paper One' with considerable enthusiasm. A knowledge of Mendel and Kepler, Debussy and Verdi seems without doubt a part of the equipment of civilised man. Enthusiasm may wane with the mythological creatures and philosophers. The two historical characters which conclude the list will, however, almost certainly make him gasp with incredulity. Mr Conquest laments that he has come on occasions when such names have been unknown even to graduates in present-day universities.

Apart from the obvious alliterative and rhythmic qualities of their names, it is hard to understand why Titus Oates and Tiberius Gracchus should have been dredged from the mass of historical characters to provide the touchstone of an educated man. Seventeenth-century Britain and Republican Rome have indeed taken a prominent place in traditional school syllabuses which were drawn up when the Whig tradition held sway. By any objective assessment, however, the claims of neither Titus Oates nor Tiberius Gracchus to immortality could seriously be put forward against those of, say, Pobedonostsev or Ito Hirobumi. Yet professors of history would be permitted to profess ignorance of the Russian and Japanese statesmen without a blush of shame.

The history teacher asks today whether there are indeed any characters or events from the past of which his pupils cannot afford to be ignorant. If Titus Oates and Tiberius Gracchus cannot be included in this category, what about William the Conqueror and Harold Godwinson? It would not be unreasonable to guess that ten times as many pupil hours in British schools are spent on the events of 1066 than on the events of 1917 in Russia. Yet the Norman Conquest is at most a fascinating part of one nation's story, while the Russian Revolution is woven into the fabric of modern life.

In previous generations there has always been a 'received' body of historical knowledge to be passed on to the next generation. This is no longer true. Robert Conquest is surely wrong when he argues that the men who featured in his history course have an unquestioned right to continued recognition. History teachers are, or should be, involved in a peculiarly acute process of self-examination. Their subject covers the whole past experience of man. They have therefore to decide which parts of that experience are relevant and interesting to their pupils.

This book does not argue any particular case. Articles are offered on particular aspects of the subject – both in academic context and teaching method – which might be borne in mind by a teacher who is reassessing his course of work. The contributors have no common point of view; indeed a few clear differences of opinion emerge. All, however, start from the assumption that history teachers must face up to change. Lines of experiment are suggested, but they are presented undogmatically. In a time of rapid change it is unwise to advocate any teaching scheme or method as a new orthodoxy.

Several contributors point out that traditional methods and syllabuses continue to be used in many schools. Leading educational publishers will testify to the fact that they still do brisk business with textbooks set out on orthodox lines.

The idea that school history is properly national history runs very deep. Plutarch recorded how Cato the Elder wrote a *History of Rome* 'with his own hand and in large characters, that his son might have in his own home an aid to acquaintance with his country's ancient traditions'. History has been used as a subject by which children are indoctrinated in patriotic and military virtues. British children have learned of the victories of Agincourt and Crécy, but were never told that the English kings were brutal aggressors in the Hundred Years War or even that the French finally won. French children, for their part, were encouraged to revel in the *gloire* of Napoleon's victories during the long years of national humiliation.

Why do we teach history? One writer presents an answer:

Our motive is the need for security, for we know – as our fathers knew when they educated us – that unless our children grow up understanding and believing in their own country, then the future is very dark indeed.

In Europe or America such justification appears highly dubious, but coming as it does in a *Handbook for History Teachers in West Africa*,[2] the old argument acquires a new significance. New countries, created in the first place by western statesmen equipped with a map and a ruler, need a sense of identity. History teachers in many African and Asian countries see their task in this conventional light, and concentrate their energies on producing a national history, such as is now being abandoned in many western schools.

Teachers in Communist countries are likewise – officially at least – free from self-doubt. History remains an indoctrination subject.

> The Soviet school differs radically from the bourgeois. Soviet history teachers have mastered dialectic and historical materialism. As we know, the historical development of mankind proceeds according to the rules of materialistic dialectics; as the result of this, historical teachers in Soviet secondary schools are able to demonstrate to their students dialectics in action over a thousand years.[3]

The non-Communist teacher may envy such certainty. Given a clearly defined theme, be it 'the triumphs of England' or 'the victory of the workers', it is comparatively easy to construct a syllabus. But, as historians become increasingly aware of the complexity of society and human motivation, it becomes increasingly difficult for them to build up a meaningful outline of the past of the human race, which can be put before children.

In the first place it yearly becomes more clear that history teaching must break out of the narrow nationalistic strait-jacket in which it has lived for so long. In a century of world-wide communications – and indeed of world-wide warfare – it has become inexcusable that teachers should continue to work from syllabuses which were designed to prepare pupils for life in a narrower environment. The following articles present the case why history teachers should be prepared to abandon the shallows where they have lived for so long and 'launch out into the deep'.

History teachers are asked to present justification why their subject should remain on the time-table of a modern school. Too often they are unable to construct any answer because the material they put across day after day is palpably useless. The justification for history teaching does not lie in the acquisition of specified portions of the sum total of fact. In mathematics or physics a pupil must master one skill before he can progress to another. Historical judgements are not built up in this way. There is no single event or historical character which rates as a *sine qua non* in a history syllabus. Some may be more desirable than others, but none are essential. The justification of the study of history at the school level, as Professor Elton powerfully argues, lies in the acquisition of breadth.

Pyschologists have studied how a child develops from knowing only 'I', to gaining a knowledge, first of his mother, then of the other characters in the world around him. Life begins as a non-dimensional point of awareness; learning is a continual process whereby the dimensions of experience are extended further and further outwards. The dilemma of the history teacher is that he realises that his task is to help in this process, yet he is unable to rid himself of the idea that he has a responsibility to be methodical and 'cover the ground'. Thus, for instance, social and economic history has been introduced as a relevant and interesting field of study; but for too many pupils this has meant in practice that, instead of learning the details of the achievements of Gladstone's Second Ministry, they sit cross-eyed with boredom, trying to memorise the levels of duty in his free trade budgets. Teachers blame examiners; the high-density compression of fact is essential, they say, from the very structure of examiners' marking schedules. Examiners blame teachers; questions which break with tradition are greeted with howls of complaint. In his article Dr Lamont suggests that the whole structure of the examination system is at fault.

The arguments in favour of world history, both ancient and modern, seem unanswerable, but it is all too easy to see how these fields of study could be reduced to the worn-out formula. To replace the British ruling houses with the Chinese dynasties is merely to juggle with the counters of learning. At the end of the day the characters of the past will still reproach us, 'if you prick us, do we not bleed; if you tickle us, do we not laugh?'

Professor Toynbee shows how the immense accumulation of historical fact can lead to a mental constipation which paralyses action. The teacher is as vulnerable as the scholar. The traditional school syllabus is already too compressed; if more is to be added, at least as much must be taken out. Faced with the problem of selection, the teacher must decide how far he is going to retain chronology. The past has been likened to a woven garment; it has both a warp and a weft, and the teacher ideally would like his pupils to see relationships both in space and time. At any particular point in his syllabus, however, he will have to concentrate on one or the other.

Mr Hallam's article presents evidence that a secondary school child can begin to grasp the idea of historical time. The great virtue of the 'kings and queens of England' approach was that it provided a child with a skeleton of historical time, readily recognisable in terms of family relationships. Few history teachers today would justify the effort spent in building up such a structure, but something else should be put in its place. A time chart on the wall of a classroom can be very useful – but many teachers are not fortunate enough to teach every lesson in the same room.

Totally filleted of chronology, history becomes an amusing, but rather pointless occupation. A project on 'Hats through the ages' may look pretty on a classroom wall, but loses its point if the words 'through the ages' are meaningless. This does not mean to say that theme teaching is undesirable in itself. Yet to divide history up entirely into themes is surely dangerous. Scholars are stressing that the barriers between 'social', 'political', 'economic' and other branches of the subject are largely unreal. This is no less true at school level. Fascinating relationships exist, which can only be seen by looking at events happening at a particular historical moment.

If the full scope of chronology is preserved on a world-wide canvas, the problem of compression becomes virtually insurmountable. Peter Carpenter has argued cogently that this problem could be overcome by studying the past in narrow bands, or eras.[4] An archaeologist begins to investigate a site by cutting trenches across it and examining the evidence thrown up in detail. By studying the past in eras it is possible to hold together the local, the national and the international scene; to study the past in breadth, and yet at the same time introduce children to the minutiae of history through the use of source material. It is possible for individuals to emerge from the past as living beings. The use of biography in history teaching has long been recognised, yet this too can become sterile unless the character is placed against the setting of his times. Most teachers at some time or another have cringed before an account of the life of some reformer, which goes into long detail on his home background and schooling, but totally fails to mention the activity which made his life memorable.

Every head of department will wish to construct his own syllabus in collaboration with his colleagues. There are few guide lines which can be laid down with any certainty, though he should be able to find help from textbooks published in the field.[5]

In so far as our pupils have studied non-European civilisations in the past, they have generally looked at them 'down the end of a European drain-pipe, or from the quarter-deck of a British man-of-war'. Indian history, for instance, has been seen through the British conquest. This has meant in practice that non-European civilisations have been studied at the point of decay, rather than at the point of strength. Professor McNeill discusses whether there is as yet any way of seeing the different civilisations as a unity. For the time being, it appears, the scholarly synthesis has not emerged. Until it does, it might be better to tackle the great non-European civilisations on their own, rather than trying to integrate them into a cohesive course.

It is surely justifiable to limit the field of study by examining eastern cultures at a particular point in time, rather than trying to plot all the changes which took place within these civilisations before they came under European influences. The distinctive feature of western civilisation is its immense potential for change. A European building or work of art can be dated reasonably accurately to within a comparatively short period. Persian musicians, on the other hand, still play works which could have been composed at any time in the past thousand years. The changelessness of eastern civilisations can be exaggerated, but children could surely get a deeper insight from a study of, say, Sung China in the early thirteenth century and Akbar's India, than from any attempt to range across the whole span of time.

Some of the contributors to this book stress the repetitive and boring nature of much history teaching, but the picture must not be painted in altogether gloomy colours. The educational revolution in primary schools is making an impact on the lower forms of secondary schools. Although many children may place history low in their order of preferences, there are many more, of all ability ranges, who have felt the fascination of the past. They have been placed within an experience, far different from that of their own environment, and are the richer for it. Although O level seems almost past hope, the

CSE offers an examination structure which can be adapted by an enterprising teacher. It is true that many official syllabuses offer only 'the mixture as before', but by using the opportunities offered by Mode Three examinations, teachers can now work out their own courses and set their own examination papers. While this is rightly subject to supervision by the boards, the potential for change is at last built into the examination system. Comparatively few teachers have as yet, however, made use of these opportunities.

History teachers are being faced with many problems besides that of restructuring the syllabus. Many find themselves working in the strange environment of an unstreamed class. The arguments for and against streaming lie outside the scope of this book. There are not, however, the same difficulties inbuilt into teaching history in mixed ability groups that there are, for instance, with modern languages. Judging by the textbooks produced for the different ends of the ability spectrum, grammar school work in the past has been too compressed and factual, while much secondary modern teaching has lacked serious content. A teacher in a mixed ability class will often find that the levels of conceptualisation of historical ideas among his pupils are not as different as paper performance seems to suggest.

The project and work sheet, as considered by Mrs Ferguson and Mr Bayne-Jardine, come into their own in a mixed ability situation. Group activities can be developed[6] in which children work at their own speed and their own level. But classroom teaching is by no means ruled out. The capacities of 'less able' children have long been underestimated. When properly stimulated by interesting material they can ask equally penetrating questions and use their imagination as vividly as some of their more academic classmates.

In recent years history teachers have also been having to look at their discipline, not as an isolated entity, but in relationship to the other subjects in the curriculum. This, again, is a natural development from the integrated school day in the primary school. Inspectors, anxious that children should not pass suddenly at the age of eleven from the security of a single class-teacher to an unlimited number of subject-teachers, are looking with favour on experiments to integrate syllabuses in the humanities.

Arguments between 'progressives' and 'traditionalists' are too often carried on in general rather than specific terms. In speech-day addresses some head teachers paint glowing pictures of curriculum reform, as if education had at last come out into the promised land.

Integrated studies become the new shibboleth, and those who express doubt are branded as reactionary.

There is everything to be said for breaking down the barriers between one subject and another, as there is for breaking down the divisions within the historical discipline. Perhaps the most important single line of research today lies in the consideration of population trends. In this field the skills of the historian are complementary to those of the economist, the geographer, the sociologist and the natural scientist. At the school level, the humanities project prepared by the Schools Council offers a fascinating avenue for development.

Yet the history teacher may be rightly suspicious of some of the schemes for integration which are being recommended to him. There are great advantages, for instance, in keeping history and geography closely linked in the early years of a secondary school, but serious problems must be faced if the two are to be linked in an integrated syllabus.[7] Clearly the geographer and the historian will both look for those parts of their own subject which can be married with the other. It is tempting to construct a syllabus which moves easily from the present to the past. Thus an examination of the industries and agriculture of modern Peru might be preceded by a study of Inca civilisation. In practice this has little to recommend it. Comparisons between civilisations so remote from one another have little meaning and the perspective is highly confusing to a child who is only beginning to recognise historical time. A historical study of Inca civilisation would, on the other hand, be greatly helped by an examination of the physical characteristics of South America. But many geographers consider that such physical geography should not normally be taught to children below the age of fourteen. When preparing such amalgamated syllabuses, the history teacher is under strong pressure to emphasise some aspects of his subject, such as voyages of discovery, at the expense of others like the invention of printing or constitutional development. As soon as the link becomes all-important both teachers lose their freedom of choice.

The strait-jacket laid upon schools by public examinations ensures that experiment takes place either in junior or in non-academic forms. But it is possible to see greater potential for collaboration between history and geography at an advanced than at an elementary level. It would be very valuable to set a sixth-form group to investigate the uses and influence of the Rhine waterway at different stages of man's development. Chronological assumptions would have some meaning, historical study of the Rhine's importance as a boundary and a line of communication could be readily linked with an examination of the physical and human geography of Europe's most important river. If the pupils really burrowed deeply into such a subject they would find themselves asking questions of the natural scientist about man as an animal – questions which the school biologist might be ill-equipped to answer; they would want to discover more about economics and social science, and would ask penetrating questions about pollution, and even the survival of the human race on this planet.

It is greatly to be hoped that subject specialists will cease to play tom tiddler's ground with their own territory. Team teaching opens out great opportunites for pooling specialist knowledge.[8] Instruction should most certainly be coordinated so that, for instance, classes going on visits into the countryside are able to make the fullest possible use of their time. But at the same time, subject specialists must surely also have the responsibility of seeing that their own disciplines do not become distorted. It is tempting to think that, because they are in process of discarding one intellectual structure for the subject, there is no need to look for another.

While in many countries the direction of the syllabus is under central control, either of the state or of representative teachers, in Britain the onus for change lies squarely on the classroom teacher. As has already been stressed, the following articles offer no blueprint for the future. They rather present some of the evidence which should inform any new thinking. In a number of chapters, academic specialists analyse the movements of thought within their own discipline.

The teacher is challenged to re-examine the scale of his syllabus. Traditional teaching has presented the subject as a national narrative, which stops well short of the present day. Professor McNeill offers a world-wide canvas. Mr Douch presents the claim of local history, studied in its own right. Dr Watt shows that contemporary history can be presented on a firm intellectual basis. Professor Cunliffe considers the particular claims of American history. Mr Hannam points out that traditional syllabuses have been underpinned by assumptions about race and social class, while Professor Hoover tells how a new history is being written about the black section of the American community, which has hitherto been neglected. He points out that this exercise can be linked with the attempt to construct the history of all under-privileged races and classes within society. Professor Mathias and Dr Wrigley show how academic historians are using statistical and analytical techniques to reconstruct the past with a greater measure of accuracy. Dr Wrigley demonstrates that there is no reason why such detailed studies as that being conducted on population trends should prevent historians from seeing the wider picture for which Professor Toynbee pleads.

Articles are also offered which consider history, not as an entity in itself, but in connection with other subjects of the curriculum. A considerable amount of work has been done on the relationship between history and the social sciences, so that Mr Heater is able to present suggestions which could be put into effect in a classroom. The relationship with biology, considered by Professor Darlington, may appear further from the situation in which most teachers find themselves. Yet the new insights of scientists like Lorenz, Morris and Professor Darlington himself, who are considering man as an animal, must have ultimate repercussions in history teaching.

Another group of articles consider the subject through the eyes of the teacher rather than the academic historian. Mr Hallam presents invaluable evidence from the research done in child study which will help teachers recognise what work is feasible at different stages. It is clearly useless to construct a syllabus which is admirable in theory, but bears no relationship to a child's level of perception.

Differences of opinion do emerge but they are not, perhaps, as clear-cut as might at first appear. While Professor Elton disapproves of teachers trying to turn children into research historians, he would probably not object to Mr Bamford's suggestion that they might be taken into a churchyard to study the inscriptions on the tombs. The claims of different branches of the subject do not necessarily conflict with each other.

The history, no less than the geography, teacher must become accustomed to handling wide varieties of scale. An Outward Bound instructor who takes a party of youngsters to the Lake District does not feel that he has failed to accomplish his purpose if his charges return home without having plotted the position of every mountain and hill in the area. He selects just a few peaks which are geared to the strength and skill of his party. His concern is to ensure that every youngster experiences the physical demands of climbing and is able to look out over the wider landscape from those few well-chosen peaks. The history teacher, faced with importunate demands from advocates of different aspects of his subject, could do worse than follow his example.

Notes

1 C. B. Cox and A. E. Dyson, 'Fight for Education, A Black Paper', *Critical Quarterly*, 1969.

2 R. E. Crookall, *Handbook for History Teachers in West Africa*, Evans, 1960.

3 M. A. Zinoviev, *Soviet Methods of Teaching History*, American Council of Learned Societies, 1952.

4 Peter Carpenter, *History Teaching: The Era Approach*, CUP, 1964.

5 Geoffrey Williams, *A Portrait of World History*, Edward Arnold, 1961–6; Phoebe Bankart, *World History in Parallel*, Philip, 1967; N. Heard and G. K. Tull, *World History in Colour*, Blandford, 1969; Martin Ballard, *Era Histories*, Methuen, 1970–.

6 As well as Mrs Ferguson's article see: Sheila Ferguson, *Projects in History in the Secondary School*, Batsford, 1967; Barrington Kaye and I. Rogers, *Group Work in Secondary Schools*, OUP, 1968.

7 Some excellent books are being produced to help teachers who are developing interdisciplinary courses in environmental studies. The problem of creating any wider integrated syllabus for the lower forms in secondary schools, however, is illustrated by the fact that, though many have tried, no one has as yet produced any cohesive course for publication. The first volumes of a new series have appeared. (Ed. Roy Pitcher, *1 The Developing World*, Longmans, 1969.) This does not attempt to 'integrate', but merely to 'coordinate' the history, geography, science and religious instruction courses. On present evidence this coordination is decidedly superficial, and the contents of the first history volume are not likely to dispel the fears of those who think that the baby is being jettisoned with the bath water.

8 D. W. Beggs, *Team Teaching: Bold New Venture*, Indiana UP, 1965; M. Blair and R. G. Woodward, *Team Teaching in Action*, Houghton Mifflin, 1966; John Freeman, *Team Teaching in Britain*, Ward, Lock, 1969; P. Worrall, R. Mitson, E. B. Dorrance, R. J. Williams and J. W. N. Frame, *Teaching From Strength*, Hamish Hamilton, 1970.

1 Widening Horizons

WILLIAM McNEILL

World History in the Schools

All, or almost all, human societies have myths to explain how the world came to be. Three – the Jews, the Chinese and the Greeks – went on to develop a running account of events, thus generating a habit of mind and a genre of literature we recognise as historical. The historical vision of each of these peoples was 'universal' in the sense that everything important, known to them, had to find a place in their historians' account. Thus the historical and prophetic books of the Old Testament explain God's purposes for men, which are, by definition, universal. Herodotus surveyed the entire circuit of the world as known to him to provide a setting for his account of the Great Persian Wars. And Ssu-ma Ch'ien, the formulator of the Chinese scholarly historical tradition, improved upon Herodotus' practice with a far more systematic survey of all that lay within his purview.

The thrust for universality lies very deep in all of us. Simple patterns, easily grasped, are a felt need in every subject of study. Detail may be infinite, elaboration vast: but what men seek is a simple principle that will allow them to fit any and all new data into a pre-existing scheme of classification, smoothly and without undue effort. From this point of view, Ssu-ma Ch'ien was supremely successful. His dynastic structure for history endures to this day, even among western scholars who deal with the Chinese past; and until 1905 Chinese schoolboys were taught history in the mode, and even from the book, Ssu-ma Ch'ien wrote in the second century BC.

No such lasting success attended the Jewish and Greek formulations of universal history. Application of prophecy to current and future events was disputed among the Jews; and these disputes were further complicated by the rise first of Christianity and then of Islam. Among the Greeks, new philosophical ideas about politics and human motivation provoked Thucydides and Polybius to recast Herodotus' heroic and episodic view of the historical process. And Christianity, of course, as it spread through the Roman world, brought the Judaic-prophetic vision of man's past into direct confrontation with philosophical-cyclical views as developed by such a figure as Polybius. Eusebius, St Augustine and Orosius did something to reconcile the two traditions, or rather to combine them by more or less systematic juxtaposition. But these efforts lacked intellectual rigour. Mundane history was not central to Christian theology. It therefore seemed enough to cull episodes (especially disasters) from pagan records and fit these into the providential frame of prophetic revelation.

Islamic history inherited the same Greek-Jewish incompatibilities, and enfolded also Arabic genealogical and Persian national traditions. From such a complicated matrix it required the genius of Abd-al Rahman Ibn Khaldun to construct anything like an intellectually coherent and rigorous pattern of world history. But by the fourteenth century, when he wrote, the Moslem world was already being eclipsed, intellectually and in other respects, by the sudden upthrust of western Europe.

Throughout the middle ages, Christian Europe paid little attention to history. Theological and philosophical questions came first. The Bible, as interpreted by St Augustine and other fathers of the Church, provided an adequate frame for the monkish chroniclers and annalists, who kept Europe's historiographical tradition alive in an age when clerics had a near-monopoly of literacy. History *per se* had no place in medieval schools. Subjects were strictly practical: reading, writing (of Latin) and arithmetic, followed by professional training in theology, law or medicine.

With the Italian renaissance and the rise of humanism, a new strand was added to European learning and education. Admiration for pagan authors concentrated particularly on their language and style, only secondarily upon their ideas. Yet the two were inseparable, so that the study of Livy, Tacitus, Herodotus and Thucydides soon revivified classical ideas of historical process among the small class of educated men who attended the new humanistic schools that spread throughout western Europe in the sixteenth century. The 'classical' curriculum, concentrating on Latin and Greek language and literature, was impractical in the sense that no definite professional niche awaited the schoolboys who graduated with a successful command of those ancient languages. A classical education therefore became a hallmark of the leisured classes, and lasted as such until the twentieth century.

History had a very limited role in the classical curriculum of western Europe's secondary schools. Patches of Greek and Roman history served as background for Cicero's and Demosthenes' speeches, and Polybius' notions of how a balanced constitution could delay the cycle of political decay seeped into eager minds along with the fine points of Greek grammar. Such ideas had little in common with Christian teachings about divine providence and God's plan for mankind; yet most of those who studied the classics in school paid little attention to such discrepancies. A few rigorous or reflective minds did struggle with the problem of how to steer a path between the pagan and the Christian vision of historical process, from the age of Gemistus Pletho and Leonardo Bruni in the fifteenth century, of Niccolò Macchiavelli and Jean Bodin in the sixteenth, through Paolo Sarpi and Bishop Bossuet of the seventeenth to the pleiad of eighteenth-century historians – Voltaire, Edward Gibbon, Johann Gottfried von Herder and others. But such efforts at synthesis and interpretation remained outside the framework of the schools, where the curriculum continued to concentrate upon classical language and literature, with some attention to Christian doctrine, along with mathematics and the new-sprung mathematical sciences.

In the nineteenth century, however, history did begin to shoehorn its way into formal curricula. Classical history became more coherent; but the great innovation was national history, pursued back to the mists of early medieval times and forward, at least in principle, to the glorious achievements of the present day. Sustaining and pervading history so conceived was the notion of progress, though the exact definition and ultimate goal of progress remained, characteristically, vague. Commonly, increase of knowledge and the growth of liberty, of individuality, and of self-consciousness were emphasised more than increases in wealth and technology which were, more or less, taken for granted.

The ease and rapidity with which European empires spread across the world seemed only to confirm the validity of this viewpoint. Europe, it seemed, was the seat of progress; the rest of mankind had been left behind, but through the efforts of missionaries, merchants, administrators and soldiers would soon be privileged to share in the benefits of modern, progressive civilisation. Superstition and ignorance might be formidable obstacles still; but in time even these would be overcome and progress become world-wide.

In the meanwhile, it seemed adequate to concentrate attention upon the favoured segment of mankind among whom progress had flourished so fortunately. Asia had its place in the earliest stages: Egypt, Mesopotamia and Israel. But with the ancient Greeks, history, conceived as the record of progress, came firmly to rest on European soil, passing the torch, with due deliberation, first to Rome, then to the Latin branch of the Christian Church, then to the nations of Europe – Italy and Spain to begin with, France and England next, with Germany (at least in German eyes) the obvious heir apparent.

This vision of mankind's past found its magistral exponent in the person of Lord Acton, whose plan for the *Cambridge Modern History*, prepared in 1898, supplied a synoptic, liberal vision – previously lacking – for the modern phase of this scheme. The ancient Oriental segment developed around Biblical studies; the classical segment around humanistic studies; the medieval segment was shaped both by national historical researches (with sharply divergent emphases as between French, German and English researchers) and by Protestant-Catholic polemics, put to the test of history. The whole remained therefore a patchwork, held together by the simple, clear perception of a linear pattern of 'progress'.

Such a picture of the past flattered western European self-esteem in general and the pride of English-speaking peoples in particular. The leading position of Great Britain and then of the United States in world affairs convinced the pre-World-War-I generation of Englishmen that all history converged and climaxed in the achievement of liberty under law – with all the beneficent consequences that flowed from this central, constitutional fact among the English-speaking peoples.

So far as I know, however, British schools as well as those of European nations on the Continent, seldom strayed far beyond a national framework for the study of modern history. The events and achievements of other European nations, like the experiences of the various non-European peoples, tended to be viewed as background for the deeds of one or another national protagonist, whether French, German, British or some other. (What did the schools of lesser nations do? Danes? Swedes? Italians? I simply do not know.)

In the United States, however, the relative brevity of the national past, and substantial isolation from the storms of nineteenth-century European history, made this kind of approach to modern history unworkable. Moreover, the ocean space between America and Europe changed perspective. American historians usually found it self-evident that Europe, over and above its national segmentation, was a whole. They even overlooked the Channel and often viewed Great Britain as part and parcel of Europe. A copious stream of European history textbooks, aimed at every grade level, from primary school to college, resulted. Until about 1930, these usually treated ancient, medieval and modern history separately, concentrated on wars, diplomacy and constitutional changes, and paid practically no attention to the non-western world.

Then in the late 1920s a new, broadened vision found its way into American schools and colleges. An entity called 'western civilisation' became the object of historical study. This kneaded ancient, medieval and modern segments of the European past into a single whole. More than that, it added social and economic as well as cultural and intellectual dimensions to the bare bones of diplomatic-military and constitutional history, details of which, from a trans-Atlantic viewpoint, seemed trifling by comparison with the more enduring cultural achievements of the European past.

Meanwhile in Europe, the shock of World War I had called earlier generations' faith in progress intensely into question. Especially from the point of view of the educated upper classes, it often seemed that instead of the progress of civilisation, its decline was taking place around them – what with the 'revolt of the masses' at home and the natives' growing restlessness in empires overseas. Classical political wisdom predicted such reversals, and it is scarcely surprising, therefore, that Oswald Spengler in Germany and Arnold Toynbee in England both resorted to a fundamentally classical, pagan, cyclical patterning of history in their famous books. They also paid the non-western world the compliment of treating other civilisations as equals – in principle at least – with the civilisation of the West. All alike were liable to rise and fall. From such a viewpoint, the liberal confidence in progress that had prevailed so generally before World War I was only a passing phase, an error of judgement and perspective. But such ideas, however appealing to public moods of the years 1920–50, did not insinuate themselves into school curricula, save in rare and exceptional cases.

This kind of inertia survived World War II. But the adequacy and intellectual soundness of all older patterns of school-taught history have been called into question since 1945 (if not since 1918) by the growing complexities of international politics which can no longer be handled by a handful of European colonial offices and the occasional despatch of a punitive expedition against rebellious tribesmen.

Newly independent states in Africa and parts of Asia set busily to work to construct their own new national histories for use in schools. Only so could older tribal, regional and other local ties be submerged into new political loyalties. In western Europe, on the contrary, the practical adequacy of a national frame for action had been deeply eroded, and the intellectual adequacy of nationalistic history seemed plainly to be contradicted by events. The idea of progress, discredited since 1914, was not revived by the technological marvels that continued to pour forth from research laboratories. Political anguish was too widespread, social strains too acute for such an optimistic vision of mankind's career on earth to have much appeal.

The resultant disarray of historical understanding is likely to prove extremely fruitful. New patterns for the comprehension of the past are urgently in demand; and it seems probable that in course of time suitable patterns will indeed be found. To be at all satisfactory, these new patterns will have to embrace the history of all branches of mankind in a far more adequate sense than has hitherto been done, either by European schools and writers or by their only intellectual rival, the Chinese.

It is not difficult to anticipate some of the lines along which this new synthesis must come.

On the one hand, there is a vast, newly accumulated knowledge about non-western peoples. This was, initially, the work of language specialists, men interested in comparative religion (often Christian missionaries or ex-missionaries) and art collectors. Within the past twenty-five years, scholars with social science backgrounds have swarmed upon the scene, asking new questions and discovering new answers at a very rapid rate. In China and Japan effective collaboration with native scholars interpenetrated western efforts from the start. With the diffusion of western concepts of social science among at least some Chinese and Japanese scholars in the twentieth century, the scale of this collaboration has become massive. Elsewhere, among Moslems and Indians, and in the regions of the world where native cultures were less highly developed before the age of European oceanic discoveries, such collaboration has scarcely begun. Nevertheless, a massive body of data has been assembled; chronological problems have been resolved with greater and greater success; the raw material for a world-wide history has definitely begun to emerge.

In addition, the labours of archaeologists allow historical reconstruction to go beyond the horizon defined by the existence of surviving literary texts – both backward in time, and laterally into regions of the earth where early written records are lacking. Art history, the history of technology, and comparative literature likewise are more and more in a position to contribute valuable information to anyone who seeks to understand the past of mankind, taken as a whole.

This kind of humanistic (in the larger sense of that word) study is matched by the development of social science, particularly of anthropology or ethnography. The primitive or simple societies that Europeans encountered in such numbers in the course of their world-wide expansion between the sixteenth and nineteenth centuries excited curiosity from the first. How did they fit into the Biblical scheme of history? Were naked savages, in fact, happier and more blessed than their discoverers? In the course of the ninteenth century, venturesome students of these communities arranged them on a scale of progress. The most influential such attempt was made by an American, Lewis Henry Morgan, whose scheme was accepted by Karl Marx and has become canonical in Communist countries since 1917. The problem such speculative schemes presented was to discover in the archaeological and fossil record evidences of historical stages that would match up with the classification (hunting, pastoral, agricultural, etc.) imposed upon surviving primitive communities. This became the preoccupation of German, French and Communist ethnologists.

In Britain and the United States, however, a school of cultural anthropologists arose, who concentrated on observing existing 'primitive' communities, in hope of discerning general principles about the structuring of human society. In the late 1930s leaders of the latter school, returning to the scene of their youthful field studies after a lapse of a decade or more, began to discover the reality of a time dimension in human societies, even very simple ones. Others undertook to study peasant communities, embedded in the matrix of a fully civilised society where written records could throw additional light on events remembered within the village itself.

In this way the boundary between cultural anthropology and history was breached, mainly after World War II. For not only did field anthropologists begin to avail themselves of archival materials for enhancing their understanding of observed behaviour, but a few historians, seeking general ideas about the processes of social and historical change, discovered useful stimulus in the theories of anthropologists about such phenomena as diffusion of culture traits, culture patterning, and the like.

Other strands and themes also played their part, for instance the flowering among the French of an old tradition of *géographie humaine* into sensitive awareness of technical-ecological-geographic parameters of the human past. Hegelian dialectic, Marxian class struggle, philosophical sociology as developed by Max Weber, Emile Durkheim, Karl Mannheim, and Freudian psychology with its emphasis upon subconscious motivation are still other, powerful currents of thought that surround contemporary historians who address themselves to the problem of constructing an intellectually acceptable world-girdling history. Only economics, with its increasingly elaborate mathematical and statistical formulations, has remained apart, since the kind of quantitative data modern economists thrive upon is extremely hard to find for distant ages and far corners of the earth.

Such a formidable array of ideas and data may seem overwhelming. Yet a number of historians have been so bold as to try to bring satisfactory order to the confusion of facts and ideas today's army of specialists is accumulating so busily. UNESCO undertook a collaborative world history immediately after World War II; the volumes that have appeared so far cull out much interesting data, but have conspicuously failed to provide any clear, intelligible pattern other than the childish bickering in footnotes between Communist and non-Communist scholars. In Germany, another collective work, *Historia Mundi*, came closer, for its editors and authors presented a loosely Roman Catholic picture of the world's past. Recent English and French efforts at collective world history have lacked the clarity and structure inherent in Lord Acton's great prototype; but individual efforts, including Arnold J. Toynbee's *Study of History*, my own *The Rise of the West: A History of the Human Community*, as well as works aimed specifically at school audiences like Margaret Lusty, *The Foundations of our Society* (designed for African students) or Noah E. Fehl, *Science and Culture* (directed towards a Chinese audience), each, in its own fashion, seeks an organising idea around which relevant data and subordinate motifs can group themselves into an intellectually comprehensible whole.

No one can be sure that a widely acceptable synthesis will emerge from such efforts. But the attempt is being made. Moreover, the felt need for an intelligible picture of world history, that will be more adequate to the facts and to our theoretical insights into how human societies function, is acute. Under such circumstances, fundamental changes are likely to take place in school curricula and in the teaching of history in European and American as well as in Asian and African schoolrooms. Two models divide the field as of now: the one cyclical and plural in the sense that a number of civilisations are treated as essentially independent of, and equivalent to, one another; the other linear and unitary in the sense that interactions across relatively large distances even in very ancient times are judged sufficient to make mankind's history a single, if loosely articulated, whole.

It seems clear to me that the segmented, pluralistic view of the human past rests mainly on literary evidences. Differences of language, religion and of learned tradition did, indeed, insulate the learned classes of one civilisation from their counterparts in other civilisations most of the time. It required a special effort for one learned élite to translate foreign literature into its own idiom. Moreover, in most cases, such an enterprise involved recognition of some serious deficiency in one's own tradition; and ordinarily only a supremely confident or direly besieged literate class could admit such a thing. But art history and technological development tell a different story. In these realms men of one cultural tradition were more ready to imitate and more open to new ideas than was true of men of letters. In so far as these evidences from the past seem important, the unitary and diffusionist viewpoint becomes more plausible.

Even if we assume that a more or less satisfactory scholarly consensus as to the shape of world history will presently emerge, there will be a necessary and substantial gap between the time at which it does so and the time when it can reach the schools. Not only do suitable textbooks and other instructional materials have to be prepared. The teaching staff have also to be persuaded that far-reaching changes in the way they have been accustomed to teach their subject have become wise or necessary. Retraining of teachers and changed patterns of teacher education are thus involved. The massiveness of existing school systems, tangled in bureaucratic red tape the world around, means that sweeping changes are bound to take a generation or longer.

Yet once a new vision has been defined, if scholars achieve rough agreement on that, the task of redirecting school procedures is

easily within reach. It would still take time; but if the will to introduce a different and more nearly adequate course in world history
holds up, means will assuredly be found. This is especially true in an
age when audio-visual media, capable of reaching millions in school
as well as out of school, already exist, available for use in formal
instruction, but as yet little exploited for this purpose anywhere in
the world.

CHARLES L. HANNAM

Prejudice and the Teaching of History

What I think of Japs. I think of the Japanese as a race of people who can build small things like radions. But they can also build big boats like the world largest tankers. Which is being built in Nip land. The truth is that I hate Japs.

1st-year mixed ability secondary school[1]

In 1952 a UNESCO pamphlet on *History Textbooks and International Understanding*[2] stated

In our judgement, the attitude of schools to the teaching of history is the acid test of the sincerity of their faith in the growth of international understanding and consequently of their readiness to tackle this vast and crucial question.

Seventeen years later with religious conflict reawakened between Catholics and Protestants in Ulster, signs of renewed anti-semitism in Russia and Poland, race prejudice rampant in Wolverhampton and Leeds, Arabs and Israelis at each others' throats in the Middle East and race-rioting in the USA, the teacher of history must be depressed at the effectiveness of his role in helping children towards detachment and objectivity and helping reduce national as well as racial prejudice. For more than half a century teachers have been concerned with the elimination of prejudice from history teaching. After World War I an inquiry into the fairness of textbooks to minority groups was begun in the United States. This was undertaken by those who wrote and used the books but the inquiry, however well-intentioned, was not very effective. The League of Nations also set up commissions to have nations examine each others' textbooks. The hopes of history teachers in most countries were great: if only nations knew more of one another, if they understood each others' customs and idiosyncrasies, war would be outlawed by common consent. Unfortunately this scheme did not flourish except in Scandinavia.

Sad disillusionment came with World War II, but even while it was going on schemes for removing national prejudice from books were again begun and since then with the help of UNESCO this work has continued and several important studies have emerged. *History Without Bias?* issued by the Council of Christians and Jews in 1954[3] summarised the difficulties that came out of this examination of textbooks. The report concluded that the teaching of good human relationships may not be the primary concern of history teaching but that nevertheless many textbooks were likely to produce this result. Surveys of textbooks then in use however still suggested that in Britain at any rate they concentrated too much on the political and military aspects of life. The ruthless selection of material that was essential in textbook writing inevitably meant that some human groups had been ignored or neglected. Most history was still written from a predominantly British point of view and what seemed adequate to the majority could easily seem inadequate and humiliating to a minority group. Jews were no more likely to be satisfied with a history of Christ that ignored the cultural contribution of their civilisation, than a Mohammedan would accept a view of the Crusades that hardly mentioned the Islamic point of view.

This list could of course be extended; no two cultures are able to view each other satisfactorily. Professor Lévi-Strauss[4] likens the process to two express trains that pass each other at speed. The amount of detail discernible depends on the speed of the trains. In *Race and History* he writes 'men whose culture differs from our own are neither more nor less moral than ourselves; each society has its own moral standards by which it divides its members into good and evil'.

From an examination of the data of ethnography and history it seems that race prejudice is not universal and is of relatively recent origin. Alexander the Great married two Persian princesses and ten thousand of his soldiers married Hindus. The main interest the Romans had in their subject people was that they should pay their tribute, and when Christians persecuted their fellow men it was on the grounds that they were 'infidels', not because they belonged to another race. The Spanish Conquistadores did not mind if their men slept with the natives, provided the women had been baptised first. Racism is neither hereditary not spontaneous. It is a cultural value judgement which has no objective basis and which in our civilisation has its origins in the work of Gobinau, Chamberlain, the imperialism of the late nineteenth century and particularly in the nationalistic creed of National Socialism. Members of the UNESCO committee, the British Historical Association[5] and many English-speaking teachers have become aware of the need for objectivity. Whenever we are up against vicious prejudice our 'liberal conscience' is outraged or at least troubled. In *Hanoi* Mary McCarthy[6] witnessed a North Vietnamese history lesson where a battle against the French in the 1950s was the subject.

> . . . it was too early to hope, obviously, that these embattled children could find in their heads a soft spot for de Lattre de Tassigny, still less for the inept General Navarre. History as taught by the French to the Vietnamese was bound to incite a spirit of revenge on the old French Empire textbooks. Mr Phan was fond of quoting, with a short acerbic laugh, from the first words of history he had to memorise as a boy: *Nos ancêtres les Gaulois* . . . Still I was sorry to find that map on the blackboard. Beyond my personal dismay and regret at what appeared to be a kind of indigence (history was richer than those children knew), I was sensitive to the fact that this lesson would be regarded as sheer propaganda. 'They indoctrinate their schoolchildren' (p. 84).

One wonders whether a lesson on the Battle of Britain in this country would be viewed with equal dismay. The instillation of direct prejudice through teaching is certainly unusual but it must be realised that prejudicial thinking can play a constructive part in the way in which we perceive situations. 'Prejudice' is a loaded word and no one would like to be considered prejudiced, and yet if it helps us as a step towards understanding it cannot be a fault entirely. In order to understand a situation or a problem we must first put it into some order in relation to other knowledge. This process is known as 'stereotyping' and this is part of the formation of prejudiced thinking in the 'bad' sense, but its useful function in the process of understanding new ideas and situations must be remembered. Because, having achieved a perspective, we can then proceed from this to make predictions, or to make decisions to find out more, or to go on to something else.

To combat prejudice which operates in the harmful and limiting way, it is not sufficient to provide more accurate information about the stereotype; prejudice in the teaching of history lies much deeper and operates on an unconscious level. No committee of 'good and true men' will do much more than eliminate obvious bias or search for it with care until it comes to the expression on the drawing of George Washington's face.[7] The attention must be directed in new ways: in the first place we must find out how the child receives information. Does the history teacher in fact create prejudice by his very tender-mindedness,[8] or does his work turn out to be quite irrelevant to the development of the child's view of his world? Like the textbook committees, teachers may perhaps have set themselves tasks which are quite beyond them. Alternatively the questions to which no answers have so far been found may need to be asked differently. In the social sciences similar concerns have been expressed and Muzafer Sherif takes them to task for their myopic approach. 'The typical research design has been constructed largely in terms of tradition or the researcher's convenience. . . . A proper framework for the study of intergroup work is imperative today.'[9] Historians are primarily concerned with group interaction and conflict. They use a different frame of reference and attempt to see a problem as a whole, while the social psychologist tends to isolate a problem in order to have a situation that can be controlled and isolated. In the field of curriculum development the social scientist can be enormously useful all the same. One would like to know from him whether there is any evidence to show how children become prejudiced, when they begin to operate in terms of national stereotypes, where they pick up ideas and whether their social class has any bearing on the criteria they use when they accept or reject information.

Here is an example taken from a child at a local comprehensive school. It illustrates the point that there are reservoirs of prejudice totally unaffected by the broadly liberal education that was provided in the school.

5th-year boy: Frenchmen are lazy. just music and wine all day long. From morning to night they sit in cafes doing – – – – all. Admittedly some work but from what I have seen they are lazey very lazey. All this gear about romance is a load of bull, and in my opinion there are very few cases of romantic frenchmen. The women are all right, but most are scruffy and dirty. All they think about is lesure and plesure.

It seems worth noting that after years of schooling so little has happened to change his outlook. The impact of French, geography, history and civics has not left much of a mark on him though he seems to have visited France.

As Toynbee pointed out in his *Study of History*,[10] the Emperor Ch'ien Lung showed that same egocentric illusion which we now meet in the West. Different cultures approach each other with identical intellectual assumptions. When the Spaniards arrived in America they killed two natives to see if they had mortal souls. The Indians for their part drowned some Spaniards to see if they were gods or would decompose like ordinary mortals. There is a western assumption of superiority, not unjustified in terms of technological progress, that western culture is synonymous with civilisation and merits greater consideration than the cultures of foreigners, savages or barbarians. If we look at the majority of syllabuses there is some acknowledgement of the debt to classical civilisations and where world history is taught there is some mention even of India, China, Japan and pre-Columbian America. What is so much harder to get across even to adults is that people little advanced technologically and with no written language – the races of Africa, the Melanesians and Polynesians, the modern Indians of South and North America and the Eskimos – nevertheless have their own civilisations, cultures which have shown powers of expansion although at this moment this power has been lost.[11] Even when teachers are aware of all this they are still faced with the problem of communicating it to the third-year isolationist who wrote:

> I don't think anything about the Chinese. I never will have nothing to say about them . . . or ever have said anything about them . . . one thing about the Chinese every one of them has the same colour hair (well nearly everyone) Chinese boys are not as handsome as English boys.

It is unlikely that the compound of beliefs, value judgements and emotions springs out of the children's minds spontaneously; it is the result of growth as much as the formation of concepts and moral judgements that Piaget has written about. To children below a certain age terms such as 'Chinese' or 'French' represent a complex level of abstraction. When other races or nations are mentioned it is not just a question of the manipulation of an abstraction but also of an infusion of strongly held value judgements. Even when there is a real contact, as with a school visit to a foreign country, both host and visitor, isolated by social and linguistic factors, will be reduced to stereotyped opinions of one another.

In *New Society* (30 June 1966) Professor Tajfel shows that preference for a particular nation begins early in the child's life. Children of six to seven, and nine to eleven, were presented individually with a set of twenty specially prepared and standardised photographs of young men, all English. The children were asked to decide whether they liked the person in the picture. A fortnight later they were told, when presented with the same photographs, that some were foreigners and were asked to say who they thought the foreigners were. The analysis of the data, which included controls and several complex mutations, showed that there was a significant tendency for children to 'like better' those people to whom they assigned the category 'English'; similar results showing preference for their own kind emerged in Austria, Belgium, Holland and Israel. Young children are certainly enormously chauvinistic and as they become older they begin to develop a stereotype of their own national group. From there Professor Tajfel proceeds to the conclusion that children 'assimilated very early the generally accepted value judgements about salient foreign countries, that this happens in almost complete absence of any factual information about these countries, and that their own national membership acquires just as early (if not earlier) an emotional significance which can trigger off a whole set of responses'. Professor Tajfel's conclusion of the article is of special interest to teachers of history. 'Thinking about large human groups in a rational and adequate manner is a complex intellectual achievement made even more difficult by the early intervention of biases.' In schools we allow children to develop these complex emotional skills almost by accident and, as the examples of children's views of foreigners quoted above show, the teaching these children have received has done little or nothing to modify their views. Indeed it would seem that a history syllabus that is entirely centred on British history will only reinforce these ethnocentric attitudes and foreigners, who only appear on the scene to be defeated, enslaved and exploited for the glory of one's own group, will hardly be seen more tolerantly when encountered in another context. If the subject does range beyond the British people in our schools we concentrate almost entirely on western/Christian civilisations and on the activities of the Caucasian racial group. This will produce a view of history that does less than justice to other civilisations.

Like feelings of national preference, we must also look at attitudes to race because brown or yellow skin and unusually shaped eyes will evoke even deeper feelings than different language and sometimes only vaguely perceptible differences in looks. According to D. Milner[12] racial attitudes develop from infancy until the early teens and then become more intense and sophisticated. In view of the fact that an increasing number of coloured immigrant children are going to be absorbed in our secondary schools it is important to note that psychological damage is inflicted on those at the receiving end of racial prejudice. White children invariably prefer the white group and reject the coloured out-group. This has been found to be so in studies conducted in the United States, New Zealand and the United Kingdom. In these studies white children rejected coloured dolls – 'he's black, he's a stinky little boy', 'he kills people'. While these attitudes may be regrettable they are not thought to be damaging to the child himself. But what of the coloured child who also rejected the coloured doll? and the Navaho Indian children who were watching a western film and were reported to be cheering for the cowboys? Moorland (1966) showed three- to six-year-old Negro children black and white dolls and asked 'which one looks most like you?' and over fifty per cent of the children indicated the white doll. These children had demonstrated the ability to recognise racial differences, and Milner comes to the conclusion that minorities suffering prejudice and discrimination in every sphere of life will produce children who reject their true identity and who aspire to the unattainable white one. He concludes that 'education has a crucial role to play in stemming the flow of racial prejudice and stereotyping from parents to children; educational material itself is not free from implicit and explicit racial attitudes and the teacher's contribution to eliminating all such determinants of prejudice will be decisive.'

Nicholas Johnson in *New Society* (7 July 1966) explores another area where the seeds of prejudice are sown: the war comic. 'How is it that primary schoolchildren have come to agree about the relative merits of various countries? Who tells them that England, Australia, America and France are to be liked while Russia, China, Germany and India are to be disliked? The answer must lie largely in what parents, teachers and other adults tell the children.' When he examines comics Johnson concludes that they are a powerful source of nationalistic references. Not only is there 'name calling' such as Jerry, Nip, Kraut, Hun, but killing is introduced in such a way that it seems sanctioned and justifiable. The heroes are usually British, but sometimes include New Zealanders (Kiwis) and Australians, and the enemy is described either by the comic or the British character as 'deadly and fanatical', 'lousy stinking rats', 'scum', 'swine' or 'slit-eyed killers' and among the ethical propositions put forward are 'these Japs ain't human beings' and 'the only good Germans are dead ones'. There is anti-Communist propaganda in American war comics: 'so we cured our Commie neighbours of their dirty little habits'. East Germany has become the area which conveniently combines the hate potential of Communism and Nazism. Apart from Johnson's interesting information on the image of war presented (perpetual, non-ideological, the sanctioning of death and violence, bullets without their real effect) it is important to look at the con-clusions of his experimental work, since there is evidence that attitudes are partly caused by the material children read and that the effect of reading war comics on young children is of some importance and may also be long-lasting.

Three points emerge from the work of Tajfel, Milner and Johnson: children already have attitudes towards other nationalities before they come to secondary schools. Racial discrimination and self-hate of coloured minorities begins early. Comics supply information to their readers which influences their preference for other nations. By the time the history teacher comes on the scene he is dealing with pupils who already have racial and nationalistic attitudes and what happens in schools does not necessarily modify previously-held views. Can it be asserted that our history teaching actually increases prejudice, or that it reinforces previously-held views? It is difficult to make a convincing claim without specific research in this area; the best one can do is carefully to re-examine our history curriculum from this point of view. Perhaps the very ineffectiveness of most teaching is a form of protection. If it had more impact there might be more reaction both from parents and authorities. We know that after generations of compulsory religious education the Church of England still loses its hold over the majority of adults in this country. If, as we suspect, the children who come to secondary schools are already full of prejudiced ideas about foreigners could the teacher not perform a useful function and use the mental processes that make the children see all the French as 'frogs' and all coloured people as 'wogs'? This could be the starting-point and the teacher could go on from there to give out detailed information which will make the previous over-simplification seem silly and inadequate to the children. A great deal of history taught is narrative rather than analytical, and controversy is far too often avoided for fear of 'indoctrinating' children. Too often the connections that ought to be made are left to the children, who are intellectually unable to make them. Is it enough to tell pupils of the dropping of the A-bomb on Hiroshima or should there be discussion of the decision and how it came to be made? Or should we go on to the problem of killing as a moral duty? The children's capacity to cope with arguments of this sort presents peculiar difficulties. At one stage they can only cope with narrative, later they can be more objective and can sort out an argument into stages and can test facts against opinions. The work done on children's sense of time and their formation of historical concepts[13] indicate times when some of the children can no more understand what the teacher or the book is telling them than a colour-blind person can tell red from green. It is relatively easy to explore concept formation when the experimenter deals with neutral terms such as 'ruler', 'nation' or 'trade'. When it comes to prejudiced views, so many factors are at work that it must be much more difficult to isolate them, particularly as fashion in prejudice changes. Textbook revision, which has been discussed before, only touches one aspect of the problem and when we wish to reconsider the very basis of the history curriculum we must begin by asking at what age children can begin to understand the points of view and values of another civilisation. The fact that a certain culture has declined, or has even been destroyed, is the equivalent of saying that it has failed. The interrelation of cultures is not often made clear enough. Again children are great 'time snobs' – what is new must inevitably be better and if another civilisation failed to explore the potential of steam, or has no television, it must be a less valuable civilisation than our own. At the moment if we begin with the stone age and end up with the present (more likely in the middle of the nineteenth century if the teacher plods through the suggested syllabus conscientiously) we have, unconsciously, set up a hierarchy because to children the most modern is best. If we draw on other cultures only incidentally we also devalue their achievements and importance: America only begins to exist when Columbus discovers it, the Australasian tribes only function to provide Cook with supplies and the Indians emerge when they are to be defeated by Clive and later when they dare to mutiny. Often there is an element of surprise that others have achieved anything. The fact that the Chinese had the compass and gunpowder and the Incas a road system is thought to be a quaint accident that pre-empted European technology.

This is not the conventional jingoism that may be on its way out, but a lack of objectivity that will ultimately lead to an inability to evaluate the nature of other cultures and civilisations. This kind of objectivity will not be provided by many of the homes, or the mass media, so the teacher will have to give some attention to the matter. Recent educational literature indicates that working-class children benefit less from their secondary education than middle-class children because they feel uninvolved in a school system that upholds the values of a class not their own.[14] Do children only want to hear about the transactions of the nobility and the professional classes, with 'the great unwashed masses' only providing a background? We present history to working-class children as we do to immigrants, as if they were no more than a minority group, and it would pay us to consider the feelings of these groups. If young immigrants despise the image they have of themselves, how will they feel if they are confronted with accounts of their civilisation that only show them as objects of conquest, exploitation or equally humiliating 'reform'? In a sense we are using other civilisations and cultures to boost our own and this must be harmful.

What can be done? There is enough evidence to show that a new look at prejudice is called for and that this in turn should change our way of teaching history in schools. We might look at another civilisation using the methods of the anthropologist rather than the historian. Bruner suggests the study of the Eskimos.[15] It may be possible to examine a society without placing it either above or below the value scales of the children. Secondly, wars might be studied not only as events in which 'we' fought 'them' but as examples of human conflict, also showing that there are ways of resolving conflict other than war and this might take the form of case studies and games rather than textbook exercises.[9, 16] Thirdly, objectivity comes late in the mental development of children and no one, not even a 'nice liberal', is without prejudice. It is therefore better to allow children's prejudice to emerge openly than to suppress it by condemnation or to pretend that it does not exist. Prejudice should be the starting-point; find out what the children feel about the 'Japs' or the 'wogs' and then produce information that undermines the stereotype. If this work is done with fervour and indignation rather than cool detachment there will be a backlash and nothing will be gained. Prejudice consists of a complex of attitudes and beliefs and it will never just disappear. It would be facile to suggest only a few practical tips to deal with it; a complete re-examination of the history we teach to children needs to be undertaken and we must try to learn how we can teach objectivity in schools in the face of so many other powerful factors.

Notes

1   This and another four extracts were produced by teachers at a conference on 'Prejudice' held by the Bristol Association of History Teachers in May 1969.

2   J. A. Lauwerys, *History Textbooks and International Understanding*, UNESCO, 1952.

3   E. H. Dance, *History Without Bias?*, Council of Christians and Jews, 1954.

4   Claude Lévi-Strauss, *Race and History*, UNESCO, 5th imp., 1968.

5   C. F. Strong, *Teaching for International Understanding*, HMSO, 1952; *English History through Foreign Eyes*, Historical Association, 1954; *Cyprus School History Textbooks*, Educational Advisory Committee of the Parliamentary Group for World Government, 1965.

6   Mary McCarthy, *Hanoi*, Penguin, 1969.

7   *The Historian's Contribution to Anglo-American Misunderstanding*, Routledge, 1969, p. 134.

8   H. J. Miller, 'The Effectiveness of Teaching Techniques for Reducing Colour Prejudice', *Liberal Education*, no. 16, July 1969.

9   M. Sherif, *Group Conflict and Co-operation*, Routledge, 1966.

10   A. J. Toynbee, *A Study of History* (Somerville Abridgement), OUP, 1946, p. 37.

11   Claude Lévi-Strauss, *The Savage Mind*, Weidenfeld & Nicolson, 1966.

12   David Milner, paper given at the BATH Conference, May 1969.

13   G. Jahoda, 'Children's Concepts of Time and History', *Educational Review*, vol. 15, 1963; K. Lovell and A. Slater, 'The Growth of the Concept of Time', *Journal of Child Psychology and Psychiatry*, 1960.

14   J. W. B. Douglas, *The Home and the School*, MacGibbon & Kee, 1964.

15   J. S. Bruner, *Towards a Theory of Instruction*, Bellknap, Harvard, 1966.

16   J. Galtung, 'Conflict as a Way of Life', *New Society*, 16 October 1969.

DWIGHT W. HOOVER

Black History

The twentieth century has more than its share of new problems which are reflected in the schools as well as in other institutions more directly connected to the contemporary scene. Perhaps the major problem in education has been created by the attempt to educate larger and larger numbers of students, many from the lower socio-economic classes. This attempt has not only placed a strain upon facilities and the staff, but also upon the theoretical base upon which school subjects rested. The discipline of history is no exception. The older history which concentrated upon the activities of a white, middle- or upper-class political élite was particularly relevant to the education of those who were to form that élite. Now, other groups are demanding a fair share of time and attention and, in so doing, are expanding the parameters of history to include those formerly dispossessed of history as well as of material success. This pressure is not likely to diminish and is now including groups, such as blacks and women, which are becoming more vocal and self-conscious.

While educational institutions seem by their very nature to be conservative they do change, however slowly this change may appear. In the United States, while compulsory school attendance laws date back into the nineteenth century, it was not until the twentieth that the comprehensive high school with its large heterogeneous population became the usual educational pattern. The serious attempt to educate the poorer children in these schools dates even later. Prior to this time, lax enforcement and lack of concern with school drop-outs, particularly in the rural South, permitted the pretence, if not the practice, of universal secondary education to survive. However, with the discovery of poverty in the affluent society of the sixties and the shrinking market for unskilled employment, the theory and practice of American education came under scrutiny. As a result, more effort was made to get and hold students in high school. In order to accomplish this feat, a more relevant curriculum was proposed, one which included a history relating to an appropriate past. Black history became part of the demand for relevance.

Beyond the structural problems of American education lay the problems of the larger society. The Civil Rights movement which came to a head in the sixties caught many Americans by surprise. The black awareness of the era, which seemed to contain overtones of threatened violence, alarmed others and produced powerful counter-reactions. The urban disturbances confirmed the fragile nature of the American solution, which had been thought so stable that few persons even bothered to articulate it. Bewildered by these events, white and black Americans alike began searching for explanations. The preferred psychological answer of prejudice did not satisfy since it did not discriminate sufficiently between what appeared to be a universal trait – categorising individuals by a number of characteristics – and a pathological condition which led to discrimination, separation, and repression. All of us differentiate; but not everyone has racial hate. The behaviourally-oriented social sciences – sociology, economics, and political science – did analyse the present scene, but their dullness and technical sophistication condemned them to a limited audience. The majority turned to history with the hope that the past would provide the key to the understanding of the present.

Black history, then, would serve two purposes: one, to help hold black students in school and develop their sense of identity; two, to tell both white and black adults why matters were as they were. These two purposes were not necessarily compatible nor were any of the audiences homogeneous. The difficulty was reflected by a semantic problem of what term should be used to describe the black man – Negro, Afro-American, or black. The two polar words, Negro and black, epitomised the differences which were composed of generation gaps, life styles, and historical conceptions.

Those most inclined to advocate radical change in America were likely to reject the term Negro as descriptive of a social role and historic past best forgotten. John O. Killens, a noted black novelist, took such a position when he declared 'The American Negro, then, is an Anglo-Saxon invention, a role the Anglo-Saxon gentleman invented for the black man to play in the drama known euphemistically as the "American Way of Life".' Implicit in the rejection of the American experience is not only a rejection of a discriminatory social system but also the genetic admixture that had occurred. Typical of those who rejected white standards of physical beauty and proclaimed the idea that 'black is beautiful' was Malcolm X. In his autobiography he said that 'the slavemaster forced his family name upon this rape-mixed race, which the slavemaster began to call "the Negro"'. The sixties in America saw a revulsion against the experience of the black man in America which differed from earlier revulsions like Garvey and his 'Back to Africa' movement in that it was widely reported to white and black audiences alike.

Black history in its most extreme form is an instrument of black consciousness and rejection of an inferior role. It is antithetical to white American history in that it is international rather than national, claiming that racial ties are stronger than national loyalties. Traditional white heroes are viewed through the sceptical eyes of black Americans who use racial attitude as a standard of greatness. Black history emphasises African origins and the achievements of African societies while reducing the emphasis on the extent to which the black man was Americanised, insisting that the New World experience did not alter the self-conceptions of black men. Black history seeks black heroes who deny the universality of western values, who rebel against restrictive white society. Black history hopes to create a third world consciousness in the minds of black people wherever they may be. As might be expected, those who advocate such an ideologically oriented history are rarely scholars and a comprehensive black history of this type that is non-mythical has not been written.

The newer, ideological black history is attempting to displace an older Negro history. This older Negro history is in the process of changing in name, if not in orientation, to black history and this creates considerable confusion. In the United States, contrary to recent claims, Negro history dates back into the nineteenth century. The first book written by a black man on the American experience is usually assumed to be James W. C. Pennington's *Text Book of the Origin and History of the Colored People*, printed in 1841. Other volumes followed, the most significant being George Washington Williams' *History of the Negro Race in America from 1691–1880*. These histories resembled white histories of the time, filio-pietistic and romantic, as they assumed a progressive, optimistic view of the future of both the United States and the black man.

In the twentieth century, Negro history became the province of professional scholars just as other branches of history were. The two most outstanding black scholars, W. E. B. DuBois and Carter Woodson, were academically trained and sought to apply rigorous standards to the discovery, evaluation, and presentation of historic data. The Association for the Study of Negro Life and History, organised by Woodson in 1915, continues to this day. The work of Woodson and other black scholars used the prevailing progressive historical assumptions of the day which were melioristic, acceptive of American values, and dedicated to the eventual goal of the full integration of black men into American society. There were heroes in this history, men who had accomplished their acceptance into the middle-class white value system – Booker T. Washington, George Washington Carver, and Frederick Douglass. The major emphasis was on black achievement in a restrictive society and black efforts to end those restrictions. The best-known college text in the field today, John Hope Franklin's *From Slavery to Freedom*, illustrates this theme with its description of the change from a servile to an independent status. Liberal in outlook, this Negro history reflected an orientation which was acceptive of social change but non-revolutionary.

In the fifties and sixties more white historians, with similar values, began investigating black history as an adjunct to the study of slavery or stratification in the United States. While Negro history was in the process of becoming black history, many of the scholars were now white. This fact caused considerable friction, as a requirement of ideological black history was that the teacher should be of like colour and persuasion. The older Negro history had been taught in predominantly black schools and colleges by black teachers, but the demands for the new black history come primarily from northern urban schools and previously white universities where the teachers were uniformly white. The older Negro history came in a Negro History Week or a Negro History Month and celebrated the achievements of black Americans. But the courses now asked for were more sweeping – African history, backgrounds, and languages – all with an eye to understanding recent movements emphasising black political and cultural nationalism.

The older Negro history was a moral enterprise, dedicated to the achievement of equality and possessed of an implicit sense of the tragic nature of the historical past. The black man strove hard and with peaceful means to win his way into middle-class America; his was not a personal failure, but was rather symptomatic of national failure. For this history, as for Marthin Luther King, Jr, the role of the black man in America was a sacrificial one. Negro history would uplift white and black alike and would provide part of the moral capital needed to achieve a just society. It would also serve to create a sense of community which would enable individuals to overcome limited circumstances. Indeed, with the exception of the tragic motif, the goals of Negro history were those of the history of the United States.

The aims of the newer black history are more explicitly psychological, as might be expected from the shift in audience to black students in urban schools and white universities. The psychological goals of black history are remedial. Black history must be taught in order to fight racial prejudice which causes lowered self-esteem and defective self-image. The informal stratification of the schools must be countered by a history which denies the inferiority of the black man. Once again the schools are asked to remedy social defects, and once again the question of the adequacy of remedy ought to be asked. Can the schools reverse the views of society unless those views are already changing? One would hardly think so; and, in a sense, to suggest that this might happen is to raise hopes overly high. There is some evidence that black history as a psychological panacea has been oversold and teachers are finding that black students are becoming less interested in black history and are questioning its utility.

Another difficulty in the increased demand for black history is a conceptual one. Black history does not fit neatly into the prevailing paradigm in American history, which holds that social mobility is universal and that countervailing power is shared in society by competing groups which achieve their goals by peaceful, legal means. The paradigm of American experience is elaborated in the history taught and, while not always consciously assumed, remains the major implicit generalisation upon which textbooks are written.

The paradigm relies upon a model of immigrant experience, one which is perhaps relevant only to the 'new immigration' after the Civil War. The model holds that each ethnic group which has come to the United States has undergone somewhat the same experience. The members of the first generation remain social outcasts, living in ethnic enclaves, subject to poverty, disease, open to political manipulation, and likely to earn a marginal subsistence as casual labourers. The second or third generations advance in skills and take on American values. By the third or fourth generation, the assimilation process nears completion as erstwhile foreigners are transformed into middle-class Americans, indistinguishable from the descendants of immigrants who had migrated earlier.

There are obvious shortcomings to this model when applied to the black experience in America. Black Americans arrived before the establishment of the Republic; their mobility has been low; their assimilation has been covert instead of overt; their middle-class status is as yet unassured. There are also similarities, enough for a number of students to insist that the model is still valid and that, to use Daniel Moynihan's words, 'Paddy' and 'Sambo' were alike.

The tailoring which makes the pattern fit changes our understanding of the urbanisation of immigrants and our understanding of their assimilation. The argument goes that while the black man has long lived in America, his migration to the cities in large numbers is essentially a twentieth-century phenomenon. A look at the 'new immigration' tells us that the story of this immigration is the transformation of the European peasant into the American city dweller, for while most immigrants were attracted to the New World by visions of cheap land, the vast majority settled in cities. The black experience in America is duplicating the process except that the black American is coming from the rural South. In this view, the black man is in the latest wave of immigration and the difficulties in the black ghetto are understandable in terms of the social dislocation in earlier ethnic enclaves. While there may be merit in this position, the data are rather limited. However, the need to explore the phenomenon is such that there have been several studies of black urbanisation. August Meier and Elliott M. Rudwick's *From Plantation to Ghetto*, the best interpretative history of the black man in America, has the process of urbanisation as part of its theme. Seth M. Scheiner's *Negro Mecca: A History of the Negro in New York City, 1865–1920*, Gilbert Osofsky's *Harlem: The Making of a Ghetto*, and Alan Spear's *Black Chicago: The Making of a Negro Ghetto, 1890–1920*, all are case studies of the black settlement in these two cities. One may expect much more attention to be devoted to black urbanisation and to the creation of a scholarly synthesis.

The second way of saving the immigrant model is to reconsider the speed and totality of assimilation. The reconsideration shows that for many Americans the immigrant experience has not led to mobility, that the belief in rapid assimilation has reflected aspirations rather than reality. Milton M. Gordon, a sociologist, shows in *Assimilation in American Life* that ethnic and religious differences persist longer than had been expected and recent studies of stratification have shown how many immigrant descendants have remained relatively fixed in social position. If these studies change our perspective on the past, we may find black history is not as much different from immigrant history as we had supposed.

Both efforts to salvage an obviously useful model reflect another basic difficulty – that of the social role of the historian. Historians, particularly in the United States, serve as secular theologians, explaining the ways of society to man. In this role, historians are conservative and success oriented, showing how changes had to occur and why these changes were all for the best. Few historians document tragedy and failure; when they do, they consider only transitory failure which illuminates present success. Populism and Progressivism died as political movements, but their spirits live on in the Democratic party. American historians have not been kind to those groups which have not achieved success in the American pattern. A satisfactory explanation of the Indians' part in the American civilisation, for example, is yet to be written. The social role of the historian has therefore not equipped him to understand black history.

Particularly troublesome is the inability to come to terms with the lack of economic and political success of the black American. A second major American paradigm is that power is gained by competition between countervailing groups. This paradigm holds that when any segment of society becomes too strong, reactive groups form to assert their own interests and to diminish the control exerted over them through either political means – the formation of a party or interest group voting – or economic means – by boycotts, strikes, consumer protest, and unionisation. The pluralistic view explains the rise of the two-party system, the creation of labour unions and the allocation of services and goods. In any case, the social system supposedly accommodates to pressures and runs on the energy generated by conflicting interests. Equilibrium constantly shifts as new groups successfully strive – in legal, non-violent fashion – for their privileges.

What this model omits is, of course, that a certain level of power must be reached before any coercion will work. Groups or individuals who are repressed to such an extent that their existence is precarious are usually unable to resist anything. Nowhere is this more clear than in the history of the black man in America. As August Meier demonstrates in his *Negro Thought in America, 1880–1915*, and in his collection of readings co-edited with Francis Broderick, *Negro*

Protest Thought in the Twentieth Century, the tactics and goals of civil rights leaders have not changed significantly from the past. What is new is that the tactics have achieved some success and the goals are receiving greater publicity. The important question now is how is it possible to go from a position of almost complete impotence to one with discernible power? Black history in this sense again asks questions regarding the very nature of society. What structural changes have worked against the continuing repression of the black man through slavery and segregation? The study of black history here touches on developments in public opinion and social values which are part of the larger whole of American history.

Ultimately, the most compelling question in black history is the origin and continued existence of prejudice. This question is one with which psychologists are struggling, but it is also one which is susceptible to historical analysis. The phrase 'institutional racism', which has become a cliché to provide a causal explanation for the lower position of the black man in America, relies upon historical evidence. While obviously over-simplified, the belief that a society is deeply prejudiced without the conscious subscription of most individuals to that prejudice has become so persuasive that it has become the consensus of the left, an article of faith which is articulated but often not scrutinised.

The concept of structural prejudice, useful as it is as a generalising device, is not without serious problems. It is too general and fails to account for differences in historical epochs and groups. It simplifies history by categorising people of unlike persuasions together, distorting the distinctions that these people themselves made. As an example, studies of the racial attitudes of white abolitionists have shown divergent views on black ability and the extent of social equality desirable for the free black man. Some of these views would be classified as prejudiced in the twentieth century, but to call abolitionist societies racist and to lump them with organisations dedicated to the preservation of slavery is inaccurate and unfair. Despite the problems, the usefulness of the explanation is perpetuating its use and more effort will be devoted to an historical elaboration of the racial assumptions of both individuals and institutions in the past.

In the United States, much of the attention directed at prejudice focuses on the institution of slavery. Struck by the seeming greater prejudice and racial unrest in the United States, historians began looking for reasons based on past circumstances. The institution of slavery became a very convincing reason. The most complete statement of the connection between slavery and prejudice was made by Stanley Elkins in his book, *Slavery*, published in 1959. Relying heavily upon Frank Tannenbaum's study of Brazilian slavery, *Slave and Citizen*, written in 1947, Elkins claimed that Latin American slavery was less repressive than slavery in the United States and that it did not lead to the creation of the Sambo stereotype. Arguing that English law did not support slavery and that English colonists, unlike Spanish and Portuguese ones, were free to define slavery in their own interests, Elkins portrayed the origins of prejudice in the debased definition of slavery which was created in the pre-Revolutionary South. The severity of the slave system, combined with brainwashing techniques later systematised by Nazi concentration camps, socialised the black into an inferior role which persisted after emancipation.

Elkins' thesis quickly became part of the conventional wisdom; and just as quickly both a scholarly and popular reaction appeared. The first attack was multi-pronged. Elkins used insights from comparative history which was just then gaining scholarly recognition. The opponents of Elkins' thesis seized upon comparative history to refute it. Perhaps the most penetrating criticism was that mounted by David Brion Davis, an historian of ideas. In his 1967 Pulitzer prize-winning book, *The Problem of Slavery in Western Culture*, and in his chapter entitled 'Slavery', written for C. Vann Woodward's *The Comparative Approach to American History*, Davis suggested that slavery shared many similar characteristics, wherever it occurred. He concluded, 'Given the lack of detailed statistical information, we can only conclude that the subject is too complex and the evidence too contradictory for us to assume that the treatment of slaves was substantially better in Latin America than in the British colonies, taken as a whole.' Davis claimed also that classical slavery resembled modern and that English and American abolitionists shared common assumptions. He viewed slavery in a larger context than the purely national one and reached the conclusion that slavery was not a peculiarly American institution.

The connection between slavery and the origin of prejudice in the United States also came under fire from another direction. Winthrop D. Jordan's *White Over Black* took a position which was admirably summarised by Moses I. Finley when he wrote that 'the connection between slavery and racism has been a dialectical one, in which each element reinforced the other.' Using both English and New World sources, Jordan presented a detailed case showing how ingrained assumptions about the word black, about Africa, and about the black man, all interacted to make the black man seem inferior and slavery seem natural. Slavery, in turn, stimulated and continued the appearance of prejudice.

Finally, the Elkins thesis that slavery created a personality type is rejected by self-conscious blacks. Refusing to accept the existence of a non-resistant slave, these persons pointed to slave revolts, sabotage, and other covert and overt behaviour to prove their contention. For present use, black men could not have submitted to the system without some attempt to subvert it.

Although the original insights of the Elkins thesis now appear invalid, much of value emerged from his study of slavery. This is particularly true of the emphasis on comparative history. The idea of studying slavery throughout the western hemisphere using data from economics, sociology, and anthropology, proved very provocative. Indeed, one would have to say that the main impetus in the study of modern slavery lies in this direction. Nor is there any reason why other institutions and ideas, such as black ghettoes and prejudice, cannot be studied in the same fashion. The comparative study of prejudice against blacks in nations to which they have been taken or have immigrated ought to be revealing and profitable in terms of historical understanding. Carl N. Degler has embarked on just such a project involving the United States and Brazil. Since much of the pressure generated for black history comes from present problems, it is not surprising to find an emphasis upon the problems of civil rights in that history. At times, this pressure can be overwhelming, as in the case of the black history course at Columbia University in the spring of 1969 which became one involving only urban problems and the civil rights movement. Part of the urgency to concentrate upon these areas is that the issues are still in doubt, so that alternative strategies can be discussed without the certitude of the historical past.

The concentration upon civil rights movements projects the dilemmas of the movement back into the past. It also calls into question the goals of the movement. Does the black man wish integration into American Society or does he desire cultural or political nationalism? Does he desire the latter as a conditional means to the former? Responses to these questions vary with the respondents and show a divided black community. Recent public opinion still holds to the goal of integration. However, the black intellectual is alternately torn between the vision of an integrated America and a separate, black community. At this crucial juncture, the belief in cultural nationalism seems to predominate in the expressions of vocal black theorists. This belief appears in different forms, sometimes in favour of political nationalism, at other times opposed to it. Alternately, it serves as a rallying-point for black consciousness.

In brief, the argument as presented by such writers as LeRoi Jones and Eldridge Cleaver is that the blacks in the world are forming a better community, one which has rejected the sterile rationalism of western white society in favour of emotion and creativity. This community could humanise white society if given the chance, a view shared by Norman Mailer, but radical transformation would have to occur. Out of this conviction came the word 'soul' which was a product of black experience, and an emphasis upon brotherhood and community among black. The belief centred in the assumption that black life styles were superior to white and, while not redemptive in the older, Christian sense, offered alternatives to the rampant materialism of the day.

As the proponents of cultural revolution become more articulate, as black music and other elements of black culture become integral parts of the world of the young and not so young, there are attempts to trace black culture into the past. Since the blues represent the core of black experience, they have been carefully studied with an eye to the factors contributing to the development of the blues style. Charles Keil's *Urban Blues*, which purports to explain this development by sociological and historical analysis, has become a minor classic. His effort tries to show how strength may come from weakness and how what, by white standards, seems odd and unstable, may be the opposite by black standards. Other questions are also being asked. Why did this cultural consciousness on the part of the black man take so long to develop? Why did black leaders reject jazz, the blues, and the masses for so long; or conversely, why did the masses not support any black leader in significant numbers until Marcus Garvey? Why did black leaders hold to white values for so long? An answer appears in Harold Cruse's *The Crisis of the Negro Intellectual*. Cruse's book concentrates upon the crucial period of the Harlem Renaissance of the twenties and blames white Marxists for diverting black intellectual attention from cultural developments to less meaningful political causes. Cruse indicates that the wrong road was taken at the time and that the cultural emphasis of the sixties might have come earlier. Both Keil and Cruse show the way for serious historical research on how the vitality of black, lower-class people finally won acceptance in the middle-class world of black and white America.

The concern with cultural change and with the lower-class black past has led others to try to write the history of the inarticulate who have left little in the way of conventional sources for the historian. The insights of George Rudé in *The Crowd in History: A Study of Popular Disturbances in France and England, 1730–1848*, certainly apply here. No one has done this in black history, yet Oscar Handlin, as Maldwyn A. Jones points out, uses the approach as his stock-in-trade in immigrant history. Also his students, of whom Sam Bass Warner, Jr, and Stephan Thernstrom are the best examples, working in urban, social history, have used sources such as manuscript censuses, building permits, and city directories which could be also used in black history. The recent interest in quantitive history is spilling over into areas which have previously seemed inaccessible to the historian.

While black history has not generated new techniques in historical research, it has helped popularise those which are being used. These techniques in historical research have supplemented the older political history and have been alternately broader and narrower. Comparative history is admirably suited for the study of the black past as it cuts across national boundaries. The methods in cultural and social history, particularly as centring upon the lower strata of society, broaden the options of historians, making it possible to study the history of social groups other than the affluent and important. These developments ought to make the historian more sensitive to the gaps which exist in written history.

Beyond that, however, black history has an intrinsic humanising effect upon researcher, teacher, and student alike, be they black or white. For the black, it engenders pride as well as an appreciation of the efforts of preceding generations. It may teach past tragedy but it also teaches present success. For the white, it offers alternative views of the past and enlarges, by vicarious means, the range of possible experiences. It ought also to lead to a greater feeling for the commonality of human life.

Further Reading

Lerone Bennett, Jr, *Before the Mayflower : A History of the Negro in America, 1619–1964*, Penguin, 1964; and *Confrontation : Black and White*, Penguin, 1965.

Arna Bontemps and Jack Conroy, *Anyplace but Here*, Hill & Wang, 1966.

Francis L. Broderick and August Meier (eds), *Negro Protest Thought in the Twentieth Century*, Bobbs-Merrill, 1965.

Harold Cruse, *The Crisis of the Negro Intellectual*, W. H. Allen, 1967.

Melvin Drimmer (ed.), *Black History : A Reappraisal*, Doubleday, 1968.

John Hope Franklin, *From Slavery to Freedom*, Random House, 1956.

S. P. Fullinwider, *The Mind and Mood of Black America*, Dorsey Press, 1969.

Thomas F. Gossett, *Race : The History of an Idea in America*, Schocken, 1965.

Dwight W. Hoover (ed.), *Understanding Negro History*, Quadrangle, 1968.

August Meier, *Negro Thought in America, 1880–1915*, Michigan UP, 1963.

August Meier and Elliott M. Rudwick (eds), *The Making of Black America : Essays in Negro Life and History*, 2 vols, Atheneum, 1969.

August Meier and Elliott M. Rudwick, *From Plantation to Ghetto : An Interpretive History of American Negroes*, Hill & Wang, 1968.

Benjamin Quarles, *The Negro in the Making of America*, Collier-Macmillan, 1964.

Richard W. Resh (ed.), *Black America*, D. C. Heath, 1969.

Armstead L. Robinson (ed.), *Black Studies in the University : a Symposium*, Yale UP, 1969.

Charles E. Silberman, *Crisis in Black and White*, Cape, 1963.

ARNOLD TOYNBEE

Widening Our Historical Horizon

In our time, educators have many tasks that are both pressing and puzzling. For instance, the increase in the number of the sciences, and the concomitant increase in the amount that there is to learn about each of them, is putting a strain on the curriculum in education at all levels. It is the same with the study of human affairs, and with the teaching of this vast and tricky subject.

The expansion of the west European peoples over the face of the globe within these last five hundred years has now knit the whole human race together, for good or for evil. Everything that happens to any fraction of mankind anywhere has now come to be a matter of concern for all the rest of us. We all now have to come to terms with each other and to coexist with each other if we are to save ourselves from destroying each other, and this necessity sets us another huge additional task of studying, teaching, and learning.

In the first place we now have to master as well as we can the most widely used of mankind's almost innumerable languages. We can no longer avoid this problem by scattering, as our forefathers are said to have done when God afflicted them with the confusion of tongues to chastise them for their impudence in starting to build the Tower of Babel. At the moment when our astronauts have out-manœuvred the Almighty by completing the building of the tower, the same impertinent human technology has reassembled us by con-juring up global communications-networks, including launching pads for unmanned missiles with nuclear war-heads, serviced by computers for guiding these deadly missives unerringly to their target. We have also to learn something about the history of the peoples by whom our innumerable languages are spoken; and this history has been written, to some extent, in the national language of every people that has succeeded, so far, in conveying its language in writing. We have to study our fellow human beings' history because we cannot know anyone adequately unless we know more about him than merely what he is today. In order to know him truly, we need to know how he has come to be what he now is; and this is just as true of human beings collectively as it is of individuals.

If this conclusion is correct, then some teaching of world history ought to be part of our educational curriculum at every stage, from elementary education upwards, and, if we concede this, it brings up the same problem as the teaching of science. In history, as in science, the quantity of things to be learnt has become enormous, while the human mind's capacity for learning remains as it has always been. Educational methods may improve, but their improvement cannot keep pace with the immense increase in the size of the field of potential knowledge.

In the domain of history, for instance, we now have to include the history of all peoples that still survive. In order to understand the history of these peoples, we have also to understand the history of their extinct predecessors; and this portion of the historian's field has also expanded. Within the last century and a half, our archaeologists have unearthed half a dozen extinct civilisations whose very existence had been forgotten. They have deciphered some of the scripts – and consequently some of the languages – in which the representatives of these extinct civilisations kept their records and wrote their literature. Meanwhile, our palaeontologists have carried our knowledge of the history of human affairs so much farther back into the past that, on their time-scale, even the earliest of the antique regional literate civilisations come to seem virtually contemporary with the world-wide civilisation of our own day. The human race – or, to speak more accurately, a tiny minority in a small number of societies – has possessed the arts of writing and reading for not more than about 5,000 years. But beyond the point at which, in our upstream exploration of mankind's past, the written records fail us, the dumb record provided by Man's tools continues to run back and back for at least 200,000 years and possibly for more than a million years.

Man's tools are, indeed, as old as man himself. The first of our ancestors who chipped a stone to make it more serviceable was the first of them to become human. Shaping tools is evidence of the reasoning faculty that is humanity's hallmark, and the early human tools have survived in far greater abundance than the bones of their makers. It is true that tools are dumb. Even the Upper Palaeolithic cave-paintings are enigmatic. We have to guess at these great artists' meaning because their accomplishments did not yet include the art of explaining their pictures by sign-posting them with captions. Consequently the amount that we can know about pre-literate Man is tantalisingly jejune compared to what there is to know about his successors who, within these last brief 5,000 years, have possessed the technique of recording, in writing, some account of their thoughts, feelings, hopes, and fears that we, their recent progeny, can decipher. Yet, though the dumb record left by pre-literate Man is relatively unenlightening compared to the self-revelations of us literates, the length of the pre-literate age of human history is so great by comparison with that of the literate age that our collections of Neolithic and Palaeolithic tools add up to quite an appreciable addition to a present-day learner's inventory of what there is to be known about human affairs. You can verify this by visiting the 'pre-history' (i.e. 'pre-literacy') wing of any modern museum.

What are we to conclude from these facts? Has the increase in the amount of potential knowledge about human affairs now condemned us to be unable to know anything about them at all? Is this plethora of potential knowledge going to stick in our throats and so make it impossible for us to chew, swallow, and digest the glut of food that has been shot on to our intellectual dinner-table, the classroom desk? This would, no doubt, be paradoxical, but that would not be evidence that the paradox was unthinkable. Human affairs are full of paradoxes; this is one of their most characteristic features; and education, which is also a characteristic part of mankind's business, is unlikely to be exempt from the danger of getting itself 'snarled' (in the expressive American usage of the word) in knots that human minds themselves have tied.

There is a warning, for present-day teachers of history, in the tragic self-frustration of Lord Acton, one of the grandest of the late-nineteenth-century historians. In Lord Acton's time the quantity of potential historical knowledge was small by comparison with what it is now, yet Lord Acton was smothered and suffocated by even that amount of 'data'. These data, in relatively moderate doses, were 'given' to Lord Acton by the progress of historical research, but the great historian was baffled by the richness of the gift. His output of published work was heart-breakingly small for Acton himself, and is disappointingly small for his fellow human beings. His contemporaries and successors realised poignantly that there died with him a wealth of unwritten books that would have been of immense value – and of permanent value too – to anyone who felt any curiosity about human history, and this whether the would-be readers of Acton's never-published *magna opera* were full-time historians themselves or were representatives of a more useful and more valuable species, the intelligent and cultivated but non-specialist public.

Why was Lord Acton so lamentably unproductive? We know why, and the reason is worth examining, because it touches the heart of the problem that is the common subject of all the contributions to the present book. Lord Acton came to grief because he had set for himself an ideal that was attainable in Dante's day, or even as late as in Goethe's day, but that was unrealistic for any historian who had had the good or bad fortune (our fortune lies, of course, in ourselves) to have been born in Lord Acton's generation. Lord Acton went to work as if he had been living in the generation of Chaucer's clerk, whose library – unusually large for that date – consisted of 'twenty bookes, black and red'. Lord Acton, living when he did, proposed to himself to write a history of human freedom based on the truth, the whole truth, and nothing but the truth – based, that is to say, exclusively on a complete mastery of all the original sources. This ideal in that age was a mirage. Lord Acton saw those illusory waters glistening on his horizon, and he plodded towards them, with all his might, through the fast-accumulating sand-drifts; but of course he could never reach his visionary lakes, any more than a galloping horseman could ever reach the point on his horizon where the rainbow appears to touch the ground.

I had an old friend of my own generation who, in his turn, made Lord Acton's mistake and who paid for it, and as Lord Acton did, made his fellow human beings pay for it. My friend, too, carried with him to the grave all but a fraction of his vast knowledge and understanding of his chosen subject. His case is more flagrant than Acton's, for my friend's chosen subject was a comparatively small and manageable one. Most of the conventional slices of the mammoth-size modern history-cake are bigger than his was, and he had pared down his own slice to the narrowest practicable thickness. He had set for himself rigid and arbitrary chronological limits. Unfortunately, however, my contemporary had also set for himself a still less realistic ideal than Lord Acton's. Lord Acton had proposed to master the original sources for the study of one thread in the history of the sum total of human affairs. My friend had set himself a vaster target in his smaller artillery-range. He had proposed to master, not only the original sources in his allotment, but also the whole of the modern published work – articles and monographs, as well as books – that had been published, apropos of these sources,

down to the moment at which my old friend was setting pen to paper
– setting pen to it, but each time leaving the sheet still blank; for my
friend's ill-advising conscience inhibited him, on principle, from
publishing anything of his own till he had mastered everything that
his confrères had published on their common subject so far. My
friend was as industrious as Acton, but he invariably found himself
falling just short of fulfilling this self-imposed enabling condition of
his; and so he condemned himself to suffer Acton's woeful defeat.

In the vain hope of inducing my friend to stand and deliver, I
used to confront him with an argument which he admitted to be
logically irrefutable but which convinced him without also moving
him to take action. If, I used to put it to him, he – the hardest-
working historian of us all – was unable to keep up with the output of
other people's published work in his field, then manifestly these
others must have failed worse than he had. Therefore, according to my
friend's own principle, these others had no more moral right to have
published anything than my friend himself had. Therefore their
published work was immoral, reckless, and worthless. Therefore,
my friend, on his own principle, had not only the right but the duty
to ignore the whole of his fellow workers' output. With a clear conscience, he could write and publish works of his own solely on the
basis of the original sources, and he knew these by heart. In his field
they are of a manageably small compass. My poor friend used to smile
but disobey. (Here, as will be recognised, I am parodying a famous
sentence in one of the versions of the autobiography of a supremely
great eighteenth-century historian who did publish a classical *mag-
num opus* in the very field in which my poor friend's life-long labours
raised only such a meagre crop.)

Ought an historian to let himself be intimidated by the learned-
ness of his modern fellow workers? I think this question is given a
conclusive answer in the negative by the argument that I have just
reproduced. And what do we mean by 'original sources'? When we
dissect these, we find that they are 'original' only in the sense that
they are at one single remove less second-hand than the pile of
modern publications that rests on them like a huge pyramid that has
been balanced precariously upside-down on a pinpoint. The most
authentically original source that we can think of is a diary, written
up once in every twenty-four hours, of an individual's actions and
experiences, and of his thoughts and feelings about these. Amiel's
Journal Intime is a classic example in real life. But how accurate is the

diarist's memory? And, however accurate it may be, how much that lies stored in it does the mind's subconscious mental censor suppress?

The most original of all the so-called 'original sources' are therefore no more than ludicrously inadequate excerpts from the sum total of the potential data, and we have now to discount, in these excerpts, the warping effect of self-regarding feelings – especially those of them that the psychic censor suppresses for the benevolent reason that, if he did not, these horrors would be too shocking for the conscious surface of the psyche to contemplate. I am still speaking of autobiographies, and of would-be candid ones. Some autobiographies, however, have been written with the deliberate purpose of concealing, instead of revealing, the truth as the author knows it to have been. Caesar's *Commentaries*, for instance, rank as 'original works' in contrast to, say, Mommsen's *History of Rome*, but it does not need a Mommsen to perceive that the apparently artless simplicity of Caesar's published works is the most artful conveyor of propaganda, and that Mommsen himself cannot be sure that he has wrung out of the *Commentaries* a thimbleful of undiluted historical truth.

However, most so-called 'original sources' are not autobiographies, honest or dishonest, and are not even records of contemporary events which could be verified to some extent by interviewing the principal actors in these events and by reading the relevant documents. Besides, the business of verification may prove disappointing. The actors may be evasive; the documents may be withheld from the public; and, even if the documents were accessible, they might be misleading; for official documents are not written in order to provide trustworthy information for historians. They are written for un-academic practical purposes – for getting something done, or, more often, for preventing any action from being taken.

And then, a large part of our 'original sources' deals with events that occurred before the author of the 'original source' was born, and his second-hand record of past history may also be the only survivor out of a number of similar works, the rest of which have perished. But, if his book is in fact the sole surviving account of a particular series of events, we cannot check his statements by comparing them with those of other historians – as, for instance, we can check some of Caesar's statements by comparing them with some of those of his un-hoodwinked contemporary Cicero.

Finally, the student of human affairs, unlike the student of non-human nature, is at the disadvantage of not being privy to the secrets of human hearts, including the secrets of his own heart. So much for 'original sources'; and 'secondary authorities' have already been sufficiently discredited.

This brings us back to the question whether the study and writing and teaching of history are possible. We have already asked ourselves whether it has been made impossible in modern times by the surfeit of 'data'. We are now facing a more fundamental and more formidable question: Is history intractable intrinsically?

This radical question is so alarming that I shall refute the logically almost inevitable answer that history is in truth intractable by producing material evidence that it is not. This was what Dr Johnson did when he was asked whether he could refute Bishop Berkeley's demonstration of the non-existence of the objective universe that a philosophically naïve mind imagines that it apprehends. 'I refute it thus,' said Dr Johnson, and he stubbed his toes by giving a kick to the nearest stone. I am going to refute my own argument that history is inapprehensible and incomprehensible by naming a pair of histories of the sum total of human affairs that have been written and published since the end of the Second World War – that is to say within the recent period in which the amount of potential information about human affairs has become virtually infinite. Each of these books is as tangible as a stone, and the earlier and larger of the two is as heavy as a small stone, so the material evidence that I am offering is as valid as Dr Johnson's.

I am referring to *The Rise of the West* (in its contents, a history of the whole world) and *World History* by Professor William McNeill of the University of Chicago, a distinguished historian of the next generation to mine. I have not revealed the name of my own contemporary who shared Lord Acton's misfortune – and fault – of being tragically and unpardonably unproductive. I am naming William McNeill because I am recommending his work as an example for other historians to follow. McNeill has demonstrated that a panoramic study and writing and teaching of history is still possible today, as it was in the days of Mommsen and Gibbon and Voltaire and Rashid-ad-Din and Juvayni and Polybius, and in the days of the two fathers of history at opposite ends of the Old World – Herodotus in Western Asia and, in Eastern Asia, Ssu-ma Ch'ien, who set the model for the long series of the histories of the successive dynasties of the Chinese Empire.

I have touched on the common reason for Lord Acton's and my unnamed own contemporary's failure. I will now mention what I believe to be two of the reasons for McNeill's success, apart from the first-rate intellectual ability which he shares with my two examples of failure. Ability alone would not have enabled McNeill to attain his objective in this modern age, as is shown by the two cases with which I am contrasting his. As I see it, McNeill has been successful because he has been realistic and because he has been brave. These two virtues are complementary to each other. McNeill has had the realism to recognise that anyone who is setting out to try to take a panoramic view of history will not be able to make a completely accurate and detailed survey of more than a patch of the vast landscape. At most, he will be able to do this in a rather small number of patches here and there. McNeill has also had the courage to take the panoramic view all the same, knowing in advance that fellow historians who are specialists on different patches (and are perhaps no more than that) will be able and eager to make valid criticisms of his survey when this traverses their special preserves. A humble recognition and acceptance of the limitations of the human mind's powers is the first of the two keys to success; the second is *de l'audace, et encore de l'audace*. I underline these two recipes for victory, because I believe that these are the virtues that all students of human affairs ought to take to heart and to practise now and in future.

A *manque de l'audace nécessaire* can be paralysing. I can illustrate this point from the case of an historian of the generation before mine whom I have known personally and whose work I admire. J. B. Bury made his deserved and enduring reputation at a fairly early stage in his distinguished career by writing his *History of the Later Roman Empire*. There was certainly *de l'audace* in this enterprise; for Bury was one of the pioneers in the study of Byzantine history. In a second edition of his *History of the Later Roman Empire*, Bury incorporated the results of the rapid increase, largely due to his own unflagging work, in the knowledge and understanding of Byzantine affairs, but in one point it was disappointing. The first edition had carried the story down to the turn of the eighth and ninth centuries, and thus had spanned the obscure but crucial and fascinating seventh century – the century in which the East Roman Empire had very nearly foundered but had finally saved itself by its own exertions, and had not merely survived but had revived as well in a

rejuvenated form. I had been particularly looking forward to seeing
how Bury, at the height of his powers, would rehandle the seventh
century – only to find that, in his second innings, he had retired at
the year 565.

Later on, I had an opportunity of asking Bury why he had not
refilled the gap. (In the meanwhile, he had already published a
separate book covering the years 802–867.) He excused himself by
pleading that the first version of his *History of the Later Roman
Empire* had been an early work in which he had been youthfully
incautious. He had ventured to write about the Arabs' assault on the
Empire without knowing Arabic and therefore without being able
to read the essential Arabic sources in the original. He had been too
old to cope with learning Arabic by the time when he had got down
to writing his second version, so this time his scholar's conscience
had counselled him to break off at the death of Justinian I. As I
listened, I felt – much though I revered Bury – that, this time, he
had made an error of judgement. In his youth he had had *de l'audace*,
and a splendid pioneer work had been the reward. In his maturity he
had become too cautious to have *encore de l'audace*, and now, in his
old age, it was too late. *Toujours de l'audace* – Danton's climax – had
been too much for Bury. He had not Danton's nerve.

  If history is philosophy teaching through example, I have been
behaving like an historian so far. Now I will play the amateur
philosopher. I will make a generalisation. I will suggest a nostrum for
treating the malady by which the study and writing and teaching of
history have been overtaken in my lifetime, so it seems to me. I
suggest that, if history is to rejuvenate itself, as the Byzantine
Empire managed to do, we historians must practise the virtues that
I have been preaching. We must have the humility and the courage
to be, and to recognise that we are bound to be, no more than
generalists in our survey of the greater part of our vast field. I will
now add that we must also have the intellectual integrity and the
scholarly precision and industriousness to make ourselves specialists
as well in some part or parts of the field, however small.

  To be a specialist in some patch or patches is as important as it is
to be a generalist in the rest.; and, like the virtues of humility and
courage, the two intellectual tools of specialisation and panoramic
vision are complementary to each other. The generalist needs to
know, to emulate, and, as often as he can, to attain, the specialist's
standards. If the generalist does not thus keep himself up to the

mark, he will be justly accused of superficiality and inaccuracy by his fellow historians, who are going to accuse him of these faults, whether justly or not, in the present climate of opinion among those historians who think of themselves as being 'professionals'. Conversely, the specialist cannot afford to be blind to the generalist's panoramic outlook. If the specialist blinds himself to this, he will not see his own special allotment as it really is; for, if he looks at it divorced from its setting, his view of it will be distorted, however minute his scrutiny of it may be. A combination, requiring a compromise, between the eagle's and the lynx's kind of vision is the *sine qua non* for success in studying, writing, and teaching history, whether generalism or specialism happens to be the historian's personal bent. A felicitous compromise, in proportions corresponding to the historian's personal genius, has been one of the causes of the success of every one of the eminent historians who have been mentioned in this essay.

Addiction to history needs no justification beyond itself. If the historian, under fire from philistines, is driven back into his last ditch, his ultimate and impregnable line of defence is that history is fun, and that fun is its own reward. However, the teaching of history is a form of taking action, and therefore two considerations that apply to action of all kinds hold good, among other kinds, for history teaching. One of these points is that there is in every case a propitious moment for taking action. This moment has to be apprehended by intuition; there is no rule of thumb for calculating it; but when the moment arrives, though not till then, it has to be seized. Taking action too late will make the work miscarry just as surely as taking action too early. The second point is that writing, like other forms of action, will be meaningless if it is not directed towards somebody for some purpose. A writer of history must address his work to a public with an eye to meeting this public's needs, and the historian's proper public has been designated in this essay already. The cultivated and intelligent but non-specialist public is the one to which the historian will address himself with the greatest profit both for this public and for himself. *Œuvres de vulgarisation*, in the ironically laudatory French usage of this French term, will be more fruitful than esoteric works that can be appreciated only by adepts in the same line of professional business. If this is good advice for writers, it must be good for teachers too. Teaching is more obviously a form of action than writing is, and the teacher's public cannot ever be a hand-picked company of middle-aged specialists.

Finally, historians – whether they are writers or are teachers or best of all, are both – have no more right than scientists have to immure themselves in an ivory tower and to get on with their work there regardless of the social consequences. History tells us that historians, like scientists, do have an impact on society, and if the historian is a teacher, his impact is direct and immediate. Nineteenth-century historians undoubtedly were effective politically. They deliberately stoked up the fires of nationalism, and the consequence is that these fires are still raging today, when we have been carried by the scientists into the Atomic Age. In this age mankind must learn to feel itself to be a single family and to live together in the bonds of unity and peace, inspired by a family-like mutual affection. The alternative, sooner or later, is mass-suicide; and there the historian – again like the scientist – has a practical responsibility. His practical task in our time is to help his fellow human beings to save themselves from the social malady with which a previous school of historians has afflicted them. The student and writer and teacher of history ought to strive now, with all his might, to widen his public's historical horizon; and, to do this, he must begin by widening his own.

2 New Emphases

D. C. WATT

Twentieth-century History

During the twenty-five years since the end of the Second World War the teaching of the history of the twentieth century, or at least of the period since 1914, has become steadily more acceptable in British universities, an acceptability which is being reflected in the growth of interest in the same period in schools and in school examinations. This growth has been greatly aided by the alteration in the Public Records Act of 1958 introduced in 1967, which is about to open to general research the records of Britain for the period of the Second World War. But that alteration was itself made in response to the determined lobbying of a group of university historians, and reflected (as does the increasing tendency of university courses to reach beyond 1945 to the middle of the 1950s as their terminal date) a new historical drive towards that ever-receding frontier of history, the present.

This is not to say that the teaching of recent and contemporary history has become completely respectable as yet. The subject still tends to be taught more in university departments of politics than in departments of history *per se*. And the older universities, on the whole, tend to lag behind the municipal universities in their attention to the advance of the historical frontier, while a number of the new 'plate-glass' universities appear to have been distracted from the pure tasks of the historian into programmes of combined studies, in which the needs and discipline of contemporary history, as well as its peculiar problems, can easily be submerged in one of the several single-valued approaches to the study of contemporary society now popular among the more progressively-minded sections of the academic community. Nevertheless the foundation of the Institute of Contemporary History, with its journal, and its international role in the coordination of study and research into the field, and the establishment of the Association of Contemporary Historians as a pressure group and as a means of communication between the various widely-scattered practitioners in the field, show that the subject has won thorough acceptance – even though part of the cost of this is that much of what passes for contemporary history is ceasing to be contemporary, while much of what is becoming contemporary history is only being very slowly opened to historical work.

In practice new ground is opened to historical study in four successive movements. The advancing frontier of the present is first explored by a mingled group of semi-independent research institutes and other less objective organisations and individuals, polemical journalists, revolutionary-minded academics operating often outside the bounds of their own discipline, writers drawn by the lure of a current controversy, politicians, soldiers, pundits anxious to establish their own version of events as a platform for future activities or as a justification of past actions. It is this mêlée of polemic and prejudice that has won contemporary history so dubious a reputation in the past; though, on the whole, the work of the university and independent research institutes, and of commercial organisations intent on providing as accurate and detailed records of events as possible, provides a shining if often neglected exception to the rest.

Behind this wave, or to vary the metaphor, this combination of genuine explorers, claim-jumpers, land and resource strippers, plain rogues, posses and vigilantes, there comes the first wave of university teachers. Their task is the establishment of a first narrative, from whatever sources are available, partly in book form, partly for use in their lecture courses. They can call on memoirs, articles, government statements, press accounts, and the like, and their academic obligations are to apply the principles and methods of their discipline to establish a body of historical hypotheses which will stand up to the demands, both scholarly and pedagogic, of university teaching.

An example of this is the history of the Suez crisis of 1956, now taught in several university courses of contemporary history. The crisis provoked a splendid outburst of contemporary polemical writing both in French and English, among which must be mentioned Paul Johnson's *The Suez War*, T. E. Utley's *Not Guilty*, John Connell's *The Most Important Country*, Robert Henriques' *100 Hours to Suez*, Randolph Churchill's *The Rise and Fall of Anthony Eden*, Erskine Childers' *The Road to Suez*. This was to be followed by others ranging from Merry and Serge Bromberger's *Secrets of Suez*, the 'revelations' of two French journalists, and Anthony Nutting's *I Saw for Myself*, the polemic of one of the victims of the crisis, to Professor Herman Finer's assault on the American Secretary of State, *Dulles over Suez*, an early example of that academic desertion of academic standards which is now so marked a feature of revisionist polemics on the cold war and the conflict in Vietnam. A marked exception to this is the American professor Leon Epstein's *British Politics and the Suez Crisis*, a dispassionate political analysis of the effects of the crisis on British politics. This was to be followed by a considerable pause, during which the memoirs of Anthony Eden, *Full Circle*, the diary of General Dayan, *Diary of the Sinai Campaign*, the memoirs of President Eisenhower, and other important source material became available. The only academic work of any respectability to cover the crisis during this period was the Chatham House *Survey of International Affairs, 1956–58*. A third stage began with the publication of two important investigations, one, *Crisis*, by the Canadian journalist, Terence Robertson, who clearly drew on extremely high-level sources in Canada and France, the other by Professor Hugh Thomas of the University of Reading, *The Suez Affair*, based on the painstaking collation of personal testimony from British and French sources. Since that date more important memoir material has become available, together with a biography of Sir Pierson Dixon, British representative at the United Nations during the crisis. One article has attempted to assess the Soviet role, Oleg M. Smolansky, 'Moscow and the Suez Crisis 1956', *Political Science Quarterly*, 1965. Any university teacher seeking to establish his own narrative for lecture purposes does not now want for material even though clearly there are a great deal of *lacunae*, especially on the Egyptian and Soviet sides of the story.

This stage must last until at least 1976 when the American publication of their diplomatic documents, *Foreign Relations of the United States*, should begin to reach the year 1956. This may be expected to provoke other documentary publications until 1987, when the operations of the Public Records Act will open British government records. This is the period of serious evaluatory research in which the hypotheses, myths, *idées reçues* and the like established over the previous two decades, will be tested and examined in the light of major primary documentation. It is the stage of the graduate student, the thesis, the learned monograph.

From this develops imperceptibly the fifth and last stage, that of the historical re-evaluation, when the crisis can be fitted into the whole history of the 1950s and the post-war period. Only then can one begin to say that it has really been seized by the historians and abandoned by the polemicists. But that is no reason for failure to study it or teach about it before.

What the historian has to face in the course of his own pioneering work is not only the technical problems of the materials available for the construction of a first narrative of events but also problems of perspective and scope. So far as the issue of teaching and research in advance of the release of official documentation under the various national and private equivalents of the thirty years' rule is concerned, professional historians are now reasonably agreed that they cannot afford to leave the field to those who used once to enjoy a monopoly of it. The absence of the professional historian does not prevent contemporary history being written, or becoming, via one of the various channels of public communication, part of the received pool of what is generally taken to be historical knowledge. It simply prevents it being written according to the accepted canons of historical probity.

Arguments of equal strength apply to the introduction of the subject into university teaching, preferably in the later stages of an undergraduate's career. The problem with the student is not one of inducing a sense of historical perspective. This problem, which looms so large in the minds of professional historians, is taken care of by the simple arithmetic of education. The third-year under-graduate of today, aged twenty-one or -two, was six to seven years old in 1956. His active span of interest in contemporary events is five to seven years maximum, three to four years before reaching university. Events before that period are as distant and unimaginable in the twentieth as they are in the twelfth century. A decade of popular neophilia has also swept away much of the sense of history and historical continuity which is so essential a component of the study of history. Conditions, political, technological, economic, strategic, have changed so radically that to a great many of today's students, history is irrelevant. This feeling, if anything, is enhanced by the failure of much teaching in contemporary history in Britain to go beyond 1940 or at best 1945. These 'finest hours' of British democracy in their external and domestic political aspects, are thus made the culminating point in British history, the history of a once-great power. Nostalgia, romanticism, escapism on both an individual and a national scale, linger and return to the period of the Second World War. Thereafter all is drab and humiliating decline to the present about which, today's young activist feels, at least something can be done. It is urgently necessary therefore that contemporary history with its emphasis on continuity as well as change should not halt in 1940 or 1945 but should advance into the post-war years.

But to do this, British historical writers have to take the lead in coming to terms with the period of decline in British power which followed 1945, with the formation of the Anglo-American alliance and the real costs paid for this by Britain, with the traumas of decolonisation and the retreat from supremacy in the Middle East and with the failure of Britain's European policy. In part this will require a realistic assessment of the degree of British decline, one that will steer firmly between the super-patriotism of the right and the exaggerated abandonment of all power by the left – one, too, that will assess clearly the psychological manifestations brought by the decline in British opinion at all levels from cabinet and shadow-cabinet members to the terms of popular debate on the mass media and the evidence of opinion polls. There are signs in some contemporary writing on Britain as a medium-rank power that the beginnings of an adjustment of thought are in progress – but the comparative absence of writings of the school of partisan approach (G. K. Young's *Masters of Indecision* is an exception) devoted to the whole rather than individual incidents in the last twenty years, suggests that we are only at the beginning of this process. There are few enough surveys of British foreign relations since 1945 anyway, so the job of teachers and providers of first narratives has clearly only just begun.

Part of the problem is one common to all history of the twentieth century, one which faces teachers of history as well as historical writers both academic and lay. This is the question of the scope of history to be written or taught, or, to put it another way, the nature of the viable historical unit to be studied, not viable in time so much as in space. Put crudely the choice is often seen as one between British history and world history. The former is no longer adequate – indeed is increasingly a misleading area for historical explanation. The latter is often so complex as to defy any breakdown into pedagogically manageable units. To teach and study British history in isolation is to become increasingly parochial in outlook and to encourage a trend towards parochialism already so thoroughly entrenched in the mass media that the pupil needs to be actively influenced against it. The division of the world, much like the divisions of Mohammedan international lawyers, into the abode of light (Britain in this case) and the abode of darkness (the remainder of the world) encourages the kind of view of the outside world as one where it should be Britain's principal aim to reintroduce morality, which is so very marked a feature of the world inhabited by the young today, deeply concerned as they are with the morals of Vietnam, Biafra, the Middle East, yet almost completely and wilfully ignorant of the politics involved.

The alternative to national history is often seen as world history, a term used to imply a universal approach that is in practice one which academic historians find extremely difficult to command. The real difficulty is to define the nature of the 'world' of which the history is being studied; a second difficulty lies in the degrees of regional specialisation imposed at the higher academic levels by linguistic and other requirements. The result is that courses in world history quickly become only very partially connected histories of separate regions or studies of revolutionary movements, militarism in politics, economic colonialism and the like which offend against every sense of the comparative approach to history, if indeed they are not clearly inspired by an ideological desire to see similarities so as to demonstrate some single-valued view of history.

The solution is not an easy one since it demands a good deal of thought as to the nature of a historical unit and the purposes towards which a particular unit is selected for study or exposition. The balance of opinion will probably settle for the study of coherent units such as western and central Europe, Soviet and eastern Europe, the Middle East, south and south-eastern Asia, mainland China and its borderlands, the United States and its Atlantic and Pacific frontier lands; schools and university departments of history concerned with general and non-specialist courses will have to make a choice of units for study between these. One would hope that the choice would light *most frequently* on the first, second and last of these units, though there are powerful forces operating in education today likely to drive choice towards the study of those units to which British opinion still feels superior because of their internal troubles, their recent emergence from colonial status, their backwardness. This view, which makes history the servant of the legitimate concerns of Oxfam, is only one instance of the particular problems which beset contemporary history, problems of choice in which moral and moral-political considerations have to be resolved.

The study of contemporary history was, for long, frowned upon by orthodox historians because of their doubts as to the possibility of objectivity and perspective. For the young, perspective, as already argued, presents no problem. But for the mature teacher and researcher it is as real a problem as that of objectivity. Both require a continuing effort to master, one which is neither easy nor particularly rewarding in terms of popularity. The true contemporary historian moves among his subject like an anthropologist among the tribesmen of Papua, neutral, detached, his professional ethics in control of his personal ones, concerned to understand rather than to condemn. He is, and must regard himself as, the vanguard of future historians. This by no means implies that he must try to project himself into the minds and values of those who will come after him. That way leads at least to Utopianism; at most, and, much more frequently, to an awful identification with the trends of the immediate present, than which there is no quicker road to obsolescence of outlook. It does mean, however, a degree of detachment from the present, a reminder that history is, among other things, one long record of man's inhumanity to man, and that the problems of power, decision, communal integration and diversification may wear different masks according to the time and place of their manifestation, but are none the less an inherent part of the human condition throughout recorded history.

The true contemporary historian has to be compared with his much more frequently encountered opposite, the man for whom history is, in the phrase of a Soviet historian, 'politics projected into the past', and who is concerned to fight again, in the light of new evidence, the battles of the past. Much past writing, for example, on the history of 1931, on the era of appeasement, and most of the work of the so-called revisionists now writing on the origins of the cold war, falls very thoroughly into this category. It is part of the motives which drive people into the study of contemporary history that they were once *engagés*, if not *enragés*, in such controversies. (It is disturbing however when they are joined by those who are far too young to have taken part in such battles, but who, like the 'instant historians' of the First World War, or some of the younger writers on appeasement, seem only too happy to adopt as their own the outlooks of their ancestors.) Such belated participants, whether *ancien combattants* or new entrants, fulfil most aptly Talleyrand's comment on the Bourbons returning to France in 1815, that they had learnt nothing and forgotten nothing. There is a very strong imperative on contemporary historians not to allow such a continuous distortion of the facts, such a misuse of the name and processes of history to such partisan purpose. This imperative requires a constant re-examination of the terms in which historical examination of the controversies is conducted, a deliberate suspension of judgement while all sides of the controversies are considered, and then, and only then, a pronouncement which in itself can only be tentative, hypothetical, conditional.

An example of this of a peculiarly difficult kind is the assessment of Soviet motives in the years 1944–5 in their approach to the question of a post-war settlement, one crucial to the revisionist controversies over the origins of the cold war. The view accepted at the time and in the early 1950s was, at most levels, a fairly simple version of one or other of the theories of Soviet expansionism, either that which saw the Soviet system as rendered expansionist by the universalist nature of its ideology, or that which saw the Soviet system as following the course of expansion set by Czarist Russia, the drive for a warm-water port, the drive to control the Danube basin, the drive to re-create, under Russian leadership, the line-up of 1815 or 1873, the Holy Alliance of Alexander I or the *Drei-kaiserbund*. The new revisionists seek to substitute for this a state inspired basically by fear of outside pressures, born of a hostile social ideology, reacting to such pressures by seeking to occupy the strongest defensive position available. Both are versions of a war-guilt thesis, both reflect an ideological position projected out of current political attitudes and anxieties. Neither is respectable in historical terms, since they clearly substitute for the historical concept of responsibility, witting or unwitting, the judicial or quasi-judicial concept of guilt.

The idea of war guilt has been the greatest boon as well as the greatest curse to contemporary historians. The War Guilt clause of the Treaty of Versailles provoked the publication of the major documentary series from the different foreign offices. The Allied determination to arraign the Nazi leadership on the charge, hitherto unknown in international law, of conspiracy to commit aggressive war, resulted in the major release of documentation on the origins of the Second World War. Historians are still far from having completely exploited the first, let alone the second of these. But the idea of war guilt also perverted historical study of the origins of the First World War for a generation or more; while the second has become one of the great historical obsessions (not only of British historiography) from which history is only just beginning to shake itself free.

The teacher of history in schools finds himself, through all this, faced with a very considerable set of pedagogical problems. The first is simply the product of the pace of historical research in areas of the greatest historical interest. The university historian himself who attempts to lecture on British or European history even in the inter-war period is confronted with a constant flow of documentation and monographs in any of the four major languages of Western Europe alone. General textbooks on the period were, until recently, ten years behind the current state of research even at the moment of their appearance. Publishers were unable to find any major academic figures willing to commit themselves to extended studies of the period, save for a few established controversialists like A. J. P. Taylor in the field of European history, or Arthur Marwick in that of British social history. This gap between research and general textbook is beginning to narrow, as the rate of significant research is beginning to slacken a little and the process of digestion of materials researched is more attractive to the new generation of historians now reaching maturity. But the problem has only moved from the inter-war period to the decade of the 1940s and 1950s. It is no nearer solution for the university or sixth-form teacher; and it is in the nature of the beast that this should be so.

This is particularly true of interpretive versions of crises. An excellent illustration of this is the Rhineland crisis of 1936, of which it is repeatedly stated that the German troops who entered the Rhineland were under orders to retreat if France sent her own troops into the Rhineland to restore the *status quo*. From this the conclusion is drawn that Hitler would have been forced to climb down, that he might well have been overthrown, and that if that happy event had occurred, there would have been no Second World War. The second part of this version of events is, of course, purely hypothetical. The first part, on which it relies, is untrue in one vital particular. Those troops which crossed the Rhine were, it is true, under orders to retreat if they encountered French forces. But it was to have been a fighting retreat, and the German military orders made it clear that the outcome of such a French action was to be war. Whether or not this would have been adhered to in practice, whether, faced with the consequences of misjudgement, Hitler would have withdrawn and his generals overthrown him, is another matter. There is, at the moment, no evidence whatever to suggest that there was an alternative regime either planned or ready to emerge, easily or quickly, had Hitler's gamble been shown to be mistaken. But it will, no doubt, take a decade or more before this version is eliminated from the textbooks. Part of the task of the contemporary historian is precisely this, the continuous removal of accepted myths, for which there is, on the whole, no evidence but their continued assertion.

Another difficulty with which the school teacher is faced is that in the study of contemporary history the student is brought up in the strongest form possible against the contrast between written history and the unknowable past. The contrast introduces a range of philosophical-logical problems about the contingent nature of historical statements, the canons of verification employed by historians, the degree of subjectivity which is acceptable or not in historical writings, which may be entirely foreign to his previous intellectual development, and with which he may not be equipped to cope, unless care is taken to provide him with such equipment. The desire for certainty is often so strong today as to induce a total rejection of history as such, or an acceptance only of those parts which can easily be accommodated into the current view of life. The student grows up, regarding the history he reads as something inherently true, or if not so, then obviously so false as to be immediately recognisable. The authority of his schoolmaster is accepted as unconsciously in this as in mathematics. By the time he has entered the sixth form he will almost certainly have been introduced to the idea that historical interpretations and attitudes can differ, and that it is up to him to decide, to make up his own mind on the facts available to him. But he will still accept that history is concerned with ascertainable, verifiable 'facts', even if he has abandoned the over-naïve view summed up in variants of the phrases beginning 'history shows that . . .', 'history proves that . . .', 'the verdict of history is . . .' and so on. The discovery that history is concerned with 'statements' which can only be judged by canons of consistency and plausibility, rather than 'facts' which are 'true', is a major hurdle that many students, in the writer's experience, have not encountered, let alone surmounted, by the time they reach university. Such hurdles are far more difficult to evade in contemporary history, where irreconcilable and contradictory statements are far more frequently encountered than in the historiography of earlier periods where interpretations rather than historical statements of an evidential kind are the main points of disagreement.

This is not to say that the student of contemporary twentieth-century history should not be concerned over interpretation or that he should concern himself simply with 'establishing the facts' and 'leaving the facts to speak for themselves'. That is, of course, an attempted evasion, which, in practice, is simply a commitment to whatever interpretation is already sufficiently established as to condition the way in which the evidence is presented to the student. One obvious theme is the intermingling of nationalist and ideological considerations in the history of the period after 1919; so that to one school of contemporary observers the main theme of international politics was a world-wide, or at least Europe-wide, struggle between the forces of populist democracy, social democracy and socialism, the cause of 'the people', against the forces of social reaction, élitist conservatism, aristocracy, plutocracy and fascism; while the others saw only nation-states in pursuit of traditional national interests clashing over the control of Europe. One thinks of Churchill's comment in 1943 that the war was becoming less ideological, and Roosevelt's reported belief that the populist nature of his government and the American system would make it easier for him to communicate with Stalin than it would be for Churchill. Behind this lies a more general contrast between conservatism and revolutionary movements, in which historians so far have devoted an altogether disproportionate amount of attention to revolutionary ideas, especially those of Bolshevism, and conservatism has been lumped together with the equally revolutionary ideas of integral nationalism in its variously Fascist forms. Social catholicism lacks any really first-class study, the conservative legal view of international relations from the establishment of The Hague Court to the European Economic Community is hardly commented upon, the conservative tradition in social welfare from Neville Chamberlain and Lloyd George's borrowings from the German Empire to the employer-based welfare of Federal Germany's *Marktwirtschaft* remains virtually unknown. The history of ideas has hardly caught up with the perspective of the 1970s; but the theme of parliamentary and legally regulated democracy, of the *Rechtstaat*, as against the arbitrary use of power for political ends, is central to any study of the internal politics of Europe between 1919 and 1970.

A second theme that emerges almost unbidden, and certainly as yet insufficiently emphasised, from the history of Europe since 1919, is the development of a common European culture, a common social, political and intellectual consciousness, examined with great skill for the years 1890–1930 by the American H. Stuart Hughes in his great work, *Consciousness and Society*, a work far too little known in Britain. As European influence in the external world waned and began to retire, so the political societies of Europe, despite, as well as because of, the ravages of two world wars, began to grow together. A European élite began to emerge, on the fringes of the underground resistance at first but sufficiently able for its non-revolutionary wing to be carried into office at the end of the 1940s throughout Western Europe. Its forerunners were the diplomatists, politicians and bureaucrats of the 1920s meeting regularly at Geneva for the League of Nations and the International Labour Office or at Basle for the old Bank of International Settlements.

A third theme is that of the rise of the super-powers each with its amalgam of ideology, revolutionary tradition, revulsion from and attraction to Europe, each to some extent professing a native political system which represents a heretical form of one of Europe's two rival political traditions, that of the constitutional and parliamentary *Rechtstaat* and that of the benevolent autocracy, a dictatorship of absolutism, of monarchy transmuted in Soviet Russia into a dictatorship of the party, each swinging between intervention in Europe and isolation, withdrawal from Europe. These are the super-powers of today lying across Europe's maritime and continental frontiers, balanced against one another around the globe by a balance of destructive capacity, yet in armed contact with one another only on European soil. The rise of the super-powers still needs to be studied in much more detail than it has been yet.

Another theme that deserves isolation is the decline of Imperial Europe and the growth of nationalism, decolonisation and anti-colonialism, the rhetoric of independence and the reality of economic aid, even the colonialist contribution to decolonisation and local nationalism, from the early break-away Christian Churches out of which have come so many variants of African nationalism through the reformist elements in Arab Islamic nationalism in North Africa, Egypt and Syria, to the British contribution to Indian independence and the French legacy in Indo-China. Indeed it is difficult to see how 'world history' in this century can be taught in any other terms.

A final theme is the transformation of world politics from the conferences of great powers of the 1890s and 1900s to the United Nations of today, with the impact of two world wars. The wars themselves have perhaps taken more than their fair share of historical attention, the just and the unjust elements in both remaining a fascinating study in the development and deterioration of international morality. As an instrument of social and technological change, war became for the first half of the twentieth century the single most important social institution. Since 1945 a multitude of small wars have replaced the world war, though without any of the developmental side-effects the world wars brought in their train. The Cold War has played its part, it is true, in promoting the movement towards European cooperation and in maintaining the uneasy leadership of the two super-powers in their respective Atlantic and Eurasian spheres of influence. It is perhaps too early to say. But the wars of the past need an infinitely greater and deeper analysis than the present debate over the justification of war can ever provide. Historians cannot simply condemn or ignore war, practising their own version of *inter armis silent leges*, or leaving total war simply to battlefield historians. The whole development of the discipline of war studies, in which historians have played so major a part in Britain, would make that impossible.

To conclude: the history of the twentieth century, of the contemporary world, is for historians and history teachers an especial challenge. It taxes their professional ethics most strongly, it demands a particular clarity about the nature of historical argument and the character of historical statements, it faces them with peculiar problems of identity and perspective. Yet it has a peculiar fascination too, that of working on or close to the frontier at which history is in a state of continuous creation, the present. The contemporary historian is the midwife of history. It is only just that this responsibility should call for particular professional care.

Further Reading

James L. Henderson (ed.), *Since 1945 : Aspects of Contemporary World History*, Methuen, 1966.

D. C. Watt (ed.), *Contemporary History in Europe*, Allen & Unwin, 1969.

D. C. Watt, Frank Spencer and Neville Brown, *A History of the World in the 20th Century*, Hodder, 1967. (To be published by Pan Books.)

Geoffrey Barraclough, *An Introduction to Contemporary History*, Watts, 1964.

Max Beloff (ed.), *On the Track of Tyranny*, Vallentine, Mitchell, 1961.

PETER MATHIAS

Economic History – Direct and Oblique

Economic history – as its hybrid name acknowledges – has always been an eclectic subject and hence much influenced by the ideas, techniques of study and assumptions prevailing in neighbouring social science disciplines. For some 'pure' historians economic history has even been cast in the role of a Trojan horse – infiltrating new subversive forces of theory into the historical camp. In reality, of course, all history relates to adjacent disciplines – medieval political history, for example, being meaningful at only a superficial level without some awareness of theology, philosophy and law. But the neighbouring disciplines which have enjoyed grazing rights over economic history – there are no sharp methodological frontiers fencing off these separate subjects even though examination syllabuses impose artificial boundaries at a practical level – have been 'political economy', economics, and increasingly sociology. Collectively they have given the subject a greater theoretical impetus and a greater commitment to quantitative evidence than other branches of history. We can predict that these two trends – a greater emphasis on theory and a more systematic search for quantification – will characterise the subject in the next phase of its growth, though the implications of the latter may increasingly challenge the claims of the former.

A consequence of the rapid pace of research which characterises economic history, as in all subjects where the frontier of knowledge is receding fast, is that new work is more likely to surface first in the learned journals than as books. With the 'problem explosion' in the subject has come a 'journal explosion', with many new periodicals being founded and economic history invading all the main journals in history and economics and having a presence in many devoted primarily to other disciplines and in the proceedings of local archaeological societies, once a curious world dominated by flints and fossils. Some short cuts through the forests are now given by sets of readings which bring together important papers previously scattered through the journals.[1]

Such collections have their dangers in presenting selected and predigested material, but teaching needs demand such instruments for bringing inaccessible material to students so that the choice is not between producing sets of readings or not producing them; but only between doing this well or doing it badly.

FACTS AND FASHIONS

Of course, much work in economic history, as in any other sort of history, remains a rather more humble brick-making exercise – adding to the pile of data that are known about different sectors of the economy. The elemental quest for new facts and case histories of little-studied areas is still active. Studies of topics like distilling, machine tools, the armaments industries, the boot and shoe industries, the electrical industries, the hydra-headed branches of the engineering industries in the twentieth century, oil and chemicals are all in train just within the limits of industrial history. The list could be greatly extended. This continuing accumulation of a larger fund of information is not to be separated from the more theoretical orientation of the subject. Old-style narrative factual history – the antiquarianism of facts for their own sake – has never taken a subject very far (however deceived its practitioners may be about the values and assumptions they bring to their search for data). At a certain level of popular interpretation the business of economic history was assumed to be to paint in the economic strokes on the general historical canvas of an age – to supply facts about the material apparatus of life at different times. Political history was to tell us that Alfred burned the cakes, and when this misallocation of resources took place. The job of economic history was to describe the kind of oven he used and the sort of flour then available. By and large social history is only just emerging from a similar condemnation to servitude by collecting 'facts' about social customs, costume, folk-lore etc. which made it a dirty word (or at least a vulgar pursuit) amongst professional historians. Economic history is not a 'bundle-subject' – a gathering of facts about an institution or an industry. It is, above all, a 'problem subject', problem orientated. As M. M. Postan said long ago: 'Economic history ends at the point at which the facts cease to answer questions . . . and the more completely the problems dominate the search for facts, the nearer is the study to the true function of history in social science.'[2]

These general assertions do not say very much about the nature of the problems which are giving new orientations to economic history: and problems are not presented to the historian naked, but clothed in the assumptions, modes of analysis and the style of research current in the disciplines that gave them birth. The influence is very much more specific than the simple truth (also relevant to trends in economic history) that work in history so often borrows its fashions from the contemporary world. With headline news given each month to changes in the gold reserves and a full armoury of state intervention deployed to curb imports, raise exports and inhibit foreign spending it is little wonder that economic historians began to question the interpretation, cast in the shadow of free-trade prosperity and the truths of classical economics, that mercantilist policies were just the result of simple intellectual confusion or a conspiracy of vested interests. Nor, with the population 'trap' in which many present-day developing countries are seen to be so plainly caught, is it surprising that the role which demographic development has played in sequences of economic change in times past should become a major topic of research. The same is true of agricultural change, 'popular' movements and riots, education and a host of newly fashionable themes. What afflicts the world of today inspires the Ph.Ds in the economic history of tomorrow.

THE SEARCH FOR QUANTITY

As influential in shaping the progress of an academic discipline as the topics upon which it focuses is the mode of research which these demand. Here the search for quantity is changing the face of economic history more than any other single influence, more particularly because this becomes itself the means to implement an intensified concern with theory. Economic history, of its nature and from its beginning, has always been more concerned with quantities than have other kinds of historiography, as almost all inaugural lectures have acknowledged. '. . . it is the obvious business of an economic historian', wrote Clapham, 'to be a measurer above other historians.' Indeed the pre-history of writings in this field, back into remote times, is cluttered with work that has little of critical value, simply because it consists of haphazard collections of quantities – jackdaw-like accumulations of figures, whose unreliability is matched only by the uncritical conclusions drawn from them. They survive as important evidence of the motivations of their authors, and sometimes as a valuable quarry from which to hack data: but quantities without structural and critical evaluation are as analytically disorientated as opinions without evidence. There is no defence in numbers alone.

In a subject concerned with outputs and prices, volumes and flows, with processes of historical change affecting populations, social and occupational groups, industries, agriculture, trades – all the facts which are subsumed in changes in the level of performance of economies rather than with the individual actors in a sequence – quantities feature prominently even where the object of the inquiry is the simple narration of change. At this level, however, a statistical series is just a piece of narrative in a different notation, not a different intellectual exercise.

More systematic quantification (even though at a much less sophisticated level) began in the inter-war years, with an international project in price history, the study of economic fluctuations and in the work of the *Institut für Weltwirtschaft* at the University of Kiel.[3] Fluctuations also provided the field for some of the early post-war research which sought to base serious theoretical discussion on a foundation of more systematic statistics – Professor W. W. Rostow making an important break with tradition with the publication of *British Economy of the Nineteenth Century* (1948). A highly-sophisticated detailed investigation is that by R. C. O. Matthews, *A Study in Trade Cycle History: Economic Fluctuations in Great Britain 1833–42* (1954). Not accidentally all these trends were led by scholars moving into economic history from an original training, and from an academic base, in economics rather than history. This was the trend of the times.

Even though figures have been deployed for the most part to produce simple, basic series of raw data and piecemeal evidence in the service of factual narrative, the flood has been enough to elicit the remark that it has become more important for economic historians to be able to count than to read. But quantification is now assuming more ambitious objectives and is becoming so different in degree that the results commonly become changed in nature. The new style of research demands knowledge of statistical, if not econometric, techniques and requires systematic data. Historical demography, for example, has become a leading field in this new-style quantification. Piecemeal or literary evidence – the observations of contemporaries, however well-informed and shrewd they be – cannot yield objective truth, save by luck, about national (or regional) rates of change of population, or reveal any of the dynamics of population growth.

Contemporaries simply did not have the means of basing their opinions on systematic data and the fact that Shakespeare (or any dramatist or novelist) made his heroines marry at the age of thirteen, like Juliet, is evidence only of what some current opinion may have been about the age of first marriage of women. Such opinion could have been widespread, and would not have been uninfluential perhaps in affecting policy, but this does not mean that it was true.

The implications for such labour-intensive (and machine-intensive) research like that currently in train with demographic history, are inescapable – the use of computers and machine processing has become a precondition for calculations on this scale. To be accomplished it is likely to need collective work by a research team, with research assistants and clerical help, enjoying considerable financial support; and to be understood it requires awareness of basic demographic and statistical techniques. These are not necessarily more intellectually demanding than other sorts of techniques but they create a new sort of technical barrier, so that comprehension is not attainable simply through the application of higher common sense. Such systematic quantitative analysis, with its consequential statistical processing, will be characterising new historical research into such topics as literacy, the occupational analysis of towns and local populations, the analysis of social origins of entrepreneurs, changes in standards of living, rates of capital formation, the measurement of productivity gains from technical change, annual values of overseas trade and the like. The hallmarks are systematic data upon which to base rigorous statistical analysis. The point is simply that many unresolved questions in economic history are such that the only intellectually satisfying answers are, by definition, quantitative. (There are many other unresolved questions where intellectually satisfying answers will remain unattainable.)

The search for quantification, let it be said, will require much *more* critical evaluation of sources – the hallmark of traditional professional historical skills – not less. The greater the extent of mathematical processing being applied to data, the greater the premium upon knowing the reliability of the sources, or the potential degree of error built into them. The new techniques rest more heavily than social scientists commonly acknowledge upon the traditional expertise of the historian: the skills of both disciplines are complementary to each other rather than substitutable. Quite apart from the question of reliability of the original data, the longer the time-span over which a series runs the greater the effect of qualitative change upon its constituent parts and the more cumulative the changes in the institutional context. When statisticians speak of 'index number' problems in series which measure accurately only quantitative change in homogeneous data they are acknowledging the historian's dilemma in seeking to assess qualitative change.

The search for quantity-comparable quantities is also creating new interests in comparative economic history. Much of this research is not heavily dependent upon theory but rests upon Clapham's elemental demands to know how much, how fast, how representative. The formidable problems of producing comparable data from the highly individual statistics of different nations (quite apart from changes in the comparability of data over time, which are daunting enough for any single national series) make this equivalent to searching for identical twins in a football crowd. Not surprisingly it has required an international research effort – masterminded by Professor S. Kuznets. For all the doubt clinging to the reliability and coverage of some of the figures at least there now exist the general silhouettes – to make no greater claims – of the evolving economies of most of the advanced industrial nations – the United States, Great Britain, France, Germany, Canada, Australia, Sweden, Norway, Denmark, Italy, Russia amongst them.[4] We can compare their changing economic structures (the proportion of the labour force, capital, contributions to total output etc. from agriculture, industry and services) over time, rates of growth, share of government expenditure and foreign trade in total spending, capital investment, productivity and the like. Equivalent comparative studies are now emerging for evolving financial structures.[5] Thus some sort of rough-hewn typology is becoming known. Analogues, comparisons of structures, relationships and rates of growth in different countries at different phases of their economic evolution will be able to be made with greater assurance than in earlier empty hypothesising about 'stage' theories of history. A new prospect of comparative history is being opened up. Statistical and structural similarities (even identities), however, do not reveal of themselves the nature of the relationships between the variables. The oldest serpent in the historian's Eden has been the injunction 'Post hoc ergo propter hoc.' Imputing causation from correlation is as injudicious in history as guilt by association in law. Again, the traditional discipline of the historian should complement the technique of the social scientist. The search for quantity is orientated by the lodestone of theory, to which we must now turn.

THE 'NEW' ECONOMIC HISTORY

The 'new economic history' so called – the word 'cliometricians' has also been coined for its practitioners (not as an insult!) – involves more than systematic quantification. This provides the necessary basis for more recondite calculations which are essentially designed to test hypotheses and 'models' which seek to reveal the way in which the different variables in a situation interact, or the relative importance of various constituents contributing to economic change. On this foundation, economic history is seen in a new synthesis with economic theory.[6] A 'model' (which can be expressed either in geometric form, or beyond a certain level of complexity in algebraic formulae) is constructed, which represents the mode of interaction of the different variables. This can be elaborated mathematically, extrapolated over time with historical data for some of the variables, and a simulated result produced for a later situation, according to the relationships built into the model. Correlations can be made to test the importance of each element – to measure the relative contribution of each to the final result. Highly sophisticated econometric techniques employing mathematics beyond ordinary calculus have been used in such formulations. It is impossible in this context to elaborate them but reference to certain studies will at once reveal the nature of the techniques.[7]

Certain of the basic assumptions necessary to this theorising have been contested; for example, that the real income of different social groups accurately states their net contribution to the total product when seeking to measure the contributions of – say – education to a particular rate of economic growth; or that, when measuring the contributions of improved transport to economic growth, resource saving can be measured by assuming that freight rates were equal to marginal costs and that marginal costs were constant. However, the central idea, when carried to its logical conclusion, provides an intriguing challenge to one of the central assumptions of the methodology of history. It has usually been said that history can never be 'scientific' in its demonstrations of proof simply because we cannot play the record over again to see what *would* have happened had one variable in a historical situation been different. A control experiment is thus impossible. No exactly comparable situation exists to provide a scientific comparison. There are no verbatim repetitions. But now the cliometricians have claimed that, in certain instances, a 'counter-factual situation' can be constructed which will allow the gap to be measured between what actually happened and what *would* have happened had a variable been different. It is this general methodological point which has brought the new economic history most specifically to the attention of historians in general. Professor Fogel, in a now famous study, undertook this exercise when seeking to measure the contribution of railways to the expansion of the American economy in the nineteenth century.[8] He constructed his model of the American economy operating just before the railways, building into it the rates of growth, demands for capital investment and labour etc., with the transport costs and efficiencies of the canal and road system. He then extrapolated the growth of this 'model' economy, reallocating the capital that, in fact, went into the railways into extra canals and making many other sophisticated assumptions. These projections were made to measure this 'counter-factual' non-railway economy in 1890. When compared with the national income of the actual American economy in 1890 (with railways) the difference would represent the resource saving, the extra growth brought by the railways – in fact a *measurement* of their contribution to American economic growth.

Quite apart from whether the answer obtained – about one per cent – is true (and many arguments will continue about this) the investigation was a methodological exercise of the first importance. Even greater argument will rage about the legitimacy of its assumptions about such things as the costing of alternative canal transport. By having to ignore the direct effects of the railways upon the mobility of people (as opposed to freight) and their indirect effects upon such things as technical change, the location and organisation and efficiency of business, growth of financial institutions and the like, 'counter-factual situations' of this degree of generality, spanning so long a time, must be robbed of significance. In this sense a precise arithmetical conclusion gives a false sense of precision to the exercise. But in terms of first principles (avoiding all the actual methodological problems about the assumptions used in the model and the operational problems of finding data to fit it) the cliometricians can argue that they are doing no more than to test, in a measured way, judgements passed by the most empirical historian.[9] When any judgement is made that railways were 'important' or 'the most important single instrument of American economic expansion', or that tariffs had a 'major effect' upon the role of growth of American industry, or that slavery was 'inefficient' or 'unprofitable', a 'counter-factual' situation is implied. One is saying that things would have been significantly different had that particular variable been changed; that one item in a historical situation was significant relative to other items as a cause of change. Whether explicit or unconscious, taken instinctively or on the basis of piecemeal evidence or by 'historical judgement', such assertions nevertheless contain assumptions about the interrelationship and order of importance of different variables.

The new techniques seek to make these assumptions explicit and to set up data and equations to enable them to be measured and tested. The 'new' economic history can thus claim to stand in the tradition of Bacon and a noble line of scientific endeavour concerned to measure, to test and to prove. Undoubtedly the search for quantity will be intensified as the years pass. The more ambitious claims of the new methodology, however, are likely to be fulfilled only within fairly restricted inquiries: the narrower the time-span, the more restricted the range of change under analysis, the more complete the data, the more limited the number of potential variables involved then the more legitimately rigorous mathematical analysis can be applied. But the potential degree of error multiplies as each of these qualifications is relaxed. And the problems of relating variables in any would-be 'general' model of development raise more methodological issues than just a critical evaluation of the raw data inputs and the logical consistency of its algebra.

THEORIES OF GROWTH

The search for quantity and the incursions of statistical and econometric techniques into economic history, which heralded the entrance of statisticians, economists and econometricians as historians, is to be explained primarily by the new interest aroused in economic history through its relevance for the study of economic growth. Since 1945 the problems of engineering economic growth in the underdeveloped countries of the world (supported by more local concern about lagging rates of advance in some 'maturing' industrial economies) have provided a profound new impetus to economic theory and, at the operational level, to development planning for stimulating economic growth. The leading edge of research in economic theory swung sharply from the study of short-term equilibrium problems to those of long-run growth. It is not accidental that the slump and high unemployment of the inter-war years in the industrial economies of the world, with the dislocations this caused for the primary produce suppliers in the international economy, should dominate the attention of theorists in that genera-tion. In motivation, if nothing else, the most abstract of theoretical economics usually relates to the practical problems of its own age.

All this is commonplace. Not quite so well known beyond profes-sional circles is the profound effect which this reorientation of economic theory has had, and continues to have, upon economic history. It has operated in two mutually-stimulating ways. Clearly, Britain, with the other advanced nations of the modern world, had industrialised in the past, experiencing a modernisation which has now become the main object of economic policy for the rest of the world. The British historical experience thus became of profound interest to economists as the first case history of industrialisation. Secondly, economists and others looking at the constraints upon growth in the present sought to understand the process of growth – to isolate the variables, analyse the various relationships involved in the development of an economy. How was an increase in population related to the process? In what ways were economies being held back by the failure of agricultural development? What role did investment play? What rates of capital formation were necessary? How profound a constraint did shortage of domestic savings impose? What was the most logical taxation policy to further growth and industrialisation? How did urbanisation contribute to economic costs and gains? Profoundly important practical decisions stood to be made in answer to these questions, which were given coherence by their formulation in theoretical, conceptual arguments. By pro-viding such a focus of interest and such a new fund of ideas and of theory, the economists made economic historians rework their conceptions about their craft. This has changed the nature of what economic history is about; it has set off research in new directions, led to new sets of questions being asked of old data and started a hunt for new material given significance by the new problems and relationships suggested.

To argue in the economists' terms of economic growth meant measurement of national income, industrial production, agriculture and trade, the balance of payments, population, capital formation and other things, for the ultimate pay-off of the infinitely complex process of growth can be expressed as a single aggregative statistic – a percentage rate of growth for the economy as a whole or a *per capita* figure – and so for sectors of the economy, individual industries etc. When interest focuses upon the relationship between one aspect of change and the process as a whole, a new incentive also exists for comparative history – of seeking, in a general way, to compare the operation of a particular variable in different contexts so that similarities and contrasts may stimulate insights into the processes of change.

To date, the importance of theory from the social sciences has lain mainly in suggesting new ideas, new relationships, new questions to be asked and new data to be sought in the light of them, rather than in any total adoption of formal models, techniques or conclusions. The shortage of data, the different context in which a historian works, the very large number of factors involved in large-scale change (some quantifiable, others not and each being responsive to the rest in some degree) preclude the employment of many techniques and the precise testing of models. Much greater precision is now possible in testing the relationship between strictly economic variables. However, the sort of evidence required for rigorous sociological analysis – which usually comes from the questionnaire and the detailed interview – is very much less available in historical data, where the inquirer must take what he can find rather than being able to arrange for the production of data to suit his inquiry. But, even so, greater precision to some degree will doubtless become available for testing the strength, or relationships, of social or psychological phenomena (such as the 'need for achievement'). These modes of analysis will still remain very different from the econometric analysis of economic variables. The intractable problem remains that of constructing a unitary analytical scheme which can comprehend economic and non-economic phenomena. In fact social science techniques on the larger historical canvas – it will be different in more limited investigations – are held at bay as much by the methodological difficulties as by the operational problems of applying them. Economic history will remain a synthesising discipline at this level. Scientific in its intentions, necessarily conceptual in its explanatory apparatus, the limitations of data and the multiplicity of influences upon change condemn it to remain a depressingly inexact science.

NON-ECONOMIC HISTORY AND THEORY

One further twist in the interplay between history and theory has widened the range of potential relationships considered applicable to the explanations of economic change. From this leads a new path which is surely destined to become a high-road for new research. The terms of reference of 'economic history' in British universities have traditionally included the words 'and social'. Often this has meant little more than studying poverty (particularly the legislation and public administration invoked by poverty), the standard of living, the institutional development of the labour movement and the impact of industrial and urban life upon the human conditions. That is to say, social changes were studied in the main as the consequences of economic change. No longer. Social and cultural relationships are now being invoked as a dynamic in the process of industrialisation, analysed in their relation to the process of growth, whether as forces for inertia or for change.

One older hypothesis has survived, much battered, into this new era of research – Weber's thesis of the Protestant ethic (though now adapted rather more to Huguenot and non-conformist, Quaker and Unitarian sects in the eighteenth century than to Calvinists in the sixteenth in order to be on stage when the industrial revolution, rather than old-style 'capitalism', began). The new concern with the social and cultural matrix in economic history is partly the search for new knowledge, particularly when so many unanswered historical questions are being thrown up by rapidly expanding research in sociology and demography. Sociologists armed with new interests and new skills have been coming into economic history, treading the same road as the economists and econometricians. History is always there, after all, inviting study by those of any professional skill wanting to follow their craft back into its past – be they scientists, doctors, lawyers, sailors, or candlestick makers, quite apart from social scientists. Historians may be forgiven sometimes for thinking that these separate histories are too important to be left in the hands of their practitioners, who not uncommonly develop an interest in their profession's history only after retirement as active members of it, and having exhausted their critical and professional energies in pursuit of their earlier careers.

A more specific impetus, however, lies behind the increased interest that economic historians now have for social and cultural matters. Not accidentally, it corresponds with new concepts in theorising about economic development. Most early 'modern' theories of economic growth (with industrialisation seen as a prime aspect in most case histories, as well as in most theories, of growth) centred upon exclusively economic hypotheses and relationships – capital, labour, resources. Non-economic variables came into the act with population growth or the entrepreneur but they scarcely entered into the analysis.[10] Like political or institutional change they were either seen as responses to economic change, being dependent variables, or as outside the terms of the theories as 'givens', 'exogenous variables'. More recently social scientists other than economists, and some economists themselves, disillusioned by the search for an illusory 'general theory' of growth in economic terms, acknowledged that the process was not to be analysed in terms of economic variables alone (even though the result was measurable in terms of increased national wealth and income per head).[11] Clearly, economic development had become too important to be left even to the economists. Some economists even declared that the main constraints upon the advance of the economically backward nations were non-economic. At the same time, others seeking to measure the contributions to total growth from different sources declared that only a modest fraction of the total rate of growth achieved could be traced to increasing inputs of capital, labour and resources – at once extending the range of potential analysis and inviting a hunt for the 'residuals', as they were called, of such contributions as technical change, economies of scale, the growth of knowledge and education.[12]

Political scientists, sociologists, demographers, education theorists, and psychologists have come into the act, on their own account and by this front door being opened for them by economists, and have demanded the use of a less specifically economic term for the subject, such as 'modernisation of traditional societies'. This is the springboard for research into the social aspects of industrialisation and economic change – social relationships affecting the process of growth in a causative way – which is now coming as a flood of 'growth-oriented' research: demography, social structure and values, family and kinship, education, law, motivational analysis, management, the growth and structure of demand (much influenced by social structure and cultural traits).[13] All these are now high on the list of fashionable explanations for growth (or absence of growth). From the entrepreneur the road has led upwards to less-embodied regions of 'entrepreneurship' and 'the spirit of entrepreneurship'. New psychological theories have been propounded about 'achievement motivation' and status attainment through economic achievement by disprivileged social groups.[14] Different ways of bringing up children, as well as the knowledge and motivations imparted by particular styles of education, have suddenly become relevant things for economic historians to discover. All these, and many other topics, studied intensively, will put more specific content into generalisations about the role of social and cultural relationships in economic growth. If economic historians have taken most of their new ideas in the past generation from economic theory, it is a reasonable prediction that they will be taking much from sociologists in the next.

MICRO-STUDIES

The demand to see processes of economic change in the round has given new life to local history and brought very much higher academic standards to it, evidenced by the establishment of a chair and a department of local history at Leicester University. Problems of manageability – the difficulties of handling so many relationships at the national (or wider) level – establish a logic of micro-studies, where processes can be analysed 'at the grass roots' in the units through which social and economic changes were being accomplished. The 'national economy' is an unreal fiction as the appropriate initial unit of study for understanding many of these processes (though for others, such as the study of economic policy, it is obviously an appropriate one). Very great contrasts existed between the fortunes of different regions and different sectors of the economy – as variations in wage-rates, prices, local population movements etc. indicate. In such a situation a 'national average' created by aggregating local data may hide more significance than it reveals. Thus, quite apart from the fact that a smaller unit than the national or industry level may be more feasible to study, it may also prove more appropriate. The accumulation of capital, labour recruitment, business leadership, demographic change, transport development and a host of other themes are being explored intensively in such micro-studies. The focus for research can be a locality, or a firm, a family or group of families, a particular occupational group.[15] Business history, urban history, transport history and historical demography are enjoying, and will continue to enjoy, great activity as a result of this. Perhaps the fastest-growing sector of all in local history is 'industrial archaeology'. Quite apart from its intrinsic attractions as a research activity, its academic results to date have ranged from pure antiquarianism – the cataloguing of local detail for its own sake – to adding a new dimension to the history of technology.

All such 'micro-studies' have temptations to antiquarianism built into them. Any single one of them also raises the questions 'how representative; how untypical?' of the wider grouping in which each 'cell' is placed – the parish within the county, or the region, the firm within its industry, the family within its social group, the canal within the collectivity of other canals. But, at best, if 'micro-studies' are undertaken with a view to investigating the wider processes of change, which operate through such local units, they will be 'microcosmic' rather than 'microscopic' in significance. And, as the numbers of local case studies builds up into representative samples, they will provide the basis for much more reputable national generalisations than have been possible to date.

We may safely predict that new trends in economic history will enhance the importance of measurement and theory; that most new ideas will probably come in the immediate future, as they have come in the past, from the neighbouring social sciences. But the historian's critical standards will remain the test of those hypotheses and the data to which they have to be applied. In history, at least, the conceptual has to be brought to the test of the empirical.

Notes

The documentation of this chapter has been limited to primary British sources.

1 As series see *Debates in Economic History*, Methuen, 1967–; *Problems and Perspectives in History*, Longmans; *Essays in Economic History* (3 vols), *Essays in American Economic History*, *Essays in European Economic History*, Edward Arnold.

2 M. M. Postan, *Historical Method: an Inaugural Lecture*, Macmillan, 1939, p. 14.

3 W. Beveridge *et al.*, *Prices and Wages in England*, vol. 1, Frank Cass, 1965; J. A. Schumpeter, *Business Cycles*, McGraw, 1939; W. G.

Hoffmann, *The Growth of Industrial Economics*, Blackwell, 1931, 1958; W. G. Hoffmann, *British Industry 1700–1950*, Blackwell, 1955; W. Schlote, *British Overseas Trade from 1700 to the 1930s*, Blackwell, 1938, 1952.

4 The main survey volume (which gives a bibliography) is S. Kuznets, *Modern Economic Growth*, Yale UP, 1966. See also, amongst many other national sudies, P. Deane and W. A. Cole, *British Economic Growth 1688–1959*, CUP, 1962, 1967; which induced as a 'useful by-product' B. R. Mitchell and P. Deane, *Abstract of British Historical Statistics*, CUP, 1962.

5 See R. W. Goldsmith, *Financial Structure and Development*, Yale UP, 1969; R. E. Cameron (ed.), *Banking in the Early Stages of Industrialisation*, OUP, 1967.

6 For discussion about the methodological and theoretical claims of the 'new' economic history see: J. R. Myer and A. H. Conrad, 'Economic Theory, Statistical Inference and Economic History', *Journal of Economic History*, 1957; R. W. Fogel, 'The New Economic History; its findings and methods', *Economic History Review*, 1966. The most comprehensive review of American research within the new style is M. Lévy-Leboyer, 'New Economic History . . .', *Annales*, 1969.

7 See, for example, R. W. Fogel and S. L. Engerman, 'A model for the explanation of industrial expansion during the nineteenth century: with an application to the American iron industry', *Journal of Political Economy*, 1969.

8 R. W. Fogel, *Railroads and American Economic Growth: Essays in Econometric History*, OUP, 1965; 'A quantitative approach to the study of railroads in American economic growth', *Journal of Economic History*, 1962.

9 As an example see A. H. Conrad and J. R. Myer, 'The economics of slavery in the ante-bellum South', *Journal of Political Economy*, 1958 – the pioneering work.

10 The entrepreneur is an exception, being taken as the active agent of change in Schumpeter's book *The Theory of Economic Development* of 1911, which appeared in an English edition in 1934.

11 See amongst a long list, W. A. Lewis, *Theory of Economic Growth*, Allen & Unwin, 1955, pp. 12–17; W. W. Rostow, *The Process of Economic Growth*, OUP, 1952, chapter 2; B. F. Hoselitz and W. E. Moore (eds.), *Industrialisation and Society*, UNESCO, 1960, especially chapter 15; B. F. Hoselitz, *Sociological Aspects of Economic Growth*, Collier-Macmillan, 1960.

12 See M. Abramovitz, 'Economic growth in the United States', *American Economic Review*, 1962; 'Resources and output trends in the United States since 1870', *American Economic Review*, 1956; R. M. Solow, 'Technical change and the aggregate production function', *Review of Economics and Statistics*, 1957; E. F. Denison and J.-P. Poullier, *Why Growth Rates Differ: Post-war experience in nine different countries*, Allen & Unwin, 1968.

13 See for example in economic history: H. Perkin, *The Origins of Modern English Society 1780–1880*, Routledge, 1969; D. E. C. Eversley, 'The home market and economic growth in England, 1750–80', in E. L. Jones and G. E. Mingay (eds), *Land, Labour and Population in the Industrial Revolution*, Edward Arnold, 1967; N. J. Smelser, *Social Change in the Industrial Revolution*, Routledge, 1959; R. Bendix, *Work and Authority in Industry*, Harper & Row, 1956; S. Pollard, *The Genesis of Modern Management*, Edward Arnold, 1965.

14 D. C. McClelland, *The Achieving Society*, Collier-Macmillan, 1967; E. E. Hagen, *On the Theory of Social Change*, Tavistock, 1963.

15 See for example of 'micro-studies' allowing intensive analysis: T. C. Barker and J. R. Harris, *A Merseyside Town in the Industrial Revolution: St Helens 1750–1900*, Frank Cass, 1959; J. D. Chambers, *The Vale of Trent, 1670–1800*, CUP, 1957; T. S. Ashton, *An Eighteenth-century Industrialist*, Manchester UP, 1939.

E. A. WRIGLEY

Population, Family and Household

In a recently published book Professor Elton remarked that the
historian 'must choose a main theme', and that 'there are two chief
considerations that really determine the main theme: the availability
of evidence, and the need to find a theme sufficiently dominating to
carry the others along with it'. In practice, he argued, political
narrative is usually the best main theme to choose. Other possible
themes, like sheep-farming or doctrinal debate, do not run 'clean
down the middle'; do not involve a large enough fraction of the
population, or relate to a large enough part of the available evidence.[1]

As an omnipresent institutional form, even the state is hardly a
rival to the family. The influence of the family in shaping men's
habits of thought and action, in furthering or constricting change,
has always been immense. In the family into which a man is born
he learns attitudes of mind, modes of conduct, ideals and taboos
which, as head of a family of his own, he will later pass on to his own
children. If the criterion of the importance of a theme to history is
the proportion of the population it involves, and its centrality to
other historical themes, then the history of the family need fear few
rivals. The practice of sociologists and social anthropologists in
their studies of contemporary communities underlines the strength
of the family's strategic position in studies of social change, class,
the socialisation process, and political and economic behaviour. Is
the slightness of writing on the history of the family due to a failure
of historians to appreciate the importance of the theme? Or is it
due simply to the lack of evidence?[2] For sources are to history what
oxygen is to the lungs. Without adequate sources interest drains
away from a topic, no matter how central to history it may seem in
the abstract.

Many historians are too little alive to the importance of the history
of the family. Unfamiliarity with the theoretical literature about the
family as an institution has played a part in making them blind to
the opportunites of analysis which their sources offer to them.[3] Yet
the evidential problem is much more important and also helps to

account for lack of interest and expertise. In this chapter I shall describe recent advances in research techniques which are increasing the volume of evidence about the family in the past, and say something about what has recently been accomplished and the opportunities and difficulties ahead.

We may first note that there is a very close tie between the surge of interest in the history of the family and the parallel growth in historical demography.[4] The connection is partly a matter of theoretical overlap and partly a result of dependence upon the same research techniques. A description of recent changes in historical demography, therefore, will serve to cover both population and family history.

Population history can be as leaden a subject as any in the whole lexicon of historical studies. Where it is a compilation of population totals and sub-totals, relieved only by quaint contemporary accounts of the onslaught of epidemics, it is seldom either fascinating in substance or intellectually challenging, or even easy to relate to the chief economic and social changes of the time and place. For many years now, however, a sea change has been coming over the subject, as social and economic historians have searched for ways in which to make better use of the available sources, moved by a conviction that population movement and characteristics were at once an excellent index of changes in economy and society and themselves at times a major cause of change. Chambers and Goubert, for example, each dealing with a fairly small area in England and France respectively, showed how vividly the use of demographic data can illuminate social and economic change, and how necessary a knowledge of demographic history is to the appreciation of pre-industrial stagnation (in the case of Goubert's Beauvaisis) or the beginnings of industrial growth (in the case of Chambers' Trent valley).[5]

Traditional population history relied upon aggregative methods, upon totals of population present, upon the sum of children born, or people dying. Its methods were those of the national census bureaus, and depended on the discovery of a source like a census and a source like vital registration. If both could be found all was well since then rates could be calculated. For example, if both the total of legitimate live-born children in a given year, and the number of married women aged 15–49 is known, a *marital fertility rate* can be calculated. Unfortunately, to find sources of both types is rare, especially before the mid-nineteenth century, and if either was lacking, the other could serve only a small number of purposes adequately.

In the middle of the 1950s, however, there was an addition to the armoury of techniques of using historical sources for demographic purposes of such importance that it enabled the subject to change gear, so to speak. The technique is known as family reconstitution. As this technique and others like it have developed, the tie between population history generally and the history of the family has grown much closer.

Family reconstitution using vital records and also some recently developed methods of analysing census material differ in several ways from traditional methods. First, the basic method is nominative, not aggregative. Information about families is built up from sources, like the parish registers, in which individuals are named. All the records of birth, death and marriage relating to a particular family are brought together and consolidated into a single record. When this has been done the fertility and mortality of the reconstituted families can be investigated in great detail, and very intricate demographic analysis is possible.[6] This is only possible, however, if father and son, aunt and niece, or for that matter unrelated people who happen to have the same names, can be distinguished in the documents and the information about them placed in the appropriate family record. Thus, whereas in aggregative work all men, women and children are faceless, in nominative only the fact that they can be identified allows the work to be done.

The second point springs from the first. Once a nexus of information about a family has been built up (the family reconstitution form, or FRF, on which this is done forming the skeleton of subsequent work) any other nominative source can be tapped and information from it concerning the family in question can be added to it. For example, Poor Law records may show the family to have been in receipt of relief or contributory to the rates. The register itself may make clear the occupation of the household head; and so on. The more the bare demographic structure is filled out with other detail, the greater the range of topics which can be explored with profit. By noting how frequently a bride and her groom came from different socio-economic groups, the nature and extent of social mobility in the community may be studied. Where nominative listings are available, the extent of the exchange of offspring as servants between households may be traced (the variation in size of the household between different groups in the community in pre-industrial England was largely a result of this exchange whereby the wealthier households employed and supported many children of poor parents whose responsibilities and resources were correspondingly reduced).[7] The same sources will show how often households containing three generations, or kin outside the conjugal family, were to be found. The relationship between, say, age at marriage and economic opportunity may be investigated; or the differences between eldest and and other sons; or the impact on individual families of harvest failure and epidemic. Nominative methods provide a descriptive framework not only for population history and the history of the family taken separately, but also for the interplay between the two in their social and economic setting.

The very first family reconstitution study carried out by Henry on the bourgeoisie of Geneva illustrates this very well. It was a purely demographic exercise in conception, but shows almost in spite of itself how nominative record linkage both suggests questions of more general interest and holds out fair hopes of solving them. Fig. 1 plots the dramatic changes in fertility which occurred among Genevan bourgeois families between about 1550 and 1750. The reason for the upsurge of fertility in families where the husband was born 1600–49 may have been the wider adoption of the practice of putting babies out to wet nurse. A mother who is suckling a baby is less likely to conceive than one who is not. At all events the average interval between births fell and fertility rose sharply.[8] For bourgeois families a sudden increase in family size brings difficulties. It means more dowries to be scraped together for daughters, more positions to be found for sons. And the standing of a family is damaged by any failure to provide a suitable start in life for its offspring. If the resources of bourgeois families are growing too slowly to provide for larger families, one solution is to restrict family size.[9]

For Henry the chief interest of the data he used lay in the opportunity it gave him to make an elegant analysis of the demographic characteristics of the Genevan bourgeoisie crowned by the demonstration of the wide adoption of family limitation in the early eighteenth century. He made no attempt to investigate the social and economic pressures which moved individual couples to adopt new habits of family formation. But he went quite far enough to show that the same framework of analysis which produced such remarkable demographic data could support equally important research into the history of the bourgeois family as a social and economic unit as well as a reproductive unit. Family papers, wills, diaries, business records, and so on, when linked to the skeletal family history brought together for demographic purposes all serve to make clearer who marries whom and in what circumstances, how property is accumulated by young parents only to be dispersed

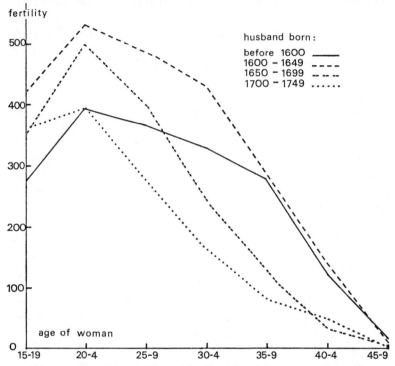

FIG. I : Age-specific marital fertility among the bourgeoisie of Geneva (children born per 1,000 women–years lived).

again among their offspring as they grow to adult years, why too large a family meant difficulties, whether the pressures in large families produced downward social mobility, what were the typical life-cycle stages through which individuals passed in the families in which they were brought up and the families which they formed by marriage, and so on.

There is a third aspect of the development of new methods in population history which deserves to be stressed: their flexibility.

This makes information collected about the family in the past relevant to much more than the history of the family, for when families are combined into groups other things may be studied. The family is a building block with which many structures can be made. If the occupation of family heads is known, the age at marriage of craftsmen may be contrasted with that of the gentry. The structure of urban households can be compared with those in the countryside. (For example, in what circumstances were resident kin commonly found in households in the new industrial towns where they would not be found in the rural areas from which many of them came?) The social, economic and demographic characteristics of migrants may be compared with those of the stay-at-homes. And so on. Until a society in a given period has been described in detail so that the nature of the differences between it and other societies are known with precision, it is idle to think of improving our understanding of the historical change. Impressionistic treatment of historical description inevitably tends to be accompanied by wayward analysis. We must push as deeply beyond easy, but often vapid, generalisation as the sources permit. What were the differences between areas of partible inheritance and those where more conventional inheritance customs prevailed? Did the property transmission from one generation to the next which took place before the death of the household head offset testamentary dispositions? How was the timing and age at marriage of sons and daughters affected? Was there a greater (or less) tendency to migrate to the nearest town? Or again, did enclosure, so much in the legislative eye and so dear to the pamphleteer's heart, lead to changes in population size, rates of growth, occupational structure, house and farm construction, etc.?

The number of historical topics which will show up in much sharper focus when examined by micro-analytic methods related to the family is legion. But one should not forget the wood in picking out some of the more interesting trees. For there is also a general issue of massive and fundamental importance to all modern European historians, and of peculiar relevance in England where the industrial revolution took place. It is the question of how similar pre-industrial western Europe was to other traditional societies. A pre-industrial society is, by definition, one in which there is little or no tendency for real income per head to grow. It is a society in which, to borrow a very convenient concept from communications engineering, negative feedback predominates. Just as a ball-cock in a cistern or a thermostat on a wall operates in such a way as to cause any departure from an equilibrium state to be offset by changes which bring the system back to where it started from, so in a pre-industrial economy incipient growth tends to provoke changes which frustrate sustained expansion. Why was western Europe able to escape this cycle of events (which Malthus, amongst others, thought inevitable)?

It is idle to expect a simple solution to so vast a problem but the study of the history of population and the family has unearthed some suggestive differences between early modern Europe and other traditional societies. In most societies a girl marries young and few are still spinsters at twenty. In western Europe in the sixteenth, seventeenth and eighteenth centuries very few girls were married at twenty and the average age at first marriage was in the middle or later twenties.[10] In Colyton in the late seventeenth century it touched thirty.[11] Men in general married still later than women. Whereas an African or Asiatic family might be shamed if a daughter was still unmarried and yet well past puberty, an English family viewed marriage in a different light. In general a man was justified in marrying only when his circumstances enabled him to set up a separate establishment (it was almost unknown for a young couple to begin married life under a parent's roof). The acquisition of property or mastery of a craft might justify marriage, but attaining manhood did not. This circumstance is linked to the remarkable number of adolescent boys and girls and young men and women in service (usually more than a tenth of the population of a parish) – the great pool of mobile labour whom Laslett has called 'the nubile unmarried'. By prevailing English habit, therefore, women passed in marriage only about half the period of their lives during which they were capable of bearing children. On the other hand a substantial proportion of their active lives was spent without responsibility for dependants. Late marriage, by reducing fertility, may have helped to preserve a relatively favourable ratio of resources to population while at the same time producing a lifetime pattern of saving and expenditure more favourable to economic growth. When more is known about these matters and of the changes in them which occurred during industrialisation, the industrial revolution, the event which made the world as we know it today, may be easier both to describe and understand. So much more than economic growth is involved in this process that an institutional form like the family which reflects a wide sweep of social and economic experience and activity, is an excellent unit to use in the study of the phenomenon.

But we must return finally to sources. They offer great opportunities, set new problems and dictate severe limits to the extension of population and family history.

The limitations which the sources impose are straightforward and seem insurmountable. The methods described earlier in this chapter can work only where there is a large bulk of nominative material, a source like the parish registers or the enumerators' books from the mid-nineteenth-century censuses. Such sources do not in general exist in Europe before the sixteenth century (English parish registers, for example, begin in 1538). Even then they are often only sporadically available, or are kept in too little detail to be helpful for many decades. Many issues must therefore be picked up in mid-stream. For example the late age at marriage which distinguished western European populations from others was already apparently common in England in Elizabethan times.[12] It would be immensely valuable to know when and how it became normal. But the absence of nominative sources of a suitable type before 1538 greatly reduces the likelihood of a fully convincing history of the establishment, perhaps even of the dating, of the new pattern of behaviour. Similarly it is much harder to discover the extent of social mobility in medieval times or the details of exchange of children and adolescents in service between households, and other indicators of family and social structure. Indeed such a gross and simple statistic as the mean size of household is a matter of lively and inconclusive debate.[13] Medieval demography is even more shot through with uncertainties and as yet there is no prospect of firm information about major demographic characteristics like expectation of life or marital fertility, still less about pre-nuptial conception rates, illegitimacy or, say, the effect on fertility of high infantile mortality.

If the history of population and family promises well, therefore, its promise is none the less circumscribed by the high threshold level of information which it requires if its most illuminating techniques are to take hold. Early modern western European history may benefit greatly, but remoter periods will gain much less directly, though indirectly they may gain rather more since a knowledge of the significance of social demography and family structure in the seventeenth century may help to introduce a more delicate shading into the discussion of parallel questions in the fifteenth century, or even the thirteenth.

Where nominative sources are abundant there is often a difficulty at the other extreme to that just discussed. For then there may be an *embarras de richesses*. The family reconstitution of Colyton, 1538–1837, for example, involved filling in 30,000 extraction slips, and the collation of the information which they contained on 5,000 FRFs, before demographic and social structural analysis could begin. To reconstitute a parish of this size by hand takes several hundred man-hours of skilled work and is expensive also in printing costs, paper and photo-copying. And Colyton is but one parish among the 10,500 ancient parishes of England. It is a prime virtue of sources of this type that they cover the entire population, not simply the well-born, wealthy and literate. But it is at first sight a virtue so laborious that it might seem unlikely to find many willing to practise it. To be oppressed by too great an abundance of information, however, is seldom as severe a trial as to search for it in vain. Indeed the problem of superabundant data is causing historians to adopt and adapt methods whose worth has been proven in comparable circumstances in other subjects.

Two of these may be mentioned since their potential importance is so great. First, the use of appropriate sampling methods can cut the labour entailed in exploiting a big body of documents to a tiny fraction of what would be necessary if each document were separately examined. For example, there may be tens of thousands of families present in a city on census night and for each family a detailed entry in an enumerator's book. Yet by examining one family entry in a hundred the characteristics of the population may be defined with only marginally less accuracy than if the whole mass were used, but only if the sampling design is appropriate (*mutatis mutandis* the same is true of any large body of documents in standard forms – farm leases, wills, tax assessments, etc.).[14] Second, modern electronic computers with random access facilities to disc packs are well able to deal with large masses of alphanumeric data. They are not just 'number-crushers' but can be made to store, structure, sort, correct, collate and process information which is a mixture of names and numbers. Thus names, dates, ages, occupations and relationships of individuals can be input onto magnetic tape (from parish registers, census records, enclosure awards, poll-books, tax records, and so on). The information can then be manipulated very much more quickly, more accurately and more exhaustively than by hand.[15]

Neither of these tools is useful only in the history of population and the family but few branches of history stand to gain more from developments of this sort. What has been achieved so far is the elaboration and testing of a set of rigorous conventions necessary to articulate all there is in the records about the vital events in the life of an individual or family. This gives precision to the investigation of the demography of populations in the past, and thus a fillip to historical demography. But it also provides a splendid foundation for the general history of the family and household structure since the same documents provide details of both and they can be buttressed by many other types of nominative record. Enough work has been done on these lines to allow some intriguing hypotheses to be adumbrated, but the body of substantive work is still in most cases too small to permit decisive conclusions. Quite enough work has been published, though, to leave no doubt that this is not work in which tedious detail is the enemy of provocative new concepts, nor unfamiliar techniques at odds with the main aims of historical analysis.

To be paradoxical it might be said that working in this vein historians are given a chance both to have their cake and eat it. It is a discipline often used to illustrate the notion of idiographic as opposed to nomothetic study, a discipline, that is to say, in which the individual event is of interest in its own right and not simply inasmuch as it conforms to a general rule. In assembling the history of hundreds of families who lived in a parish over several centuries, or in examining long lists of families in censuses, we are kept close to the raw stuff of everyday life – the cycle of birth, marriage and death, the arbitrary, individual horror of famine and disease, the pressures of poverty, the decision to prefer wealth to lusty youth in a spouse, the birth made legitimate by a marriage celebrated long after the foetus had first quickened into life. But this intricate and exhaustive inquiry into the minutiae of family life goes hand in hand with the opportunity to understand better the changes which separate our world from Shakespeare's and to do so in terms which further the understanding of social and economic change generally. Changes in the family as an institution were never sudden, simple and striking. But the family was, and largely is still, so squarely at the centre of social, economic and demographic activity, and reflected the activity so sensitively, that it is folly to neglect any way of measuring its characteristics and understanding how it functioned. The history of population and the family may falter because the problems involved prove so intricate, but it will not fail because they are too trivial to deserve attention.

Notes

1 G. R. Elton, *The Practice of History*, Sydney UP, 1967, pp. 136–7; Fontana, 1969.

2 A sociologist, W. J. Goode, in *World revolution and family patterns*, Collier-Macmillan, 1963, has emphasised how many assumptions about the history of the family, even during the last century, are based more on speculation than hard fact. He stresses how valuable it would be to know more – see pp. 366–7.

3 A good illustration of what is possible when a scholar is well equipped in this respect is afforded by G. C. Homans, *English villagers of the thirteenth century*, Harvard UP, 1942.

4 See E. A. Wrigley, *Population and History*, Weidenfeld & Nicolson, 1969, especially pp. 10–14.

5 J. D. Chambers, 'The Vale of Trent 1670–1800', *Economic History Review*, Supplement 3; and P. Goubert, *Beauvais et le Beauvaisis de 1600 à 1730*, 2 vols, Paris, 1960.

6 For details of this and of the operations involved in family reconstitution using English parish registers see E. A. Wrigley (ed.), *An introduction to English historical demography*, Weidenfeld & Nicolson, 1966.

7 See P. Laslett, *The world we have lost*, Methuen, 1965, for a very illuminating discussion of the part played by servants in pre-industrial society in England.

8 See L. Henry, *Anciennes familles genevoises*, Institut national d'études démographiques, 1956, especially pp. 77–8, 94–110, and 127–42.

9 See J. A. Banks, *Prosperity and parenthood*, Routledge, 1954, for a description of how middle-class English families met a similar problem in the later nineteenth century.

10 There is a brilliant discussion of the significance of the late age at marriage of women in western Europe in this period in J. Hajnal,

'European marriage patterns in perspective', in D. V. Glass and D. E. C. Eversley (eds), *Population in history*, Edward Arnold, 1965.

11 See E. A. Wrigley, 'Family limitation in pre-industrial England', *Economic History Review*, 2nd series, XIX, 1966, pp. 82–109.

12 The additional analyses now becoming available at the Cambridge Group for the History of Population and Social Structure support this view, but it is too early to be dogmatic on the point since the parishes analysed so far may prove not to be representative of the whole country.

13 Though the problem of the mean size of household in medieval England is not resolved, much more information is available about this statistic in more recent centuries. See especially P. Laslett, 'Size and structure of the household in England over three centuries, Part I', *Population Studies*, XXIII, 1969, pp. 199–223.

14 See the chapter by R. S. Schofield, 'Sampling in historical research', in E. A. Wrigley (ed.), *The study of nineteenth-century society*.

15 The capacity of electronic computers to perform work of this type and their mode of operation is described in R. S. Schofield, 'Population in the past: computer linking of vital records', *Bulletin of the Institute of Mathematics and its Applications*, 1970.

ROBERT DOUCH

Local History

The study and teaching of local history have been constantly recommended in England since the end of the Second World War. In some respects this movement is a recent one, but in others it represents the extension of a well-established tradition.

Between the late nineteenth century and 1945 the universities showed little interest in local history. Several outstanding historians from J. R. Green through F. W. Maitland to A. L. Rowse worked in this field, but they regarded themselves primarily as historians of England.[1] The only relevant academic appointments were made in the University Colleges of Reading (1908) and Hull (1930) and the University of London (1921).[2]

More interest was shown in local history in school. After the 1902 Education Act, history became a compulsory subject in both elementary and secondary schools, and between then and 1945 this school history, at first mainly political in character and taught orally or from a reader, underwent a series of important changes. A surprising number of these were closely associated with local history. Some, such as the increasing emphasis on social and economic history, the rising interest in archaeology, and the developing stress on citizenship, concerned the content of the syllabus. Others were the outcome of changing views on educational theory. As the ideas of Pestalozzi, Froebel and Dewey spread, the significance of first-hand experience, realism and concrete examples, and the value of activity and individual work came to be appreciated, thus stimulating study of things near at hand.

The reasons given for teaching local history and the place accorded it were not always the same. During the first half of the period its value was said to lie in the fact that it could supply vivid illustrations to enliven the generalisations of national history. The first handbook for teachers in elementary schools, published in 1905, stressed that 'striking events of local history should be included', advice which was repeated in all subsequent editions.[3] 'Constant reference to the history of the locality as illustrative of the general history' was also the course advocated in the first circular issued by the Board of Education on the teaching of history in secondary schools.[4] In the same way, members of the Historical Association early in the century regarded local history in school as 'a magazine or storehouse of vivid and pregnant illustrations of the general course of national history'.[5] These illustrations could be of two kinds. They might refer to the outstanding personalities and happenings of national importance connected with the neighbourhood or to ordinary features and articles, such as buildings, customs and dress.

It was the mid-twenties before many people in England began to argue that local history should be studied and taught in its own right and as a point of departure for more general inquiries. The first writers to develop this approach in relation to history teaching were F. Clarke and J. J. Bell.[6] Older children began to be involved in the movement at about the same time as the value of local surveys came to be recognised and promoted, especially in studies of citizenship and planning. A full survey would embrace study of the locality from all points of view, but the method could also be restricted to historical studies.[7] Significantly, in 1925 the Historical Association established its Village History Committee, rechristened a few years later the Local History Committee.

By 1939, therefore, two approaches to local history in school had emerged – the 'illustrations of national history' and the 'local survey' methods. These were examined and recommended by Eric Walker in his review of the place of local history in school.[8] How far practice supported theory and how many schools were employing either or both approaches, it is impossible to say. However, while a contemporary survey of the teaching of history in English schools mentions local history, it certainly does not give the impression that a great amount was then being studied or taught.[9]

Since 1945 new developments have profoundly influenced local history studies at all levels. Perhaps the most significant event was the establishment in 1947 of the Department of English Local History at University College, Leicester. Here was a university institution recognising local history as a respectable branch of academic study. The first two heads of department, Professors Hoskins and Finberg, defined the province and purpose of the study of local history as tracing the origin, growth and, perhaps, decline and fall, of local communities. This immediately linked the subject and environmental approaches in a fundamental way which, while inherent in the local survey approach of the thirties, was still new to most students of history.[10] The content of historical study was also enlarged by the work of the Leicester school as its members, and others, took up previously neglected aspects. Thus the fifties and sixties saw more academic historians interested in field work, the inclusion in archaeological studies of remains from the recent past, and a new interest in vernacular architecture. Fresh areas of inquiry (such as urban and labour history and demography) were also developed. These advances were greatly helped by the way in which local documentary sources became available after the war through the widespread establishment of county and county borough record offices. While museums and museum services have not been extended in comparable fashion, the foundation of specialist and open-air museums should not be overlooked. Amateur interest and participation in local history also increased enormously. The number of local history and archaeological societies has multiplied. A new periodical, *The Amateur Historian*, launched in 1952, is now published as *The Local Historian*, by the National Council of Social Service, an organisation which sponsored the formation of a Standing Conference for Local History in 1948.

Other subject specialists, interests and organisations have also become much more interested in the environment in recent years. The geographer has developed field studies. The sociologist has stressed the varied effects of different environments on those who live in them. The chemist has become more aware of pollution. The biologist has emphasised conservation. The engineer and the architect have realised the importance of public participation in town planning. A Centre for Environmental Studies has been established, and group work and inter-disciplinary inquiry have become more common.

The work of educational institutions has been affected by the changes just described, and to a lesser extent has contributed to them. The influence has been most marked in adult education groups and in colleges of education. The schools, particularly up to the mid-sixties, were continually encouraged to study local history. Many writers still saw the locality mainly as a source of illustrations for national history, though local history was also recommended in its own right.[11] Even such a keen local historian and teacher as V. H. T. Skipp wanted local material related to topics which were included for other than local reasons and 'for the most part . . . put over by means of brief oral intrusions'.[12] The integrated or environmental approach has also been recommended for both primary and secondary schools, though geographical and scientific aspects have usually been much more prominent than local history in such work.[13] Environmental study has become even more popular in junior schools since the publication of the Plowden Report in 1967. At secondary level the immediate post-war impetus of the local and social studies movements was largely replaced early in the fifties by emphasis on traditional and examination work.[14] Some local history has been introduced into Certificate of Secondary Education programmes since the establishment of that examination in 1965. The publication of the Newsom Report and some of the Schools Council's work, such as the humanities and environmental studies projects, have also encouraged further interest.

In the course of post-war developments, a third method of using local material has been more clearly identified and emphasised, namely the study of an aspect or aspects of the locality in depth, perhaps for the intrinsic local interest or perhaps as a lead into a topic of more general significance.[15]

Just as it was impossible to estimate the amount of local work in history which was being undertaken in English schools in 1939, so no accurate assessment can be made of the present situation. However, there is little doubt that, while local history studies have increased in the last twenty-five years, less work of this kind is attempted than should be. Archivists compare the large number of students with the small number of practising teachers who visit record offices. Environmental work, as has already been remarked, often seems to pay insufficient attention to the past. Examinations still restrict experiment in secondary schools. And, since the mid-sixties, world history has replaced local history as the aspect of studies most frequently recommended as indispensable.

How is this situation to be explained and what might be done to remedy it? The answers to the second question help to account for the first; more teachers need to be convinced of the real meaning and significance of local history and more help needs to be given them in finding suitable local material and in using it with children of different ages and abilities.

In order to appreciate the real importance of local history, many teachers must look afresh at their conception of history. Throughout the century views on the nature, content and methods of school history have, to a large extent, been transmitted downwards from the university. History was always to be approached objectively.

Its content was British history, at first political, constitutional, military and ecclesiastical, to which social and economic and other aspects were subsequently added. The history of other areas, Europe, the Empire, the USA, for instance, was included as changing circumstances decreed. In this way the syllabus expanded continually. Special periods for detailed study appeared only slowly alongside the long outline sketches. With both, factual knowledge, usually unrelated to the pupil's own experience and committed to paper and memory through teachers' talks and notes, provided the staple learning. Thus history in school has been obsessed with a procession of events in time and has been learned rather than understood. It has been too verbal, too general, too intellectualised. Lines of development, patches, individual and group work have obviously made their mark. Nevertheless, the work of many schools, particularly at the secondary stage, still consists of the outlines of British history treated in chronological sequence and often divorced from the present. As Mary Price wrote recently, 'There are the strongest reasons for supposing that in a great many schools it is excruciatingly, dangerously, dull and what is more, of little apparent relevance to the pupils.'[16] Many boys and girls agree.[17]

The place of the study of the past in the education of children needs, therefore, to be reconsidered; all will become adults and citizens, few will become historians. It may well be that the purpose and methods of studying history at different levels should not be the same. In any case, many university historians now interpret the subject very differently from their predecessors.[18]

The main purpose of studying the past in school should be to enable children to know themselves and their world better and to live in it more satisfyingly and more effectively. The emphasis should be on the present and the future with the past being used both to help to explain the present and to contrast with it. There can be no fifty-year gap between 'history' and 'now'. The idea of change is a much more important, and less difficult, concept than that of time. Children need to be involved in history, to see it, not as a film which they simply watch, but as a continuing play in which they themselves are actors. Usually, the starting-point should be the children, their world and their interests, with attention frequently focused on the tangible and observable and with the children constantly challenged to find out for themselves. Historical studies should be much more concerned with the specific and should afford opportunities for individual involvement in the appraisal of evidence. They should seek to encourage imaginative insights along and across the past-present-future continuum. It is this historical attitude and awareness that we should be seeking to develop.

Advocates of environmental studies have long been convinced of the strength of some of these arguments, and of the more general psychological and educational reasons in favour of such work. The problem has been, and still is, that many environmental studies enthusiasts know little history and relatively few history teachers have seriously questioned the traditional approach to their subject or have experimented with environmental studies. If the arguments outlined above are accepted, then aspects of the local, national, European and world scene will all need to be investigated and explained. But they will not best be tackled by the kinds of pre-ordained syllabuses which are so familiar at present, and they will be complementary to, and not, as is often suggested, competing with, each other. In such a scheme the importance of local history work is clearly fundamental.

Whether or not one agrees with the above ideas on teaching history, the remaining problems which are identified and the remedies proposed are relevant to all studies involving local history in school. A major weakness at present is the lack of suitable courses of instruction for intending teachers. The lead given by Leicester in promoting local history has not been followed by many other universities.[19] Environmental studies courses offered in colleges of education vary in content and effectiveness. Students who choose history as a main subject are likely to spend much more time on a special study involving detailed knowledge of limited source materials than they are exploring the opportunities and sources of local studies in general. Is it too much to expect that all students should have some knowledge and experience in this field and that those with relevant subject specialisation should be familiar with, and knowledgeable about, its local implications?

The varied nature of the source materials of local history and the fact that often there are few general guides or particular local examples available constitute another obvious difficulty. Since the war the supply of books for the teacher has improved considerably. Inspired by Professor Hoskins' *Local History in England*, and armed with the bibliographies published by the Historical Association and the Council for British Archaeology, he should be able to find reliable background reading on most aspects of interest.[20] Similarly, the supply of books for children on topics such as churches, roads and social services, has been revolutionised since 1945. It is the shortage of books and other materials on specific localities which is so noticeable. Such publications will not often be commercially profitable, but they can be produced, as some valuable pioneer efforts prove. Bibliographies, like those for Dorset or Oxfordshire, are an essential prerequisite. Surveys of the resources of the neighbourhood are invaluable.[21] General series of pamphlets, such as those published by some local branches of the Historical Association, local history societies, museums and city corporations, are helpful. Area guides to field remains, like that for Durham, would be most useful.[22] A considerable amount of documentary material has been reproduced, some in book form, some as collections of photographed material, some duplicated. The types of publications issuing from the Essex and Kent Record Offices could be copied elsewhere, as could the best of the many archive teaching units which have been compiled.[23]

Another problem in the past has been the marked lack of cooperative effort in sharing experience and in producing materials. Teachers of different subjects in individual schools need to get together: so do teachers from different schools in the same area. The work of adult classes would often be relevant. College lecturers could organise long-term schemes with students and with local teachers. And all tutors and teachers should have close relationships with local librarians, museum curators and archivists. Together these various parties could begin to help solve each others' problems, make local materials generally available and publicise successful work done in school. The fast-growing number of Teachers' Centres being established by local education authorities and the increasing number of field centres provide ideal bases for such cooperative ventures. Discovering local history would still involve a teacher in considerable preparation, but the task could be much less daunting than it often is at present.

What can be done in school? Clearly there can be no universal prescription since environments, schools, teachers and children all vary. But all teachers of history should ask themselves about the nature of their local environment and the broad opportunities it offers, not for historical research, but as a means of educating. Ideas can be obtained from the increasing number of examples, now being published, of work undertaken at various levels.[24] 'Local' must mean that material or those experiences which lie in the neighbourhood and which are already known to the children or which can become known to them as a result of the work being undertaken. It is the first-hand quality and reality of this material which is its vital characteristic. If it loses this, it loses its special appeal and special impact. Thus we need to appreciate what may be local to children of different ages and in different circumstances. The history of the area immediately surrounding the school, for example, is often neglected with young children and, where local history is used for illustrative purposes, the area from which examples are chosen is frequently much too wide. Teachers of history should also ask why such material needs to be utilised: sometimes it will be to help children's personal or social development, sometimes it will provide situations for the exercise of certain skills or be part of the subject, history. Frequently, only the last has been much considered by the history specialist. The more general consideration will lead to a discussion of the relationship between history, humanities and environmental studies throughout school courses and the place of local history in each. Such discussions, on both a school and an area basis, assume even greater importance in the light of the current reorganisation of primary and secondary schools. What kinds of approach, content and method are best suited to particular age and ability groups? What will environmental studies and humanities courses embrace and how will the study of the past figure in them? At what stages and for what reasons should history be treated as a separate subject, and what will it include? Some of the answers will vary from place to place, but the questions must be discussed. There is need for cooperation, imagination and preparation.

The resulting content and treatment of material from the past may be very different from what they have traditionally been. There will be more concern with familiar things and with the present and the recent past, though this is not to say that the relevant long ago and far away will be neglected. Topics, themes and problems should provide the broad framework: some of these may directly concern time sense, sequence and duration, but these factors should certainly not condition the entire arrangement of work. Sometimes the topics or problems will be treated generally, sometimes from a more specifically historical point of view. Where an historical period is studied locally, this may well be regarded, not as an illustration of national history, but as something vital in its own right, study of which could lead to some understanding of a national situation or a general development. Perhaps the most vital contribution of local material to studies of the past is that they provide an opportunity, often the best opportunity for a wide age and ability range, to experience the two main characteristics and aims of historical study. First, material remains permit the study of evidence in a variety of forms, archaeological, oral and written, leading to an understanding of historical method. Secondly, they furnish one of the best means of kindling historical imagination.

In many ways the situation in which history teachers now find themselves is fundamentally the same as it has been on several previous occasions. They are being challenged to re-think the contribution of their subject to education. In earlier, and current, discussions of curriculum change, teachers of history have been the most conservative subject group. They have either tended to ignore many of the changes going on around them or have adopted an essentially defensive attitude towards them. They must now re-appraise the significance of their subject and argue for it, and for themselves, from a position of strength. In such a reappraisal, the local past ceases to be illustrative and becomes indispensable.

Notes

1 But see A. L. Rowse, *Tudor Cornwall*, Cape, 1941.

2 H. P. R. Finberg and V. H. T. Skipp, *Local History: Objective and Pursuit*, David and Charles, 1967, p. 2.

3 Board of Education, *Handbook of Suggestions: for the Consideration of Teachers and Others concerned in the Work of Public Elementary Schools*, HMSO, 1905, p. 63.

4 Board of Education, *Teaching of History in Secondary Schools*, HMSO, 1908, p. 5.

5 W. M. Childs, *The Teaching of Local History*, Historical Association Leaflet no. 11, 1908, p. 3.

6 (Sir) F. Clarke, *Foundations of History Teaching*, OUP, 1929, and J. J. Bell, *Living History*, Philip, 1928. Cf. Board of Education, *Report of the Consultative Committee on the Primary School*, HMSO, 1931.

7 See for example C. C. Fagg and G. E. Hutchings, *An Introduction to Regional Surveying*, CUP, 1930, and Board of Education, *Village Survey Making; an Oxfordshire Experiment*, HMSO, 1929.

8 E. C. Walker, *History Teaching for Today*, Nisbet, 1935, pp. 96–148.

9 Olive E. Shropshire, *The Teaching of History in English Schools*, Columbia UP, New York, 1936.

10 See Finberg and Skipp, *op. cit.*, p. 10: for discussions of this definition see several articles in *The Amateur Historian*, vol. 6.

11 See for example Ministry of Education, *Teaching History*, HMSO, 1952; W. H. Burston and C. W. Green, *Handbook for History Teachers*, Methuen, 1962, pp. 77 and 89; D. W. Humphreys, *Local History in School*, National Council of Social Service, 1954, rev. ed., 1965; and Incorporated Association of Assistant Masters, *The Teaching of History in Secondary Schools*, CUP, 3rd ed., 1965, pp. 17–19.

12 Finberg and Skipp, *op. cit.*, pp. 104 and 116.

13 See for example G. A. Perry *et al.*, *The Teacher's Handbook for Environmental Studies*, Blandford, 1968, and M. F. S. Hopkins, *Learning through the Environment*, Longmans, 1968.

14 Ministry of Education, *Local Studies: Near Home*, HMSO, 1948, and E. Layton and J. B. White, *The School Looks Around*, Longmans, 1948.

15 See for example M. S. Dilke (ed.), *Field Studies for Schools*, Rivingtons, 1965, p. 45, and R. Douch, *Local History and the Teacher*, Routledge, 1967, p. 5.

16 M. Price, 'History in Danger', *History*, vol. LIII, no. 179, October 1968, p. 344.

17 Schools Council, *Enquiry 1: Young School Leavers*, HMSO, 1968, pp. 55–83.

18 See for example M. Bloch, *The Historian's Craft*, Manchester UP, 1954, and J. H. Plumb, *Crisis in the Humanities*, Penguin, 1964, pp. 24–44.

19 B. Harrison, 'History at the Universities, 1968', *History*, vol. LIII, no. 179, October 1968, pp. 371–2.

20 W. G. Hoskins, *Local History in England*, Longmans, 1959; *English Local History Handlist*, Historical Association, 4th ed., 1969; *British Archaeology: a Book List*, Council for British Archaeology, 1960.

21 See for example R. Douch, *A Handbook of Local History: Dorset*, University of Bristol, 1962; T. Booth and H. A. Carnell (eds), *Local History in Bedfordshire*, Bedfordshire County Council, 1960; and N. J. Frangopulo (ed.), *Rich Inheritance: A Guide to the History of Manchester*, Manchester Education Committee, 1963.

22 *History Field Studies in the Durham Area*, Durham University Institute of Education, 1966.

23 See J. Fines, 'Archives in School', *History*, vol. LIII, no. 179, October 1968, pp. 348–56.

24 For some examples, see R. Douch, *Local History and the Teacher*, pp. 119–97; J. West, *History Here and Now*, Schoolmaster Publishing Co., 1966; *Teaching History*, vol. 1, no. 2, Historical Association, November 1969; D. G. Watts, *Environmental Studies*, Routledge, 1969, pp. 72–109.

MARCUS CUNLIFFE

American History

It is sometimes said that the tertiary (university) level of British education determines or ought to determine the secondary (school) level. Universities, after all, are supposed to be the centres of innovation in ways of viewing our world; and from a more practical if not cynical consideration, schools concerned to get their pupils into universities would be advised to attune themselves as far as possible to the tertiary trends.

Within the field of history, the study of the United States has certainly become a significant feature of British university curricula. In 1945 there was only one British chair of American history – at University College, London – though there were visiting chairs, subject to annual rotation, in Oxford and Cambridge. A quarter of a century later there is no British university that does not offer courses in American history. Americanists occupy chairs, some of them quite new, at places including Birmingham, Edinburgh, Glasgow, Manchester, Oxford and Sussex. Several universities have introduced departments or programmes of American studies, in which the history of the United States is associated with the nation's literature, politics, geography and so on.

DRAWBACKS?
Such growth has been less evident in the schools. A number have managed to institute at least some provision for American history. A few have been quite ambitious. The majority have not so far taken the plunge. Naturally, I write as an advocate of the field. But before making out a case, it is important to identify reasons for this apparent inattention. One argument, perhaps the weightiest, is that the school curriculum is already crowded. History undergraduates are not able to cover anything like the entire range of options open to them. No one in three years can hope to acquire even a superficial familiarity with, let alone a mastery of, ancient, medieval *and* modern history; of political, economic, social, cultural and psychological aspects; of the complex evolution of society in Africa and Asia and Russia and North America and South America, as well as that of Britain and Continental Europe. Indeed in an era of increasing

specialisation very few university teachers are themselves equipped to survey mankind from China to Peru. If the teachers cannot do this, how can the taught be expected to? And if universities cannot solve the problem, how can secondary schools?

Some order of priorities seems essential. It can be plausibly contended that in the schools the pupil should first gain a knowledge of his own locality and of his own country – both because he *ought* to, and because his immediate environment offers materials to hand. Second, we may feel that at the other extreme he should be exposed to 'world history', perhaps with particular reference to the twentieth century. World history would obviously include the United States, but would not allow any detailed concentration on purely American affairs. Indeed spokesmen for world/contemporary history such as Geoffrey Barraclough, who believe that historians have been far too Europe-centred, suggest that seemingly larger conceptions like that of an 'Atlantic Community' embracing North America and western Europe, harbour a new type of historical parochialism. One would still be confining the young mind to a study of the white world, to the exclusion of the vast realms of the non-white world. Moreover, to Barraclough the very idea of an Atlantic Community is historically dubious: a recent invention, politically and strategically motivated. Whether or not he is correct, one must admit that scholars have shown a good deal of perplexity in deciding whether the American hemisphere can be fitted into a European scheme of things. Analysts of the emergence of the 'Third World' have for instance usually left Latin America out of their account, while conceding somewhat sheepishly that it no doubt ought to be brought in. Cultural historians sometimes appear equally uneasy, when they deal with such abstractions as the Enlightenment or Romanticism, about allotting (or denying) a role to the United States.

The problem has in a way been intensified by the outlook of most American historians, at least until recent years. As expressed in the average American textbook of national history, and as implied in monographic work, the main outlines of American history depend upon a principle of contrast, which in turn carries an assumption – often unwitting – of American superiority. The United States is presented as a new, active civilisation, repudiating and superseding the old, static, parent culture of Europe. Growth, success, democracy are portrayed as its achievements; and even its difficulties or shortcomings (over industrialism, urbanisation, ethnic prejudice and the like) are usually suggested to be on an altogether grander scale than those of western Europe. The unconscious chauvinism conveyed in these interpretations arouses and clashes with our own, British brand of chauvinism. In American versions, we lose the Revolutionary War; we are thrashed in the culminating battle of the War of 1812, at New Orleans; and we are accused of having behaved badly as a biased neutral in the American Civil War of 1861–5. In short, if the history of the United States is a large-scale affair, then the very scale of activities, pedagogically speaking, may appear to diminish the appeal of British history. Our industrial revolution is eventually dwarfed by America's; our native textbook view of the establishment of political and social democracy is reduced, if not nullified, by the record of American advances towards liberty and equality. In other words, to dramatise American history, to fasten upon main themes, might seem to entail making *British* history less significant, less palatable, to our own teenagers.

Two further objections may be mentioned. There is the notion that American history need not be formally taught because it is recent, 'easy' and already accessible to us through films, television, newspapers and magazines. Presidential elections, for instance, are prominently featured by the BBC: why go over the same ground in the classroom? An opposite objection – also expressed in the comment that the United States is too recent a creation to *have* a real past – is that the texture of American history is often complicatedly drab: a welter of issues like land policy, tariff schedules and anti-trust legislation that defy bold analysis. As one who never studied American history at school, I can well recall my own initial bewilderment when I was an undergraduate and read a book about the American Civil War: I knew there were two sides to the war but was slow to grasp which was which, when one was labelled 'Federal' and the other – almost identically, it first seemed to me – as 'Confederate'.

Let me reiterate that in seeing the force of some of the points raised above I do not accept them as vital. They are considerations rather than absolute barriers – reasons for proceeding sensibly, not reasons for declining to proceed at all. The case for American history rests on a broader base; and this justification indicates a method that might be followed in launching classes. The case is that in a genuine sense, not the current jargon-sense of the word, America's past is 'relevant'. America's present-day preoccupations have for the most part a long heritage. Some of them are of the very essence of modern history – that is, of the world of the last two hundred years. Like any country, the United States has evaded or mishandled some of its problems. But certain of these problems remain unsolved because they are insoluble: not fatally so, yet necessarily so, because they raise fundamental issues in a recurrent drama of choices. A marked feature of American historiography has been the inability to settle upon an agreed interpretation of any major element. Every ten or twenty years there is renewed controversy, leading to a revision of the previous revised version. This in itself testifies to the aliveness of American history. Figuratively, the terrain's distinctive features turn out to be active volcanoes. The American past stays alive and constantly challenges the present, because it encompasses the aspirations and dilemmas of modern man.

SPECIMENS
American history possesses a curious resonance. *It may therefore be approached via the present day.* Here and now we can fasten upon a debate – over civil rights, say, or the limits of presidential authority, or the shape of American foreign policy – that is both timely and fundamental. Moving back from the present, we can usually trace the origins and developments of the debate. Not all issues are of course equally resonant: I would not recommend an investigation of tariff schedules on this score. Sometimes the situation closely parallels that in Europe; sometimes it anticipates a European predicament; sometimes it appears intriguingly different. The point is that, whether in history or in general studies classes, we may legitimately appeal to the pupil's interest in contemporary America as the way into a historical discussion; and that such an approach is perhaps best organised thematically, instead of proceeding chronologically on a broad front.

To illustrate this suggestion, I offer a brief outline of nine themes:

1 Puritanism
2 Plenty
3 Population
4 Prejudice
5 Nationalism
6 Government
7 Democracy
8 The World Outside
9 Dissent

They hang together, or can be made to modulate from one to

another. But each could be treated in isolation. Not all need be used. Other possible thematic topics will readily occur to teachers. Mine are merely specimens.

1 *Puritanism* Starting with the material of today's news media, one might note an apparently contradictory phenomenon. America is in many respects a 'permissive' society. In literature as on the stage it would seem that anything goes. Public figures, especially politicians, are exposed to derisive criticism. Yet according to a public opinion poll, the three people whom Americans most admired in 1969 were President Nixon, Vice-President Agnew, and the evangelist Billy Graham. This presumably was the vote of the 'silent majority', who approve their government's policy in Vietnam, who regard their police not as 'pigs' but as bulwarks against crime and riot, who believe in hard work and self-improvement, and who associate church-going with Americanism. So we see two Americas in conflict; their mutual antagonism, starkly dramatised in the clash between students and police in Chicago during the summer of 1968, is a crucial factor in the divisive tension of the contemporary United States.

The origins of American irreverence and lawlessness may be left to later discussion. For the purposes of this topic our interest centres upon the pervasive and continuing force of a moral code that we may call 'Puritanism', and may consider to have a double quality – negative and positive.

The negative side is hinted at in a sarcastic definition of 'Puritanism' offered fifty years ago by H. L. Mencken: 'The haunting fear that someone, somewhere, may be happy.' That is of course not an adequate definition of a word that has had many meanings since its first usage in sixteenth-century England, and which still had a fairly precise and honorific application when it passed to the seventeenth-century settlements of New England. But Mencken's joke reminds us of the pressure of American public opinion – a pressure leading at various times to intolerance, censorship, and moralistic campaigns (notably the one which established Prohibition in the 1920s, with disastrous consequences). The religious sanctions of this seemingly hypocritical censoriousness deserve to be understood. They could be given a historical dimension if a class were to investigate the Salem witchcraft trials of the 1690s – the episode on which Arthur Miller formed his play *The Crucible*.

The positive side likewise takes us back to the seventeenth

century. It includes respect for education, intensity of individual effort, a belief in philanthropy as a moral obligation, and a growing readiness to conclude that practical piety is the way to wealth. Such psychological dynamism – the Protestant or Puritan Ethic – may also have its unlikeable features: witness the attack on Benjamin Franklin in D. H. Lawrence's *Studies in Classic American Literature* (1923). In the strict sense Franklin was not a Puritan. Yet his *Autobiography* is a fascinating eighteenth-century document, a midway stage between the Bible commonwealth and the world of Samuel Smiles.

2 *Plenty* This is the theme explored in David M. Potter's *People of Plenty: Economic Abundance and the American Character* (1954). Potter's concern is to relate the American national character to the economic largesse provided by the American environment. The one, he maintains, derives from the other. His view is worth discussing, in the context of the idea of 'national character' as such. Another approach, possibly more rewarding at the introductory level, is to start from the phenomenon of contemporary American affluence; to review in outline the growth of American economic power; and to seek to explain the rapidity and extent of this growth. How much did it depend upon the Protestant Ethic; upon libertarian impulses inherited from the mother country; upon a slave labour force in the South and European immigration in the North; upon the availability of investment capital from Europe; upon the quantity and variety of natural resources – land, timber, minerals; upon launching an industrial revolution later than the mother country? Today, the word 'environment' has begun to carry ominous overtones of waste and pollution. Is this the price belatedly paid for the speed and energy of America's economic development? Why did some other nineteenth-century nations – Russia for example – fail to develop at equal speed? Did certain disadvantages in the American situation stimulate enterprise? In the terms of Arnold Toynbee, was there a 'challenge' that inspired a 'response'? New England displayed a great deal of economic vitality. Yet the region's soil was poor; iron, coal and other resources were lacking. Answers to some of these questions are suggested in *The Great Experiment* (1955), by the English historian Frank Thistlethwaite, and in Daniel J. Boorstin's *The Americans: The National Experience* (1965), a highly unconventional general history of the United States between the Revolution and the Civil War. New England, he remarks, consisted largely of ice and granite. The New Englanders

turned these unpromising materials to profit: they exported blocks of ice to areas with hot climates, and sold slices of granite for paving-stones.

3 *Population* The present population of the United States is over two hundred million. At the time of the Revolution it was around four million. In national and ethnic origins the United States is amazingly polyglot. How much was population growth due to natural increase? How did this compare with population figures in other countries? How many millions entered as immigrants? Where did they come from? How did they come; and why? Except for ending slave importation, and for prohibitory steps to bar Chinese and Japanese immigration, the United States maintained a policy of virtually unrestricted immigration until the 1920s. Who favoured this policy, and on what grounds? Hector St John de Crèvecœur's *Letters from an American Farmer* sketched an idealistic vision of the 'new American', a product of all nations, as early as 1782. His picture was more or less duplicated at the beginning of our century through Israel Zangwill's metaphor of the 'melting pot'. How far did the pot in fact melt? What strains did multinational immigration impose upon the United States? What objections were expressed? Why were immigration quotas introduced in the 1920s, and with what results? Did they represent the betrayal of an ideal, or simply a realistic recognition that nations, like smaller communities, cannot hold together if they become too diverse? Was the effort to 'Americanise' immigrants an expression of bigotry, or a sensible and necessary reaction, or something of both? How far, and in what ways, did the United States remain 'British' – in language, culture and institutions? (Note that Herbert Hoover was the first President to bear a non-British surname.) How far did WASPs (white Anglo-Saxon Protestants) remain dominant? (Note that John F. Kennedy was the first non-Protestant President, and that even he was the Harvard-educated son of a millionaire.) What part have religious affiliations played in the story? To what extent have successive layers of immigration supplied an American version of a class-system? What is the significance of organisations like the Daughters of the American Revolution? Again, there are some admirable and fairly inexpensive books: *The Uprooted* (1953), by Oscar Handlin, a boldly impressionistic interpretation of the immigrant experience; *American Immigration* (1960), a crisp and knowledgeable work by the British historian Maldwyn A. Jones; and

Beyond the Melting Pot (1963), by Nathan Glazer and Daniel P. Moynihan, an imaginative sociological account of 'the role of ethnicity in the tumultuous, varied, endlessly complex life of New York City . . . The point about the melting pot . . . is that it did not happen. At least not in New York and, *mutatis mutandis*, in those parts of America which resemble New York.' Was this a tragedy for the United States, or – in balance – a gain? The relevance of such an inquiry for contemporary Britain does not need stressing.

4 *Prejudice* Any such inquiry naturally leads into a consideration of racial and religious prejudice. Present-day documentation is abundant: in newspaper descriptions, for instance, of the Black Panthers or the revival of Red Indian 'nationalism', or in such books as *The Autobiography of Malcolm X* (1965), Richard Wright's *Native Son* (1940), Ralph Ellison's *Invisible Man* (1952) and John Hersey's *The Algiers Motel Incident* (1968). What were the origins of the white man's prejudice against men whose skin had a different colour? For the first inhabitants of North America, we may consult two well-conceived collections of historical documents: *The Indian and the White Man* (1964), edited by Wilcomb E. Washburn, and *The Indian in America's Past* (1964), edited by Jack D. Forbes; Alvin M. Josephy, Jr's, *The Patriot Chiefs* (1962), which studies the lives of nine Indian leaders; and Thomas Berger's brilliantly sympathetic and ironical novel, *Little Big Man* (1964). The beginnings of white racialism, of course, lie in Europe. While it would be silly to indict Shakespeare as a bigot, students might be invited to consider the figure of Caliban in *The Tempest*: how much does Shakespeare see him as a man, and how much as a monster? A serious inquiry, at sixth-form level, should include Winthrop D. Jordan's long and learned *White Over Black: American Attitudes Toward the Negro, 1550–1812* (1968), from which it would appear that colour prejudice was transmitted to the New World as an item in the emotional and intellectual baggage of the first English settlers. Why and how was it institutionalised into slavery? Why has it persisted in American life a hundred years after the end of slavery?

From the start, America was implicitly regarded as a white man's country. To what extent was it also a white *Protestant* country? Were non-Protestants in effect second-class citizens? (Note that religion was only one factor in the sum of prejudice. When permitted to do so, Negroes readily became members of the various Protestant denominations.) In the twentieth century the spectrum of prejudice is indicated by the manifestoes of the revived Ku-Klux-Klan of 1915–25, which was anti-Catholic and anti-Jewish as well as anti-Negro. These religious prejudices also might be traced back to the mother country. Guy Fawkes' Day could be linked with recent disturbances in Ulster; and – again with reference to Shakespeare – a discussion of the role of Shylock in *The Merchant of Venice* could be rewarding. A fascinating American development, in the 1840s and 1850s, was the temporary emergence of a political party, the 'Know-Nothings', based almost entirely on anti-Catholic (or anti-Irish) sentiment. It is worth stressing, however, that religion as a criterion of prejudice has almost vanished in the United States. In *Protestant, Catholic, Jew* (1955), Will Herberg shows that American religion has become a sort of tripod: each of the three faiths has been accorded an 'official' standing. If this reveals a marked decline in one form of prejudice, how impressive are the signs of a decline in colour prejudice?

5 *Nationalism*   The United States began as a group of British colonies, achieved independence through armed resistance, and went on to become a 'nation of nations' – though, as we have seen, with considerable disagreement as to whether its polyglot population could or should be fused into one homogeneous mass. Other aspects of nationalism, as a central theme in modern world history, may be illuminated by studying the phenomenon in the United States.

Several lines of inquiry are opened up in Boorstin's *The Americans: The National Experience*, and Seymour Martin Lipset's *The First New Nation: The United States in Historical and Comparative Perspective* (1964). What are the problems of new, 'ex-colonial' nations? Having made a revolution, how do they restore the principle of authority and persuade their citizens to respect the newly instituted government? Why do their military leaders tend to assume power as political leaders? This happened in the United States, or seemed about to happen, when General Washington became President Washington (see Marcus Cunliffe, *George Washington: Man and Monument*, 1958). Many new nations fail to achieve a stable, representative government: why did America succeed? Old societies such as England or France may grow into nationhood over several centuries. With new ones the process is telescoped, and may strike outsiders as artificial, forced, even absurd ('the following tradition will take effect as from next Wednesday . . .'). The symbols of nationality – anthems, flags, patriotic myths – have to be rather urgently manufactured. What were the American symbols? How quickly did they take on life?

A feeling of political identity is sometimes more easily arrived at than a feeling of cultural or psychological identity. Ex-colonial nations often go back into their pre-colonial past for this purpose. It may provide them with a name (Ghana, Zambia) and a national language, and with native costumes, heroes and legends. But the United States had no language but that of the mother country, and the primeval Americans were not white men but 'Indians' – defeated and dispossessed. There was not even a suitable indigenous name for the new country. 'The United States' is a constitutional description rather than a name; 'America' refers geographically to an entire hemisphere of which the US is only a part. The struggle for a national culture, repeated subsequently in nation after nation, long perplexed the writers and artists of the United States.

Most nations fall into regions, each with fairly distinct characteristics. 'Regionalism' is usually regarded as an enriching form of diversity. But what when regional loyalties harden into 'sectionalism', hostile and possibly separatist in spirit? What if one section has so strong a conviction of its own identity that it wishes to break away altogether? Such was the situation of the slave states of the American South that seceded in 1860–1. Was the Union, which itself had broken away from the mother country, justified in refusing to permit secession? Was the Civil War which followed the South's action in some ways a final stage in American unification, akin to the wars of the same period that resulted in the unification of Germany and Italy?

6 *Government* American government and politics crowd upon our attention. A book like *An American Melodrama: The Presidential Campaign of 1968* (1969), by Lewis Chester, Godfrey Hodgson and Bruce Page, reminds us that they are both diverting and enormously important. Starting with today's world, one might discuss with a class the position of the US president, as compared with that of the British prime minister. In Britain the formal role of head of state is filled by the monarch, leaving the prime minister to act as head of government. In the United States the president is required to do both. How far is this feasible? He is isolated from Congress, quite unlike the prime minister. Does this mean that the president has more leeway than the prime minister, or less? Some Congressmen

complain that an ambitious president such as Lyndon B. Johnson ignores the legislative branch. Some MPs say the same thing about the prime minister and his cabinet circle. What are the similarities and differences? Is either system preferable?

In order to answer such questions it is necessary to look at the evolution of the American governmental system. (Relevant books by British scholars include Max Beloff, *The American Federal Government*, 2nd ed., 1969; Marcus Cunliffe, *American Presidents and the Presidency*, 1969; and Malcolm Shaw, *Anglo-American Democracy*, 1968.) The debates of 1787 and succeeding years over the new constitution might seem more the province of a history special subject than of a general survey. But it is fairly easy to pick out a few main themes. The crucial issue was how to establish a national government which would be both sufficiently powerful and sufficiently responsive to the popular will. Another issue was to decide on a proper balance between the authority of the national (or 'federal') government and that of the individual states. In both cases the constitution is somewhat ambiguous, partly because the delegates to the Philadelphia convention were far from unanimous. With the first issue, an ideal solution eluded the delegates also because efficiency and representativeness are to some extent incompatible. With the second, federalist issue we may point to the histories of Canada, Australia and Nigeria to indicate the problems inherent in federal systems. An interesting experiment, also germane to the next topic in my specimen list, would be to get a class to draw up a constitution, possibly for Britain or – more modestly – for their own school. Such an exercise ought to lead to a consideration of the aims of government (to get some things done? to stop some things from being done? to promote the general welfare? to protect minorities and underdogs?) It might, too, raise the question of whether written constitutions are desirable. Should one generation bind the next generation? How can documents of this kind avoid becoming obsolete?

Many worthwhile schemes will suggest themselves. The whole history of states rights is one such. It could be placed in a contemporary context by discussing criticisms of American government: for example, that the administration is too autonomous and has proved this by committing the nation to an undeclared war in Vietnam; or, more broadly, that the 'power structure' is materialistic and brutal. How and why did the federal government, and the presidency, become more powerful? Ought their power to be diminished, perhaps by decentralisation? If so, does the history of states rights suggest that state governments would be more humane? The historical role of the Supreme Court could in itself supply material for many discussions. Its recent activities in defending civil rights seem to contradict the view that central government is necessarily repressive. Is it possible to maintain a welfare state without a strong central government, and a numerous bureaucracy?

7 *Democracy* This topic has links with *Puritanism* as well as with *Government*. British antecedents, e.g. in John Locke and the Bill of Rights, are worth stressing. So are the natural rights assumptions of the Declaration of Independence of 1776. 'All men are created equal': what did this mean at the time, and how has it been interpreted subsequently? The 1787 Constitution laid down that there should be no monarchy, no titled aristocracy, no religious tests for office. In the next half-century, property qualifications virtually disappeared; for adult white males there was universal suffrage. The press was free – scurrilously so, in the eyes of most presidents and many foreign visitors.

Yet conundrums remained – difficulties attesting to the fundamental dilemmas of democracy, and also to the incompleteness of the American doctrine of equality. Alexis de Tocqueville's *Democracy in America* is too complex for quick reading. But certain passages could be taken as texts – notably Tocqueville's commentary on the danger that public opinion, even where expressing the majority will, could become a form of tyranny. John C. Calhoun, the spokesman for the slave states, argued that minority interests ought to have a veto power. Was his view tenable?

Other difficulties involved the relation of politics to democracy. Eighteenth-century American constitutionalists like Thomas Jefferson were worried that government would fall into the hands of a self-perpetuating élite. To guard against this they insisted that the activities of government should be simple enough to be understood and performed by any average citizen. There should be frequent 'rotation' in office to break up élites and bring ordinary citizens in. But with the development of political parties 'rotation' became a method of rewarding adherents with jobs: 'to the victors belong the spoils'. And as government grew more complicated the argument for training and experience grew stronger.

Another vexed question was that of education. If all men are

created equal, all should benefit equally from educational opportunity. But *are* all men, or all children, equal in intellectual ability?
What if parents, or their children, do not *want* to continue schooling?
Even Jefferson, in devising a three-tier educational scheme for his
own state of Virginia, constructed something that looks as much
meritocratic as democratic. The history of American education is
full of lessons on the consequences of the democratic principle that
schooling is a natural right.

'All men are created equal.' If this is accepted as a nation's creed,
how can it also accept the exclusion of some of its citizens from the
practice of democratic rights? One answer, put forward by Calhoun
and other defenders of slavery, was to deny the truth of the dictum.
Men, he argued, are manifestly *un*equal. Another common response,
with relation to Negroes either slave or free, was to deny that they
were men – or human beings – in the full sense of the term. The
queer logic and quasi-scientific theorising employed to reinforce this
contention are as absorbing as they are depressing. Somewhat less
grim examples of chop-logic are provided by the problem of whether
'men' also meant 'women'. As in Britain, where women likewise
did not have the vote in the nineteenth century, the question was
often answered with the argument that women differed from men
not through being inferior but through being superior – finer
creatures who would be degraded by contact with such sordid male
preserves as politics.

The historical resonances of these debates are manifold. The
franchise may be a *sine qua non* of civil rights: but what else is needed,
and how can it be guaranteed? Did the enfranchisement of women
have any significant effect upon the political system? At what age
does a man become a man? Does 'all men are created equal' include
children? Nineteenth-century European travellers complained that
American children were spoiled and insubordinate. Was this another
way of saying that they were already benefiting from the Declaration
of Independence? Did John Dewey's ideas on progressive education function as a gloss upon that Declaration?

8 *The World Outside* There would seem to be little continuity of
heritage between the early America and today's super-power, so far
as foreign policy is concerned. Critics of that foreign policy sometimes draw the contrast, and assert that the United States has forgotten its own basic intentions. When we examine these, however,
the matter proves not to be clear-cut. Long before the Revolution,

the Puritan colonies spoke of the special meaning of their theocratic society. They were 'as a city upon a hill' (a phrase cited by John F. Kennedy in one of his speeches), occupying a proud and exposed situation, watched by the rest of mankind. The new nation extended and secularised the idea of itself as a society with a special destiny to fulfil, a society in some ways set apart from others, and especially from the corruptions of Europe. Washington and Jefferson, in words repeated again and again by American orators and essayists, warned their countrymen against entangling alliances. Certainly they were to trade with other peoples; but commerce was one thing, the risk of war quite another. In the first decades of independence Jefferson was one of the Americans who compared his country to China. Both, it was felt, were peaceable, agricultural, inward-looking, geographically and spiritually remote from Europe. Suspicion of Europe and the determination to steer clear of its machinations were revealed in the Monroe Doctrine of 1823. This statement of American principles warned European nations not to intervene in the affairs of the American hemisphere, and indicated that the United States was equally indifferent to the power-balance of nations inside Europe. As such the Monroe Doctrine was one of the first of many signs of American 'isolationism'. Not until the Second World War did the United States enter into a full-scale alliance with any other power. In the prelude to both world wars of this century a sizeable body of public opinion aligned itself in favour of neutrality; in neither case did the United States enter the war at the outset.

Nevertheless, it could be said that America *has* been involved in every world conflict since 1775 – or even earlier if we include colonial history. Why? In part because, as the Napoleonic wars demonstrated, trading nations cannot easily maintain neutrality. In part because of the rapid growth of American power; at the end of the nineteenth century, when the United States was beginning to acquire bases overseas, the contrary fate of a helpless China seemed an object lesson. Possibly also because of economic and ideological ties with Europe – the so-called 'Atlantic Community'. And finally, perhaps, because American isolationism had always run hand in hand with a counter-tendency towards ideological if not actual expansionism. In effect the Monroe Doctrine had staked out the whole American hemisphere as a US sphere of influence – to the bitter and continuing resentment of the Latin American nations. In the context of 1970 it might seem that, from the first, American idealism carried a latent assertion of a 'manifest destiny' to extend the American dream across the globe. According to taste and the particular historical circumstance, isolationism and internationalism could both be interpreted as virtuous impulses, or as vicious ones. Recent books like Noam Chomsky's *American Power and the New Mandarins* (1969) and David Horovitz' *From Yalta to Vietnam : American Foreign Policy in the Cold War* (1969), in dwelling upon the vicious side, overlook some of the truly painful ironies of well-meaning American behaviour.

9 *Dissent* The books by Chomsky and Horovitz are instances of a great quantity of root-and-branch indictments of present-day America. Works by Norman Mailer amplify the record; other examples include Ronald Segal, *America's Receding Future : The Collision of Creed and Reality* (1968). It is of course possible that such scarifying predictions are correct. To minimise America's problems would be foolish.

Yet they serve to raise an issue of a more general sort. The bulk of current critiques of the United States assert that the situation is unprecedentedly bad. They are unhistorical both in not being concerned with history, and in the less acceptable sense of not being *aware of* history. But it does not take much digging into the American past to discover that at several previous points a tone of acute dismay and disaffection has apparently prevailed. Predictions of disaster have been frequent. So have denunciations of American materialism and mindless vulgarity. Politicians have long been unpopular (cf. Artemus Ward: 'I am not a politician and my other habits are good.') So have the police, who were portrayed as 'pigs' nearly a hundred years ago in a cartoon by Thomas Nast. Successive waves of reformers and radicals, each probably unaware of previous precedents, have repeated surprisingly similar arguments. 'All proclaim their disgust', said George Santayana of the restless students of 1922, 'at the present state of things in America, they denounce the Constitution . . ., the churches, the government, the colleges, the press, . . . and above all they denounce the spirit that vivifies and unifies all these things, the spirit of Business.'

Several valuable lessons may be learned by studying the historical patterns of dissent. One is that history supplies a perspective. It tests the truth of generalisations that rest merely upon the evidence of one moment in time. It enables the student to perceive more reliably what factors in a given situation *are* genuinely novel.

Another lesson is that by looking for comparable material at different periods we may become aware of certain patterns or trends that shed light on the underlying nature of a society. Arthur Schlesinger, Sr, indeed suggested that there was a cyclical tendency in American history: reform movements of roughly the same duration alternated with eras of 'reaction' or indifference. It is undeniable that there have been several eras of reform in the United States, and that each has lost its momentum. Why? Because reforms were achieved? Because people lose their enthusiasm for any movement after a while? Because of something spongy in the fabric of American life that absorbs and deadens indignation? Because the tradition of American dissent has tended to indulge in wild exaggeration? To what extent, historically, has dissent been a matter of generation-conflict, a manifestation of youth? These are only a few of the topics that could be explored within the theme of *Dissent*, and by ranging between present and past.

CONCLUSION

It is easy to think of other thematic treatments organised around the same approach: present-day problems, historical origins, developments, wider applications. *Violence* would be an obvious possibility. Though no ideal introduction to the theme is available, there is a long and informative paperback compendium, *The History of Violence in America* (1969), edited by Hugh D. Graham and Ted R. Gurr. *The Myth of the Cowboy*, approached initially via film westerns, would be another rich vein.

The permutations and combinations of curricula in American history are almost infinite. In every case, to reiterate, the appeal lies in the resonance of the subject. The subtitle of Ronald Segal's book – 'the collision of creed and reality' – hints at the reason for this appeal. All societies experience a tension between *ought* and *is*, between an ethical imperative and the consideration of what is possible or expedient. To an unusual degree among nations, the United States has proclaimed an attachment to the ideal, and a belief that the ideal is attainable. Like the rest of mankind it has fallen short of its own aspirations. But this discrepancy has generated controversies of extraordinary weight, acuteness, pathos and sometimes hilarity. They are the stuff of American imaginative literature; and novels such as *Huckleberry Finn* or *The Great Gatsby* supply an additional element of historical truth. American history can be taught drearily, or naïvely in the 1776-And-All-That mode. Yet it offers a marvellous challenge to the lively teacher.

Note

All the items mentioned in the essay are available in Britain, most of them in paperback editions. A further useful work is H. C. Allen and C. P. Hill (eds), *British Essays in American History*, Edward Arnold, 1957. There are convenient and up-to-date historical atlases of the United States by Martin Gilbert (*American Historical Atlas*, Weidenfeld & Nicolson, 1968), and by D. K. Adams and H. B. Rodgers (*An Atlas of North American Affairs*, Methuen, 1969).

3 Across the Disciplines

DEREK HEATER

History and the Social Sciences

Throughout the English educational system, guardians of pure history may be found courageously defending their chosen subject against the undermining influences of social studies: ivory towers are under siege from the social scientists, while in the blackboard jungles guerrilla warfare is engaged with the social studies cadres. At the same time, an increasing number of historians and history teachers are – treacherously in the eyes of the traditionalists – seeking positive forms of alliance. In the academic world, when established traditions are challenged in this way and a condition of uncertainty supervenes, the problems are inevitably thought out in print. It is scarcely surprising, therefore, that in the 1960s a number of particularly thoughtful publications were produced on the relationship between history and the social sciences (or studies). In chronological order there came firstly Mr Burston's pamphlet, *Social Studies and the History Teacher*;[1] then two or three articles in special numbers of *The Times Literary Supplement* devoted to 'New Ways in History';[2] there then followed two particularly penetrating articles from Leicester University: Dr Holloway's 'History and Sociology: What History Is and What it Ought to Be'[3] and Mr Bernbaum's 'Sociology and Contemporary History'.[4] But before leaving this brief bibliographical survey particular mention must be made of an American book, Professor Krug's *History and the Social Sciences: New Approaches to the Teaching of Social Studies*,[5] and the section entitled 'Rivals' in Professor Elton's *The Practice of History*,[6] since they are particularly germane to the present discussion. These references have been given, because it is impossible to do justice to the details of the debate in one short article: the interested reader must go to the originals. The purpose of this chapter is rather to sketch in quite briefly the arguments for and against an intellectual and pedagogical apartheid between history and the social sciences; to demonstrate the utility of close cooperation between the two sets of disciplines; and to detail a syllabus-model based on this premiss of cooperation.

One further introductory note is necessary before developing this argument. Three terms – social studies, social sciences and sociology – have already appeared and we cannot proceed without providing definitions of their meanings and usage. Sociology is, of course, now a clearly defined academic discipline. But it is also the core of a whole family of disciplines known as the social sciences, embracing also economics, politics, anthropology and psychology. In this chapter, the term social sciences will be confined in its use to these identifiable disciplines at whatever level they may be taught. A distinction can therefore usefully be drawn between the clearly defined social sciences and the more amorphous social studies as taught in some schools. Frequently taught through the medium of 'topics' (e.g. race, the family), social studies lessons may often draw upon geography, history, religious studies, literature and biology for their material as well as the social sciences proper.

History is a well-established subject in both university and school curricula, consolidated by a good half-century as the recognised academic discipline for the study of man in society. It should not be surprising therefore that the emergence of relatively new disciplines – the social sciences – to study the same subject-matter has provoked a reaction of some hostility. History, after all, has refined its techniques of study and provides a well-tested way of understanding its material. Moreover, to be quite blunt, there are thousands of teachers in our educational institutions (including the present writer!) trained in the discipline and with a vested interest in maintaining its status. We must nevertheless ask what the main arguments are for retaining history as an autonomous discipline.

Firstly, there are what might be termed the standard arguments in support of history's place in the curriculum. They are basically three. History, it has been said, provides the student with a sound political education: hence the traditional political and constitutional bias of the syllabus. Also, because of its basic preoccupation with the dimension of time, history has taught its students to realise that all is in flux – that the future will differ from the present as the present does from the past and as one age in the past differed from any other. Man is not fully self-aware without this temporal perspective. Moreover, because history leads the human mind on journeys of inquiry to societies distant from our own in time, it is a liberating influence and thus a liberal education in itself. By the middle years of the present century historical studies had become the substitute for classics in the county grammar schools and in redbrick universities.

Such arguments are continually marshalled in defence of history. More recently, however, they have been reinforced with the proposition that history performs the unique educational function of developing an appreciation of the value of evidence and at the same time a scepticism in weighing its validity. Increasing emphasis on 'the historical method' at all levels from primary school to undergraduate teaching is a practical indication of this shift of the centre of gravity in the arguments surrounding the value of historical study. One further positive argument in favour of history must be noted, though it is a difficult one to handle. To be brief and bold – history is interesting. To describe history as interesting might be counted as bold because of the considerable contrary evidence from our secondary schools that history is seen as one of the least interesting subjects.[7] Yet the narrative and biographical elements in history have an immense interest potential – witness the great popularity of books, serialised magazines and television programmes which use such material. Skilful teachers, of course, are also capable of realising this potential.

So much for the positive arguments in favour of history. Let us now sketch in the arguments used by historians against social studies and social sciences. At the academic level two main issues are usually raised. Firstly, the social scientists are accused of a myopic focus upon the present: using the past merely to understand the present, studying the present as an end in itself. Such activity, it is argued, leads to anachronistic thinking and can even become self-defeating, since a distorted view of the past provides misleading data against which to check the social scientist's general theories about society. This leads to the second objection, namely what is felt to be a naïve reliance on general laws and the accompanying disregard of evidence that might undermine or contradict the generalisations. Turning to the school level, many history teachers have also yet to be convinced that social studies can be properly articulated into an effective teaching syllabus. Ghosts of the post-war social studies programmes, child-dead within a decade, still haunt common rooms and teachers' centres. Nor are the newly-born social *science* courses in secondary schools yet sufficiently strong or widely adopted to exorcise the spirits of their half-siblings.

The historian has a cogent case; how does the social scientist's compare? Let us look at the positive side first. It will be convenient to consider, first of all, two minor arguments mainly relevant to the school level only. Social scientists are at pains to remind their critics that their subjects stretch across a wide range of study – sociology, economics, politics, anthropology, psychology. And since, therefore, every aspect of society provides the subject-matter of the social sciences, they, like history, can stake a claim to being a proper vehicle for a liberal education. By this last third of the present century the social sciences are gradually coming to perform the role of history in the comprehensive schools and in the new universities. The second minor argument centres on the natural interest that any reasonably educated person might be expected to have in the society in which he lives. A scholarly, analytical approach to the structure and problems of present-day society, it is argued, is preferable to the subjective and haphazard response of the citizen innocent of the social sciences. However, the weightiest argument concerns the utilitarian nature of the social sciences which sets them in such sharp contrast from the humanities like history. The social sciences seek to understand society, but in understanding they lay bare the means whereby society might be changed. The utilitarian value of the social sciences derives from their techniques of quantification, classification of data and the drawing of general laws – from those very characteristics, indeed, upon which are founded their claims to be sciences. Furthermore, this utilitarian value has given the social sciences a peculiar relevance to the present pragmatic generation, whose interest has been catered for by a considerable expansion of study facilities in higher education.

History, in contrast to social science, has little evident utility – a view certainly widely shared by pupils in English secondary schools. To many of the modern generation, history, like God, is dead. Many history teachers are, of course, well aware of the decline of interest in their subject,[8] and are altering their syllabuses and teaching methods (as many other contributions to this book show) in a great variety of ways in an effort to reverse this tendency. 'A *desperate* effort' some social studies teachers would say – for they see in the great variety of changes (e.g. contemporary history, world history, the use of archive material) not the vigour of reform but rather the frantic search by a dying body for a revitalising elixir.

One might summarise the differences between the two sets of disciplines by defining history as a study of unique events in the past and the social sciences as the study of general laws about the present. If one then consolidates this distinctiveness by demonstrating the lack of sympathy between the teachers of the two subjects, any hope of cooperation in a common syllabus must appear to fade as a pipe-dream. Moreover, since both history and social science (or social studies) occupy the same broad area of the curriculum – namely social education – they cannot coexist as separate entities in the time-table of any given class: the law of the conservation of the curriculum, to use Lord James' phrase, simply will not allow it. They would thus seem to be forced into a posture of competitiveness: history *or* social studies.

Yet one must not exaggerate the differences – either the differ-ences in the nature of the disciplines or the differences that might divide their practitioners. It is perhaps more profitable to regard the historical and social science methods and perspectives as comple-mentary rather than contradictory. The social scientist can learn from the historian to be more tentative in his generalisations and to test his hypotheses against the rich evidence of the past. The his-torian, in his turn, can learn to handle the techniques of quantifica-tion and be less reticent about drawing generalisations from his material. If the scholars in the two fields can respect each other, can learn from each other, can even perhaps become indistinguishable (as Dr Holloway advocates[9] and has personally achieved – is he an historian or a social scientist?) then the way may be open for coopera-tion at the school level. Since coexistence is impracticable and since competitiveness is likely to lead to the elimination of one or other of the subjects together with all the characteristic values listed above, cooperation would seem highly desirable. How can such a desirable end be achieved in terms of syllabus construction?

Two methods are already being employed – basically each side borrowing from the other. Social scientists and social science teachers are bound to draw on the past for at least some of their illustrative material – even if they do confine their attention to the recent past. (It is doubtful, after all, if 'the present' has any meaning at all that can distinguish it from the recent past.) It is true, of course, that content is, in the context of our discussion here, not as important as the way in which the material is used. Economic history is different from historical economics, for example.[10] Never-theless, many courses in economics contain an element of economic history just as those in sociology embrace social history and those in politics, political and constitutional history. Social scientists have always acknowledged that a study of the past in some way is necessary for a full illumination of the present. In contrast, however, it is only comparatively recently that historians have recognised the usefulness for their own work of the techniques of study developed by the social scientists: indeed, the work that has been the product of this recognition has been called 'the new history'. Keith Thomas analysed this new approach in an article in *The Times Literary Supplement*.[11] He distinguished three elements: firstly, the consciousness of the need to define terms with greater clarity (for example, class); secondly, the adoption of quantification techniques (for example, in demographic studies); and thirdly, the use of analogies, especially from anthropology, to cast a clearer light on societies studied by historians. Even if the article has become 'notorious' (Beloff[12]) and even if it is 'shot through with an engaging arrogance and historically invalid assertions' (Elton[13]), it none the less states the facts of academic life: historians are increasingly using with effectiveness the techniques and ways of study of the social scientists. And, it can be added, some teachers are following suit.

This mutual exchange of methods of working takes us some way along the path of cooperation. But we still have two sets of subjects – historical sociology and sociological history, or whatever the mixes might be termed. They are, indeed, in chemical terminology, mixtures, not compounds. Is there any way of achieving, at the school level at least, a coherent, organic syllabus compounding elements of both history and the social sciences? I believe that there is and I believe that the key lies in a clear understanding of the nature of concepts and the way in which they can properly and effectively be used in curriculum construction.

One of the most influential books published in recent years in the field of curriculum development has been Jerome Bruner's *The Process of Education*,[14] in which he pronounces the now famous, wide-sweeping statement that 'any subject can be taught effectively in some intellectually honest form to any child at any stage of development'.[15] The foundation for this belief is the faith placed in the 'spiral curriculum'. The argument briefly is as follows. Every subject is susceptible of analysis into a limited number of basic concepts. All teaching material should be organised and presented in such a way that it is seen to illustrate these concepts. But the material must also be presented so that the concepts are illustrated in increasingly sophisticated ways as one moves higher up the age and ability scale. Concepts are constantly returned to but at a higher plane of sophistication – hence the spiral image. The simplicity and apparent effectiveness of this curriculum model easily explain its popularity. By compartmentalising information, the subject-matter of any given discipline is more easily comprehended than by its presentation in a random or fragmented way; and by the constant reference to the basic concepts, learning is being continually reinforced.

It is all very neat and convincing; and the search for the magic concepts has been on ever since the publication of Bruner's book – for the stair-well must be constructed before one can build up the treads of the spiral staircase. It is all very neat and convincing, but I suspect that there is a catch. The perception that Bruner (or rather the committee of which he was chairman) had of the curriculum is capable of realisation only if the word 'concept' is taken to mean 'a transferable explanatory principle'. It must be transferable to different situations in time and space in order that it might embrace all the possible illustrative material and in order that it might be employed at every level of the spiral. This rather abstract argument will be developed later. The point that I wish to make immediately is that not every subject is susceptible of analysis into concepts defined in this way; and consequently not every subject can be moulded to fit the spiral-shaped syllabus advocated by Bruner's committee. There are subjects that have clearly defined structures – the subjects, indeed, whose very *raison d'être* is the formulation of general laws. And here, surely, lies a vitally important distinction between history and the social sciences. The fact that sociology and its neighbouring disciplines are pretenders to the title of 'science' places them in the category of structured subjects analysable into basic concepts, which in turn may be built into a Brunerian spiral. History, on the other hand, is primarily concerned with the uniqueness of events (*pace* Arnold Toynbee) rather than recurring patterns. To those who would argue that they have, in fact, discovered historical concepts I would answer that these concepts are either social science concepts (e.g. class, leadership) or that they are non-transferable descriptions (e.g. the Reformation) which, however useful they may be as 'containers' of certain historical information, are unique to the historical situation under review and therefore irrelevant to the task of constructing a spiral syllabus.

The denial to history of discrete constituent concepts is by no means intended as a denial of its value as a subject for study. On the contrary, I would wish to argue that history is *more* than a subject (in the usual, time-table meaning of this term and in the sense that economics, for example, is a subject); and furthermore that a clearer understanding of what is probably the most natural relationship between this broadly conceived history and the social science subjects would lead easily to a coherent curriculum in this sphere. My argument is as follows. History should be perceived not merely as a subject, but rather as a mode of thought: all subjects can be studied historically. Nevertheless, history has traditionally been used particularly as a means of social and political education, with consequent emphasis on the social and political aspects of history; the histories of science and art, for example, have rarely featured in any important way in syllabuses. If the argument has been sound up to this point, the conclusion that one must draw is surely that history should be taught in such a way that it is used as a vehicle for the basic social science concepts. The social sciences, in other words, will be used as ways of articulating the historical mode of thought. There are, of course, problems in such a scheme. For example, despite the belief of Bruner already quoted and notable work like that of the Margerisons in Bradford,[16] it is doubtful whether it is a suitable curriculum model for English primary schools, where a much freer association of material in topic work is a well-tried and successful tradition. It may also inhibit, in some small measure, the development of similar project work in secondary schools.[17] Nevertheless, at the secondary level the light constraints imposed would be a small price to pay for the gain of a firm, supporting structure. Moreover, the overall gains would be enjoyed mutually by history and the social sciences. At the moment, too many history syllabuses are either overloaded in content or the material is selected in a rather haphazard way; while in the social sciences the material is too frequently somewhat abstract and lacking in vivid interest. By fusing the two groups of subjects in the way suggested, history provides the vitality and colour of its narrative and biographical matter while the social sciences supply a coherent learning structure. The syllabus would be constructed in the normal ways of history syllabuses – chronological outline and/or sequential 'patches' – but the material would be selected for its usefulness in exemplifying the social science concepts as well as for its interest potential and inherent historical significance. And, in addition, the teacher would handle the material so as to develop in the pupils the facility to recognise the concepts in whatever historical situation they were studying.

Clearly there is room for manœuvre in the practical implementation of this syllabus-plan. There is room, too, for differences of opinion concerning the basic concepts that should be taught: indeed, the process of identifying concepts has barely started in England. One must recognise also that major concepts themselves consist of a network of lower-order concepts and just how far one takes a class into the complexities of any given concept must naturally depend on the intellectual capacity of the class. For example, sociology might be broken down into the four fundamental concepts of institutions, socialisation, organisation and stratification. One must recognise, however, that organisation, for instance, embraces such sub-concepts as anomie, bureaucracy and alienation, or that stratification includes class, status and power.[18] In economics, too, four basic concepts might well be identified, namely, scarcity and choice, production and distribution, specialisation and interdependence, and fluctuation in and control of economic conditions.

In order to pursue this syllabus-model of historical exemplification of social science concepts, let us work out in some depth a framework of concepts in political science with suitable illustrative material drawn from twentieth-century history. The following would provide a useful list of concepts: leadership, decision-making, role of the individual, ideology, international relations (conflict), international relations (resolution of conflict). Let us take each of these concepts in turn and see how they might be developed and illustrated.

Firstly, leadership. Biography, especially of intrinsically interesting people, is always a popular approach to history; and the twentieth century can provide a rich variety of interesting people who might be used to illustrate the nature of political leadership in a variety of situations. Lenin, Hitler, Churchill, Gandhi, Nkrumah, Hammarskjöld and Kennedy would be a useful list. Questions that might be asked could include the social origins of these leaders, how they rose to power, how they exercised and retained power, the influence of charisma, the importance of the mass media in the exercise of leadership and the importance of a party organisation or similar mass-backing.

Examples of decision-making could be gleaned from situations ranging from those that are very near to the pupil's experience, such as the comprehensive-school programme, to remote, high-level decision-making, such as the Bolshevik decision to seize power in November 1917, the operation of Churchill's war cabinet, the problem of the exercise of the veto in the UN Security Council and Kennedy's agony in the Cuban missile crisis. The part played by individuals, the institutional framework, the processes of giving and taking advice and the power to take decisions are all embraced by the concept of decision-making.

The role of the individual might be exemplified by the activities of CND, the American Civil Rights movement and a detailed study of the most recent British election. Questions about the political socialisation process, sources of information for the citizen, lobbying, pressure groups and elections are all involved in this concept.

Ideology, of course, is more difficult to teach. Nevertheless, topics like communism, national self-determination, nazism, apartheid and the Hindu v Moslem issue in the Indian sub-continent are important enough for the teacher to persevere to make them comprehensible. The study of ideology might involve the philosophical bases of the theory, its origins in a particular historical situation, the changes wrought by the acceptance of the ideology and the relationship between the existence of an ideology and the exercise of power.

The study of international relations involves the understanding of two basic concepts, namely, conflict and its resolution. International conflict may occur as the result of several different kinds of quarrels – ideological, an arms race, economic needs and jealousies and the processes of colonisation and de-colonisation. Resolution of conflict may be achieved by bilateral agreement, the intervention of great or super-powers, the work of a supranational authority or by the quarrel being rendered obsolete by new events.[19] International conflict could be illustrated by the Second World War, the Cuban missile crisis, the India-Pakistan conflict, the Suez crisis of 1956 and the Vietnamese war. The resolution of international conflict might be handled through the Versailles peace-settlement, the nuclear test-ban agreement, the granting of independence to rebellious colonies and the operations of the UN peace-keeping forces in the Congo.

The illustrations that have been given have not been chosen entirely at random: they represent rather the exemplification of a manageable number of concepts within the framework of ten fairly obvious topics of twentieth-century world history. The pattern may be most readily explained by means of the table on page 144.

The full exposition of the thesis presented in this chapter would, of course, require a vastly extended table to cater for earlier periods

	Russian Revolution	Versailles Settlement	Nazism	Second World War	Cold War	USA since 1945	India	Africa	UNO	Modern Britain
Leadership	Lenin		Hitler	Churchill		Kennedy	Gandhi	Nkrumah	Hammarskjöld	
Decision-making	Seizure of power			War cabinet		Cuban missile crisis			Security Council and the veto	Comprehensive schools
Role of the individual					CND	Civil Rights movement				General election
Ideology	Communism	National self-determination	Nazism				Hinduism v Islam	Apartheid		
International conflict				German and Japanese wars	Cuban missile crisis	Vietnamese war				Suez crisis
Resolution of international conflict		Peace settlement			Test-ban agreement			Decolonisation	Congo	

of history and its projection into a third dimension to deal with the other social science disciplines; though it must be admitted that it is doubtful whether anthropology and psychology (as well as sociology, politics and economics) can be handled through the historical medium.

As educationists we have learned to bandy about the words 'literate' and 'numerate'. Yet *social* education is just as pressing. The 'generation gap', the multi-racial society, incomes and prices policy, enfranchisement at eighteen – these are all matters of urgency. They impinge on young people's consciousness through the mass media, and need to be taught in such a way that the young citizen can come to grips with them within rigorously defined frames of reference. The young person needs help to understand the society in which he lives and to place that society and its problems securely in a time perspective. Social science provides the teacher with the tool for the job, but he must not forget that 'history is and must be the very shank of social science'.[20]

Notes

1 W. H. Burston, *Social Studies and the History Teacher*, Historical Association, 1962.

2 K. Thomas, 'The Tools and the Job', *The Times Literary Supplement*, 7 April 1966; E. Shils, 'Seeing it Whole', and P. Temin, 'In Pursuit of the Exact', *ibid.*, 28 July 1966.

3 S. W. F. Holloway, 'History and Sociology: What History Is and What It Ought to Be', in W. H. Burston and D. Thompson (eds), *Studies in the Nature and Teaching of History*, Routledge, 1967.

4 G. Bernbaum, 'Sociology and Contemporary History', *Educational Review*, vol. 20, 1967–8.

5 Mark M. Krug, *History and the Social Sciences: New Approaches to the Teaching of Social Studies*, Blaisdell, 1967. Professor Krug's argument is very similar to that adopted in this chapter, though I had developed the basic idea before reading his book.

6 G. R. Elton, *The Practice of History*, Sydney UP, 1967; Fontana, 1969.

7 See, for example, Schools Council, *Enquiry 1: Young School Leavers*, HMSO, 1968, chap. 3.

8 See, for example, Mary Price, 'History in Danger', *History*, vol. LIII, no. 179, October 1968.

9 S. W. F. Holloway, *op. cit.*, p. 21.

10 See Ralph Davis, *History and the Social Sciences*, Leicester UP, 1965.

11 See note 2 above.

12 Max Beloff, 'On thinking about the Past', *Encounter*, October 1969, p. 48, n.12.

13 G. R. Elton, *op. cit.* (Fontana edition), p. 18, n.5.

14 Jerome S. Bruner, *The Process of Education*, Harvard UP, 1963.

15 *Ibid.*, p. 33.

16 See Vincent R. Rogers, *The Social Studies in English Education*, Heinemann, 1968, p. 47.

17 See the chapter on 'The Project Method' below.

18 This is a simplification (and perhaps distortion) of an analysis by my colleague, Mr R. Skelton.

19 I owe the basis of this analysis of conflict and conflict-resolution to Professor F. S. Northedge.

20 C. Wright Mills, quoted in Asa Briggs, 'Sociology and History', in A. T. Welford *et al.* (eds), *Society: Problems and Methods of Study*, Routledge, 1962.

C. D. DARLINGTON

History and Biology

HISTORIAN AND BIOLOGIST

Those of us with an historical sense naturally want to use this sense to understand the past and in turn to use this understanding as a guide to the future. The discovery of causes is the means to this end but how are the causes to be discovered? Ancient teachers could have no idea of the extent of time or of space in which man had lived and in their interpretations they were bound to rely on beliefs in myth and in magic, beliefs from which we are only now in process of escaping.

If this is true of history it is no less true of biology. For only at the beginning of the nineteenth century did biology begin to pull itself together and to give its parts a single name and purpose. It was only then that the desire to discover common and remote causes made itself felt and the necessary conjectures took shape. When this happened it was easy to see that a biologist like Darwin, collecting evidence and testing hypotheses, was doing a job that overlapped with the work of an historian. Both disciplines required the same patience in studying the long-lasting changes of living things.

As teaching subjects, no less than as research subjects, history and biology have common problems. Both have to be taught to non-adults; but their success in this direction is an obstacle to their development. The appeal of written history to tribal instincts or to anecdotal interest retards its maturity, for such impressions mean that the serious intention will be disregarded just when it is later most needed. So it is with biology. Both these sciences indeed demand a sense of time, of development, and of connectedness which only a few individuals are capable of acquiring. These gifts or faculties need to be discovered and selected: they cannot merely be instilled. Incorrect teaching will therefore fail in the very special purpose of discovering the vocation in life of the future historian and biologist.

In teaching history or biology, however, we have another common danger. The young are bound to pick up ideas on both these subjects from newspapers, politicians or even parents – ideas inconsistent with one another or with what we might wish to teach. As the

American writer, Artemus Ward, once said: the trouble with most folks is not so much plain ignorance as that they know so many things as ain't so.

Nor are these merely the mistakes of youth, for the mature historian and biologist are quite capable of borrowing one another's discarded ideas. For example, writers are bound to use the everyday names for peoples like Jews or Romans. Such names suggest the biological character of races; correctly so. But at the same time they suggest the unbiological character of not undergoing evolution; incorrectly so, for these peoples, these races, have all undergone evolution. Similarly the name of family is given to a group of male descent, connected with the inheritance of rank and property. But all families depend for their character equally on female parents. The legal or political comes to be confused with the biological. Sometimes this is right; sometimes it is altogether wrong.

A mistake of a different order happens when ideas are borrowed from the social sciences. For in general their origin may be traced back to Herbert Spencer. The biological opinions of this philosopher are widely followed today not by biologists but outside biology. It seems to be thought that because he introduced the word evolution to biology he knew how evolution happened. Whereas unfortunately, like Lamarck, Spencer thought that habits and ideas could impress themselves on heredity. Merely by education (or perhaps by reading Spencer) one might change one's race and improve the character of one's descendants.

Much the gravest fault, today, however is one found among biologists, or supposed biologists. It lies in the assumption that at some point in time man ceased to be an animal and acquired a mind or a soul. At that moment biology changed into history. Since that unrecorded day, so the story runs, human society has developed without genetic change and by processes unrelated to those which governed his earlier and baser animal life. I have even been asked by an eminent but innocent physiological colleague when I thought this first of all D-days was to be dated. When was it, he asked, that natural selection had ceased to operate on man and social processes had taken control of culture, of civilisation and of the future of our species?

One does not need to be much of a biologist or a historian to see that man must have developed in a continuous succession from father to son over some millions of generations. The passage from *Homo erectus* to *Homo sapiens* we can see was no heroic jump; it was a straight exercise in procreation. Nor was the passage from pre-history to history, from excavation to documentation. Nor is the passage from white man's sociology to black man's anthropology. These represent shifts in methods of study but not in the principles or properties that are being studied. The barriers between them are simply the academic obstacles invented by the collective ignorance and timidity of specialists. Any child can see this if adults will allow him to do so.

THE MEETING-PLACE

If we agree that the historian and the biologist are not forever set apart and that there is common ground for discussion between them, we have to ask ourselves at what point this discussion should begin. Clearly the whole of mankind is our common interest. But what is to be our scope in time? Surely we can compromise with eternity. We need not take the whole of evolutionary history but we ought to go back to the great watershed from which all the later growth, movement and multiplication of man has flowed.

Where is this watershed? It stands at the origin of agriculture ten thousand years ago. From that moment man himself and the crops and stock he bred both began to multiply and to diversify with a speed and to an extent unknown in his or their ancestors, unknown indeed in any organism before that time. A transformation began which is now, happily or unhappily, reaching its climax. To be sure there followed five millennia of silence from the point of view of the documentary historian. But they were millennia which carried new races of peasants and pastoralists across Europe, Asia and part of Africa; there they proceeded to beget the peoples who were to make history in each region.

Although these are early years, years dated only by the archaeologist with the help of Carbon-14, nevertheless the historian wants to know how a few cultivators, beginning in Anatolia, could in 5,000 years transform the mode of life of men in three continents. He will want to know how they could do so without destroying the racial differences between their peoples or, above all, their fitness to live in quite different climates. The answer is by hybridisation and by selection. The men picked up plants and animals of new species to breed and grow and use for their food and clothing. For themselves they picked the native women of the new lands. In a hundred generations new races had been bred from these new genetic combinations, selected for new climates and also for the new arts of husbandry. This process has been repeated throughout history with vital effect. Whether we are teachers or pupils we can see it happening around us today in many parts of the world where advanced and primitive peoples meet.

When we come to the period of the five thousand years of recorded history, there arise a choice of questions that the historian may ask of the biologist. Let us begin by taking a general rather than a particular issue. Historians have long been impressed by the apparent cycles of success and decline that befall dynasties and empires. It is easy to draw the conclusion that pride comes before a fall and that this moral principle is a law of nature. But this answer gives us no explanation of the past and no guidance for the future. For these we have to examine the behaviour of people, their mode of breeding and their control of their environment in each of the diverse historic situations concerned. We then find a number of rules whose operation we can grasp and use as a basis of prediction. Three of these will show what I mean.

First, the progress man has made in controlling his environment since long before his invention of agriculture has always tended to destroy this environment. The prosperity man extracts from the earth damages the earth in a way he has never been able to foresee. His failure to foresee danger (which still persists) has wrecked one civilisation after another.

Look at what happens in detail. The slash-and-burn farmer spoils his land and moves on to a new site after five years. The fixed peasant may stay a whole millennium. But then he generally finds that he has exhausted his soil, silted up his canals, felled his forests and worked out his minerals. What does he do then? Once the prosperity of a district or country is destroyed the rulers and the craftsmen have always moved away. The mass of the peasants, however, have usually stayed and starved. In these respects what happened in Babylonia has happened in Britain; and it is happening today in many parts of Africa, both black and white.

Secondly, all families which prosper by some invention of their own have arisen by normal human processes of outbreeding. But once established in their prosperity they begin to set themselves apart. They form inbred tribes, castes or guilds which include their kindred and exclude strangers. In short, they set up a closed shop.

They then cease to be capable of adapting themselves to new conditions which they themselves may have helped to create. It is an immemorial practice but, again, we can see it around us today.

Thirdly, these inbred castes serve a useful purpose in transmitting the knowledge and skill on which they are based, that is in transmitting culture. The disastrous effect of inbreeding which comes later, is felt first by the families of kings. For these families or dynasties being the smallest, and most exclusive of all, carry their inbreeding to an extreme – often indeed to the point of incest. And being the most powerful families they can, more perfectly than the rest of us, protect themselves from the effects of natural selection. The combination of these two circumstances in the end often ruins them.

A wide range of historical inquiry can be devoted to illustrating these situations and showing their effects on both the rulers and their subjects. But to enjoy this pursuit, and to profit by the exercise, the historical teacher and his pupil need to know a little of the ideas of biology. They need to take note of the behaviour of animals as well as humans. They need to consider its relation to the choice of habitat, the choice of occupation, and above all to the choice of mate. They need to see the connection between these things and the properties of heredity and variation. For these properties are the common connecting link in any living system.

THE PARADOXES OF HEREDITY

Mendelian theories taught to the young student of biology for some seventy years have not usually helped him to understand human beings. Indeed they have often put him off for the rest of his life. Mendel chose to breed peas because the few hundred garden varieties are self-fertilised; they are absolutely uniform and predictable and they breed absolutely true – 'as like as two peas'. But human beings are not self-fertilised. They are not even mated brother-to-sister. They do not breed true. They are all of them different, thousands of millions of them covering the earth through the whole of history; including even brothers or sisters who have the same parents and same ancestors. This then is the chief paradox of heredity: it means quite different things with different methods of breeding. This is something that the biology teacher expounding Mendel's laws rarely if ever thinks of telling his pupils. And they probably wouldn't pass their exams if he did.

Now biologists, all this century, have been more and more concerned with following the clue given them by Mendel. This is the clue which has led to the finer and finer understanding of how heredity works. It has taken them down to chromosomes, genes, DNA and the genetic code, all of which are of far-reaching importance. But this deep concentration of interest has meant that they have never bothered to think out the practical consequences of heredity for ordinary people. To do that is a formidable task, and perhaps a moral as much as an intellectual one. For it requires nothing less than cutting out the jargon. Can it be done? I believe so.

The essence of the thing is the contrast between heredity and variation, which turns out to be almost the same as the contrast between inbreeding and outbreeding.

On the one hand, inbreeding gives pure breeding. It gives heredity pure and simple. Even if it is only as close as first-cousin marriage, if continued for a few generations in a small group which remains small, inbreeding gives a pure race. There are (if UNESCO will allow me to say so) many such pure races among living peoples today. In such races the communities are homogeneous and harmonious, stable and stagnant. Equality is practicable. Justice is natural. The children are like the parents. They even tend to agree with them. In consequence they invent nothing. They keep everything. They merely transmit the culture they received. The whole system is predictable.

Outbreeding, on the other hand, gives variation. It can occur only when there is a large group brought together by movements of tribes, families or individuals, movements which make it possible for unrelated people to mate and to multiply. It produces children that are unlike their parents and unlike one another in form and habit, in capacity and belief, in health, in fertility, even in speech. Inequality and injustice are naturally generated. Families and the communities they form are inharmonious and unstable. They produce misfits but they also produce innovators, men and women with new habits and new ideas. They thus destroy and also create culture. And the system as a whole is unpredictable.

Between these two extremes lie most of humanity. Between them most of history is enacted. But above all, perhaps, the great persons and great events of history are connected with the transitions from the one to the other, from inbreeding to outbreeding. If the historian is on the look-out for this connection he will be able to discover how the principle operates, how it is to be modified or limited, how far it applies to kings or priests, merchants or craftsmen. And if he is able to contradict it he will have discovered a new biological as well as historical principle capable of altering the prospects of mankind.

If the historian does inquire on these lines he is bound to learn something about the creation of culture which is, after all, the real stuff of history. He will find that inventions and discoveries are sudden events, the work of individual men and women; or a succession of such people.

It does not seem to matter whether invention concerns the extraction of a metal, the measurement of an angle, the foretelling of a flood or an eclipse, the framing of a phrase, or the use of such new ideas and methods in winning the respect or securing the government of a community. Whichever it may be, such events, formerly rare and obscure, now common and observed, are the steps by which history is made and culture created. But this does not happen until the discoverer has shown another individual how to imitate and repeat what he did. Only at that point is culture transmitted.

All teachers are experimenters with living beings in this very field of the transmission of culture. And one of the things we learn first from our experiments is that some individuals can understand a discovery when it is explained to them and others cannot. This we attribute to differences in their character, their native wit and judgement, or their intelligence. The transmission of culture thus seems to be a test of intelligence; and a test of something connected, we understand, in some way with heredity.

Here the historian may well take the same view as the biologist. Indeed he may well see more easily than the biologist that history is a continuous performance of ability tests, total brain and body tests to which mankind has been submitted from the beginning. They are tests which are ruthless and cruel in discriminating between individuals and families, communities and races. We find there is no substitute for ability, and ability is always in short supply.

These are processes to which Darwin gave the name of selection. Isaiah called them winnowing. And Matthew just spoke of the shepherd dividing the sheep from the goats. But when we look at the facts of history and the experiments of biology together we find that they include more activities than the biologist or historian could have separately imagined. Let us draw the outlines of one of these.

MIGRATION AND CULTURE

Animals and human beings alike have some choice of environment. As individuals, families, or tribes they move to where they find life easiest and best. The dramatic aspect of this movement is what we call migration. What are its biological causes and effects? We do not know with certainty or in detail where the Cretans went to or where the Etruscans came from. But if we study Europe during the last millennium we may make good guesses, for in Europe we know what has happened with certainty and much detail. And from this we can arrive at some principles.

In Europe, as everywhere else, migration is selective. The peasant depends on his land, on the understanding of his land and what grows on it, for his survival. He therefore loves his land – which is incidentally the genetic and psychological basis of serfdom. If he migrates, he cannot take his land with him. So he does not migrate if he can help it. But townspeople, whether they are governors or craftsmen, priests or scholars, can pack the tools of their trade in a bag and move where they choose. And it is their activities which are the crux of civilisation.

Careful study allows us to connect the movements of these people with both their causes and their consequences. Alexander's conquests in Asia, and the cities he built, created a system in which townsmen could and did move as never before in history. The Hellenistic kingdoms opened channels through which technically advanced people all over the ancient east could flow, mix and interbreed. The mode and the limits of their interbreeding were set over many centuries by two agents: the Greek language and the Jewish religion. These were the two channels which allowed the genetic wealth of the older nations to flow westward into Europe. It was a flow which was cut off from Asia, and even more from Africa, by deserts and disease. After the break up of the Roman Empire, those channels became the Latin language and the Christian religion. It was they which carried civilisation to the limits of the Continent, and turned Europe into the intellectual and cultural powerhouse of mankind.

Thus we reach the principle that civilisation is carried by the migration of civilised people. It is carried by people from the anciently evolved centres of civilisation; that is by a brain drain which, according to its amount, may or may not impoverish the parental communities. It is never carried in any other way. And anyone can see how it is being carried (or not being carried) in this way today.

The historian may examine these questions on different scales of inquiry. On a medium scale he may compare two contemporary societies like those of Athens and Sparta or he may look at the different stages of development of one society like that of the Ottoman Empire or of the Venetian Republic. In any of these examples he finds differences in the detailed breeding relations and consequent evolution of different social classes. These diverge in character and in behaviour, broadening or narrowing, standing still, or gaining or losing by migration, or – what is in effect the same – by religious conversion.

If the historian now wishes to look at events on a larger scale he can see a picture that is no less instructive. If he turns to India he sees the strengthening of religious control over the formation of castes in the interests of the priestly caste itself. He sees repeated attempts and repeated failures to break down the rigidity of the system. And he sees the result in the nearly perfect transmission of culture and slowly increasing integration of habits and beliefs from generation to generation for over two thousand years. But when he turns, on the contrary, to Europe, where the geographical diversity was greater but the racial diverisity less, he accordingly finds a different balance of events. The fall of the Roman Empire meant the break up of a large part of the class structure of western Europe. A wave of outbreeding broke the continuity in the transmission of culture. And in the resulting confusion much was lost. But after a few generations, new peoples, new geographical groups or nations, sorted themselves out and picking up the threads of the ancient culture, in part by immigration from the east, began to make new inventions, to invent new modes of government, and create new cultures. All these changes went with the formation of new social classes, kings and nobles, scholars and priests, merchants and artisans, above the largely immobile and subservient peasantry. But none of these classes were fixed. All were recruited from below and recruited from outside, recruited by selective migration, selective mating, and selective conversion to new religions.

These are only some of the ways in which processes of selection which Darwin used to explain the evolution of wild plants and animals are elaborated and diversified when they act on the more complex situations of stratified and civilised human societies.

THE PARADOXES OF HISTORY

These things may appear to the historian as paradoxes. They are, I believe, some of the basic paradoxes of history because they are inherent in its biological foundations. But there are many other paradoxes known to the historian which are not at all clear to the biologist.

The historian can see that originally different social classes are derived from different races of people who preferred to work with one another rather than kill one another – itself a remarkable discovery. He knows that kings and priests made it their business to keep the peace between social classes by dictating their exact rights and duties and, above all, prescribing how they should or should not breed together. These kings and priests had discovered that marriage makes history. It was again a remarkable discovery, based, we may suppose, on observation of its social and political consequences. But the mode of control, which had to be accommodated to instinct, religion and law, had far-reaching and unforeseen consequences. It led to the formation of castes in all ancient societies and in India today; it guided the development of city states in Greece; it led first to Roman survival and then to Roman dominance in Italy; and it led to the evolution of governing classes, military or priestly, everywhere.

The first and greatest paradox of history is therefore that rules devised for short-term political purposes have long-term biological effects which, like the environmental effects of civilisation, were not at first foreseen. Societies which discover how to change their rules to suit new conditions are the ones which achieve long-term success. But of course it is not society as a whole which learns anything: it is particular classes, groups and individuals which have the wit to make the discovery and the strength to apply it.

INDIVIDUAL AND COMMUNITY

A second paradox which confronts the biologist and the historian perplexes them separately but can be resolved by them together. It concerns the relations of the individual with the community.

The biologist investigating causes has to separate what comes from *inside* and what comes from *outside* the organism. He separates nature and nurture, heredity and environment. They are the two opposed and perhaps independent factors in deciding how an organism will develop and what it will do. He notices, to be sure, that animals in part choose where they will live. They choose their environments so that their environment is to that extent subordinate to their heredity. But what is he to make of man in society? He observes that men have been creating their own environments in creating civilisation. And in a stratified society each social class has found and partly made its own environment, that of the community in which it lives. Here the historian can help. For these present environments have been created by men in the past. They depend upon an accumulation during earlier generations of invention and interaction, teaching and learning, in which different individuals and classes have played different parts, owing to their differences of genetic character. These are differences which in the long term dominate the history and the evolution of society.

How this happens can be seen most neatly in the development of the rules of behaviour and the rules of speech which we use to describe our morals and our language. In both these fields the individual learns first from his nearest kin, his family. Later he learns to accommodate himself to a whole tribe. And in a stratified society the tribe has become a class. Either group has its local beliefs and practices and its local dialect. The class may also accommodate itself to other classes, the lower orders respecting, or pretending to respect, the opinions, accents, or usages of the higher orders. In all these reactions the environment is genetically conditioned by processes to which we may apply Bagehot's term *deference*. Or we may ascribe them to the *imprinting* which Konrad Lorenz discovered in geese. Or again we may relate them to the *herd instinct* of Wilfred Trotter. The biologist may ask the historian whether *snobbery* is not one of their expressions and the *establishment*, both secular and religious, one of their products.

At this point the historian may explain that all the processes of developing civilisation have to be screened in respect of their social origins. The steps in the development of agriculture were taken by men and women who learnt to store grain and to sow it, to reap grain and to thrash it, to hoe land and to plough and water it.

The arts of government, just as much as those of agriculture and industry, were the results of sequences of individual discoveries taught and learnt and accumulated by the kindred and descendants of the discoverers. These arts, whether kingly or priestly, whether relying on force or fraud, were always practised and always survived by the activities and the breeding of very few and by the acquiescence of very many. They have always depended on genetic differences and on certain ancient properties of largely instinctive behaviour.

The growth and organisation of society depend on the appearance of groups of men who could exploit the properties of animal behaviour possessed by their fellows. The first men to do this were kings of whom we know nothing beyond the fact that they were pastoralists who undertook to manage the peasants. The most recent, we may see, have been the Communist thinkers and leaders. We can watch them taking a century to perfect their more sophisticated but still clumsy techniques, trying to suit them to modern conditions and to different races, societies and situations.

Between social classes, however, conflict and cooperation always exist together. Although the pages of documentary history are filled with the record of conflicts it was cooperation that came first, leaving much evidence for the archaeologist, and still matters most.

Many debatable questions we may leave to be answered later. But we must be aware of their existence. We must bear in mind that the problems of the individual existing in a stratified society lie at the root of his religion. The individual needs to accommodate himself to the demands of the community. He needs to adjust what is instinctively necessary for him to what is rationally absurd and unjust in the heterogeneous family. Such needs lead to those unconscious conflicts in the mind of the individual which are relieved and exploited by the witch doctor and the priest, the ruler and the politician.

Methods of study change but what is studied always has a certain common character. And that character depends on the evolutionary fact that the reasoning part of the brain has been imposed on a non-reasoning, unteachable, instinctive part, a directly genetic part, that was there first and is still necessary for the working of the whole outfit. The unconscious conflict between the two has been exposed by the rapid development of complex societies. Notably it underlies the methods invented by prophets and used by priests and rulers to protect as well as to make use of the people they guide or govern. It also underlies the processes by which the people submit. In this way we may understand the barriers of deception, the credibility gaps, between the governors and the governed, and also the sudden revolutionary shifts in the behaviour of the governed when they discover what has been happening.

THE WORK AHEAD

It now begins to appear that the connections between biology and history are more varied than we might at a first glance have guessed. It is rather obvious and commonplace to point out that the applications of biological techniques in statistics or ecology, medicine or agriculture, can give solutions to detailed problems in history. So modest a proposal requires no argument and will meet with no resistance. What is less easy to see is that a second and deeper approach, the introduction of biological methods and ideas into historical teaching and research, requires in the next fifty years a breakdown of barriers between fields of descriptive study. This is the same kind of breakdown which, in the last fifty years, has accompanied the growth of biology. It will, no doubt, meet with strenuous resistance. Language and religion, economics and technology are, however, inextricably entwined as causes and consequences with race and class, mating and fertility. How the causes and the consequences are related is a matter which in these circumstances some historians will be prepared to examine as hypotheses. Is this not just what the teacher needs to make his subject develop in the minds of his pupils as they meet the situations of real life?

A third approach is to learn from the pervasive parallelism of these two immense fields of study. To give an imaginative reality to the teaching of history any practical teacher will agree that it must be presented on several scales of space – local, national and world – and on several scales of time – contemporary, historical and archaeological. Each of these, it must be obvious, is paralleled in biological studies, paralleled simply on account of that living and developing character of the science of history and of the science of life which makes them continually illuminate one another.

A part of this parallelism is due to the attachment of both disciplines to the physical world. The shape of the earth, its contents, its changing climates all influence, and in the longest term control, the evolution of organisms and the development of civilisations. But above all the evolution is tied to a causal framework which it has been the business of genetics to discover. We now see that history is a demonstration of genetic processes, immensely elaborate processes which cannot in fact be studied except through observing history and treating it as a grand experiment of nature. Or, if you wish to say that it is the grand experiment of man, we need not argue the point.

If we propose to use history and biology as means of studying one another, if we wish to regard history as the climax of biology, there is one last point that we need to be clear about. Throughout the study of both subjects and vitiating their development there has been the desire to discover, if not the millennium, at least a happy ending; and if possible to discover it post-haste. There will always be a wish to tell a moral tale and to reach a quick and comfortable conclusion; to show that men, or at least common men, do what they ought to do, and usually succeed by doing so. There is a wish to show that mankind is all the time getting wiser and the world men live in is getting richer and better by the mere passage of time. This Panglossian philosophy can go with the view that change is always bad (the reactionary view) or always good (the progressive view). But if history and biology are to have one philosophy they must agree to leave this moral colour out of their story and show it, however reluctantly, uncorrected in black and white. May we not agree to leave the colour, for the time being, to the artists who will follow us?

Further Reading

C. D. Darlington, *Genetics and Man*, Allen & Unwin, 1964; 'The Genetics of Society', *Past and Present*, 43, 1969, pp. 3–33; *The Evolution of Man and Society*, Allen & Unwin, 1969.

T. K. Derry and T. I. Williams, *A Short History of Technology*, OUP, 1960.

Konrad Lorenz, *King Solomon's Ring*, Methuen, 1952.

Desmond Morris, *The Naked Ape*, Cape, 1967.

A. Wagner, *English Genealogy*, OUP, 1960.

F. M. Wilson, *They Came as Strangers*, Hamish Hamilton, 1959.

4 The Teacher's Opportunities

R. N. HALLAM

Piaget and Thinking in History

Since the 1920s Jean Piaget of Geneva University has been investigating the thought processes of children and adolescents. He has provided an invaluable service to education by demonstrating once again that children think in very different ways from the adults who surround them. At first he was concerned with young children's thinking, but the publication with Barbel Inhelder of *The Growth of Logical Thinking*[1] showed his interest in adolescents' thought processes.

Piaget's early training as a zoologist is seen clearly in his initial assumption that at any level development is a process of adaptation to the environment. This adaptation can be subdivided into two interrelated components, assimilation and accommodation. On a simple level, for example, chewing food is assimilation while opening the mouth is accommodation to the external. On the cognitive plane assimilation is 'taking in' information from the environment. One need not have a correct grasp of this new fact or experience. This frequently happens with children learning abstract concepts in history. They assimilate in an egocentric manner without real understanding; hence the many 'howlers'. Accommodation occurs when one's established thinking skills grapple with new data in the environment and are thus modified. The imbalance between one's thinking skills and the new demands of the environment is called equilibration by Piaget.

One of the most controversial aspects of Piaget's views is his belief that there are certain stages in the development of logical thought.[2] The stages, however, are not to be conceived as 'immutable realities' but more as an aid to understanding the development of children's thought. The criteria for each stage were derived from observing how children dealt with physical and mathematical experiments. Young children, for example, were given two balls of plasticine which they agreed were equal in size. Then, in front of the children, one ball was altered into a 'sausage'. Children below the age of six years tend to say that, 'There's more in this (sausage, ball) because it's (longer, thicker) than the other one.' Somewhere between six and eight years, they might appear insulted to be asked such a simple question because obviously the amounts do not alter. More complex experiments involving the use of a balance, pendulum and so on are described in *The Growth of Logical Thinking*.[3] From his investigations, Piaget concludes that there are three main stages in the development of thought: pre-operational, concrete and formal operational stages. Detailed criteria for each stage are described on pages 164–5.

It is not yet certain which factors determine a child's progress through the stages. Important ones must be heredity, maturation, social and cultural conditions, the type of physical and intellectual stimulation received and the type of material being studied. Piaget has emphasised that an adult in western society can operate at varying intellectual levels during the course of one day. When his own car went wrong Piaget, for instance, operated at 'empirical trial and error on a very low level. . . . At other times I go even lower and almost give way to magical behaviour.'[4] Thus a schoolchild might be able to operate successfully in a relatively simple context such as the manipulation of basic number but have great difficulty in the next lesson when asked to grapple with, say, sixteenth-century religious changes.

Whether it is feasible or not to apply Piaget's criteria for logical thinking to historical thinking can be considered in another way. Are different types of intelligence needed for reasoning in history and in Piagetian experiments? Vernon[5] decides that Spearman's 'g' factor or 'the eduction of relations and correlates' affects all types of thinking. Vygotsky[6] states that intellectual development is unitary: 'the psychological prerequisites for instruction in different school subjects are to a large extent the same.' Piaget himself has explained that there should be a connection between reasoning using physical apparatus and verbal reasoning. For Piaget, verbal behaviour is an *action* 'which simply replaces things by signs and movements by their evocation, and continues to operate in thought by means of these spokesmen'.[7] At the present stage of research into thinking it would seem likely, though by no means certain,[8] that the thought structures postulated by Piaget are 'also invoked in other learning and thinking situations, say, involving verbal interpretation as in history',[9] although there will be a time lag in the appearance of the three main operational stages.

Following the example of Goldman[10] in religious thinking, I used Piaget's criteria to assess the answers of 100 pupils aged eleven to sixteen years on three historical passages: 'Mary Tudor', 'The Norman Conquest of England' and 'The Civil Wars in Ireland'.[11] These were selected, after a pilot survey using a number of historical passages, as the passages which gave a wide range of answers. Each pupil answered a total of thirty questions, ten on each passage. All the answers on each story were used in the main statistical analysis but only answers to individual questions will be quoted.

As the investigation proceeded, two facts became evident. The type of replies which Piaget had discerned with younger children could also be seen in secondary school pupils' answers to questions on history. Secondly, the children were reasoning, in general, at a lower level than had been expected, reaching, for the most part, the formal operational level at a chronological age of 16:2 to 16:6 years and the concrete operational level in their twelfth year. The following answers would seem to illustrate Piaget's criteria at each level.[12]

The following criteria were used to assess the operational level of children's answers.

I PRE-OPERATIONAL THINKING

Not relating the question to the information provided
The children's opinion of Mary Tudor, after having read an impartial account of her, was often only hazily – if at all – related to the information in the passage. A subject aged 13:11 years with an IQ of 115[13] said that Mary 'was too harsh and too ready to kill somebody. She didn't really mind who it was. She didn't have many friends.'

Isolated centrings on one feature only
A boy of 16:9 years with an IQ of 128 seemed particularly influenced by a passing reference to the Domesday Survey. He decided that William was a cruel man since 'it was twenty years before he sent around to see how the country was. Anyone who really cared for the country would have sent around before then.'

Transductive reasoning – moving from one element to another without considering all the factors involved
A pupil of 13:3 years with an IQ of 118 decided that Mary Tudor liked 'fancy clothes'. When I inquired why, since there was nothing about this in the passage, he replied: 'With being a member of the Catholic Church the priest has very expensive vestments and [so]

she liked very expensive clothes and also to have jewels and other decorations on her.'

2 CONCRETE OPERATIONAL THINKING

The ability to give an organised answer but limited to what is immediately apparent in the text
A pupil aged 16:1 years with an IQ of 115 explained that William destroyed the north of England 'because the Danes had come down and attacked the Norman garrison at York so he'd gone to drive them back and revenge himself on the English'.

'Was it right to carry out such a severe punishment?'

'Well, it was no point taking it out on the English when it was the Danes' fault. They did all the fighting.'

'Did it say that in the passage?'

'Not completely. It was not necessary to take it out on the whole population. There must have been some ringleaders; he need not take it out on the English'.

3 FORMAL OPERATIONAL THINKING

Realising a multiplicity of possible links. Envisaging all possible explanations, finds out through logical analysis which are true. Hypotheses are postulated and these can be confirmed or not by the data. The child 'commits himself to possibilities; there is a reversal of direction between reality and possibility'.[14]
This is the answer of an exceptional pupil aged 14:8 years with an IQ of 127 to the question: 'Do you think the people of England . . . would have thought that not having women as rulers was a good policy (idea) after the reign of Mary Tudor?'

'I should think so because she had to marry a foreign ruler in order to stabilise her throne, which in turn had caused her to join England in a war against France which brought no benefit to England though it was probably a good thing in the long run. Further, unlike her father, she had burnt men for being heretics as opposed to her father who had burnt them for being traitors. Burnings for being heretics would be opposed by most people since they would understand executions for political reasons but not for faith – especially the many simple people who were executed. Most people would not be devoutedly Catholic or Protestant – they would go with the wind, but they would object if things got too violent.'

After reading the passage on the Norman Conquest of England the subjects were asked if they thought William of Normandy was a cruel man. This pupil was the only one of the hundred who started his answer with an hypothesis: 'It depends what you call cruel. If the definition of cruel is to . . .'[15] Inhelder and Piaget stress the importance of 'equilibrium structures' in adolescent thinking. Peel[16] explains that this is the ability to 'think in terms of opposing and balanced forces and in terms of cancellation of forces and their compensation by other forces'. This particular subject's answers were unusual in that he showed a consistent ability to oppose, balance and compensate variables in an historical context. Only one other subject was able even to approach such a developed level of thinking.

The results do not support the ages which Piaget suggests for the beginning of each stage. Piaget's subjects were, however, experimenting with concrete materials. Furthermore, research workers in England[17] using experiments taken from Inhelder and Piaget suggest that the logical thinking of most fifteen-year-old pupils is likely to be at a lower level than Piaget suggests.

That formal thinking develops later in the study of history would seem to be confirmed by other investigators who have tested children's understanding in history. Bassett[18] found that only 9·5 per cent of his 13+ age group, taken from a sample of above-average intelligence, were able to appreciate reciprocity in recorded human action. Coltham[19] discovered the most typical response of subjects ranging from a mental age of 9:1 years to 16:0 years to six commonly used historical terms. Only two terms were typically described at the concrete level and none was typically described at the formal level. Booth[20] discovered that able fourth-year pupils were not answering at the hypothetico–deductive level on many occasions. Recently, I examined very able children aged 13+ years on a number of historical passages. A preliminary investigation seems to show that most of the answers were at the concrete level. That thinking skills develop relatively late in history need not cause any great surprise. Not only is the action far removed from the children's immediate world but they can be faced at the hypothetical level with inferences and moral dilemmas which can perplex the most intelligent of adults.

Piaget's experiments on the development of a concept of time have been mainly concerned with physical time. Two dolls, for example, started and finished a 'race' at the same time, but one went faster than the other. Only at seven to eight years did children admit that the time of movement was the same for both dolls. Lovell and Slater[21] report that children realised that time did not alter with changes in speed first in a water experiment and then later with the dolls. They postulate that time is a specific concept, not developing in all situations and in all media at the same age.

An experiment by Michaud[22] shows children's difficulties in dealing with abstract time. About half of his thirteen-year-old subjects decided that putting the clock forward in spring made them older. An early study by Sturt and Oakden,[23] 'replicated and substantially confirmed twenty-five years later by Bradley',[24] showed convincingly the difficulties children have in understanding historical time. It was not until eleven years old that three-quarters of the children understood the basic implications of historical dates. In dealing with historical epochs, those most remote from their own time were most easily distinguished because they could be most negatively characterised when compared with the twentieth century. The appeal of the distant past to children was found by Musgrove,[25] who discovered among 228 children 'a consistent average preference for history remote in time. This was so at all ages between ten and fifteen, with boys equally with girls, and in secondary modern as well as in grammar streams.'

Jahoda explains that subsequent research in various countries has substantially confirmed the main conclusions of Sturt and Oakden, 'in particular, the view that somewhere around the age of eleven tends to be a turning point in the development of concepts of historical time; it is only after that age, for instance, that the past becomes differentiated into various historical periods'.[26] A full understanding of chronology, however, may not develop until sixteen years of age.

Two investigators tried to improve children's concepts relating to historical time. Pistor[27] used an experimental and a control group from the ages of nine to eleven years. There were no significant group differences, 'which would seem to suggest that the increase in historical understanding is more a function of mental maturation, coupled with the widening of general experience, than of purely formal teaching . . . [but] . . . such a finding must be treated with some reservation.' Vikainen[28] taught a class of eleven-year-olds so as to give a chronologically clear presentation of historical events.

There was also an attempt to make the children interested in measuring historic time. Two classes acted as controls. After one year the experimental group was superior in their performance on problems involving time memory as well as mathematical time conception. The average performance of the experimental group on the historical material was slightly superior. This last research indicates that it may be possible with the right methods for teachers to improve their pupils' understanding in history.

Such insights can be brought to bear on the planning of a syllabus. The majority of secondary school pupils up to a mental age of sixteen seem to be at the concrete operational level of thought in history. Some clever children, however, will be reaching the formal level. The syllabuses should therefore be reorganised to take account of the limitations in most pupils' reasoning. If material is too advanced for the children they will either reject it, and possibly history as well, or assimilate it in a meaningless way.

History, therefore, for nearly all the pupils under fourteen years of age should not be over-abstract in form, nor should it contain too many variables. Even such a sympathetic writer as Bryant[29] seems to expect too high a level of thought among average children. Among topics which she recommends for a two-year course for pupils aged eleven to thirteen are 'parliamentary reform' and 'the business methods of trading companies'. If these were dealt with in the abstract, it is unlikely that average children would be able to understand them in any depth. Bryant suggests 'themes' for the first two years at secondary school since the traditional chronological syllabus is a 'millstone'. A chronological syllabus need not, however, necessarily mean a wild rush through the ages. Used wisely, topics in such a syllabus can be arranged so that the younger children learn the less detailed history of early times, while the history of recent years, which contains important yet complex topics, can then be taught when the pupils are able to reason at a more mature level.

The way in which the syllabus is organised must obviously be left to the individual school. Dividing each year's work into a number of patches, as explained by Lewis,[30] allows time for thorough work, discussion, reflection and thereby a possible improvement in pupils' thinking skills. Bareham et al.[31] have selected certain vital periods in history and used these to give an imaginative introduction through a historically accurate story, followed by factual material and assignments which exercise the pupils' thinking skills. A term's work on pre-history, possibly based on Place's *Prehistoric Britain*,[32] can give pupils of all types of ability an insight into the work and methods of an archaeologist. For pupils mainly at the pre-operational – that is, illogical – stage the 'themes' (Bryant) or 'lines of development' (Jeffreys[33]) have much to recommend them provided that the material is 'concrete' – for example, transport, clothing, homes.

Whatever plan is adopted, the material must be so selected that it 'matches' the pupils' schemata or thinking skills. Hughes[34] remarks that 'even more enlightened teaching methods cannot ensure success unless the existing schemata are sufficiently developed to deal with the situation'. The material should be of such a standard that it helps the pupils to improve their reasoning powers. A great deal of ancient history can be taught as a concrete subject: the homes, daily life, industries, agriculture and trade of the prehistoric period; the pyramids, calendar, writing and annual inundations of Ancient Egypt; the material achievements of the Greeks and Romans, and so on. With more intelligent children, in the early years of the secondary school, it is possible to include some abstract ideas in a simple manner, but it is preferable to link them with the pupils' everyday life. Democracy in Athens, for example, can be understood if the children have tried to discover how democracy works in their own country. Some of Plato's ideas can be grasped if they are connected, however crudely, with the educational system in Britain. In narrative work there should be constant attempts to give concrete examples of the events described verbally. Apart from the obvious use of diagrams, maps and illustrations, a few pupils defending the door against an imaginary Persian host at Thermopylae, or the collection of the names and denominations of neighbourhood churches before a lesson on Martin Luther, can help pupils to assimilate new ideas far more easily than through verbal exposition. McLaughlin's suggestion[35] that the concrete operational stage could be equated with the ability to hold four concepts simultaneously has interesting implications for narrative work. Presumably no more than four variables of the same type should be used for any one story. One would deal only with the essential characters, for instance, in the early colonisation of Virginia: Raleigh, Smith, Pocohontas, Rolfe. Recently, children of just below average ability found it difficult to distinguish the voyages of Diaz and da Gama because of the similarities.

Following such a seemingly restricted course for the first two or three years, depending on the operational level of the pupils, need not mean that the traditional values of studying history are lost. The teaching of history is often recommended in the hope that children's imaginative fields will be widened. Pupils learn to contrast their present society with other civilisations and this should lead to the questioning of familiar values. Younger pupils will achieve this far more through the study of 'concrete' history than by trying to grapple with abstract topics. The study of Tudor houses, for example, could lead to a discussion of the differences between Roman, Tudor and modern houses, and might conclude with a realisation of the rapid changes in the last four hundred years compared with the period from AD 410 to the sixteenth century.

Nor, if children are dealing with material that is largely concrete in nature, will they necessarily lose the intellectual values commonly associated with the study of history. Statements will still need to be queried and confirmed. Simple cause-effect relationships can be appreciated in studying such topics as the development of lake villages or the punishments meted out to sixteenth-century criminals. Relevant information still has to be gleaned from the textbook. The most worthwhile result of learning history, the cultivation of an inquiring spirit, is easier to stimulate in younger pupils through the study of concrete topics such as writing, houses, entertainments, clothing, transport and so on than in trying to force them to understand abstract political, constitutional and religious changes.

Most children in the third year should find no difficulty in dealing with the evidence before them, provided that the vocabulary is not too difficult. They should be able to tackle the more abstract type of history presented in a simple and possibly graphic form. More variables can be introduced into narratives, but even then for all but the most intelligent there should not be more than six variables and usually only four. It is amazing how often writers will give such a thorough and detailed account that they end in merely confusing the children.

A minority of secondary school pupils may have reached the formal operational level at 14+ years. These pupils will often be sitting for external examinations. In the past examination questions have seldom demanded more than the repetition of learnt facts and opinions and thus allowed teachers to rely on dictated or copied notes for successful results. Boards recently do seem to be setting questions which demand inferential thought, but their syllabuses are often over-crowded and so much ground has to be covered that little time is left for reflection or discussion during the lessons. A compulsory section on historical documents might give examination candidates the opportunity to exercise their historical judgement and thus avoid excessive dependence on memory work.

Whether it is possible to accelerate children's logical thinking is being strongly debated at present. How far does the development of thought depend on maturation and how far on interaction with the environment, both social and intellectual?[36] Do we have to accept that certain chronological or mental ages are essential before children can reach the concrete or formal levels, or is it possible to arrange the learning situation in such a way that the children's thought processes are so challenged that they have to adapt to the new, more complex material? The evidence is by no means complete or conclusive but a teacher's task is obviously to try to develop thinking skills as far as is practicable. Inhelder and Piaget[37] explain that the beginning of the formal stage 'may be, beyond the neurological factors, a product of a progressive acceleration of individual development under the influence of education and perhaps nothing stands in the way of a further reduction of the average age in a more or less distant future'. The suggestion that it may be possible to accelerate thought processes has been eagerly adopted in the USA – perhaps over-eagerly as far as Piaget is concerned. He has recently explained[38] that while it may be possible to accelerate these stages 'there is not much to be gained by doing it beyond a certain measure'. Worthwhile aims in accelerating thinking in history would seem to be to eradicate as quickly as possible pre-operational thinking among younger children and to help the older pupils to progress at least to the lower reaches of the formal stage before they leave school.

Both aims would possibly be realised if teachers asked children to hold and balance seemingly contrasted facts or views. With children who often think pre-operationally, the teacher should point out two aspects of the historical character or situation. For example, despite Mark Antony's courage, how he was outwitted by Octavian; how Cromwell could seem sincere in his beliefs and yet be ruthless; how Galileo's beliefs about the Universe were more like ours than those of the Roman Catholic Church; present-day and past attitudes towards education, poverty or crime. This idea of making a pupil move from one fact or idea to another and then return to the original

fact or idea stems from Piaget's explanation of how children understand that quantities do not alter even if the shape is altered. The
process is called 'equilibration', meaning the temporary imbalance
between the child's partially established thinking skills and the new
demands of the environment.[39]

Progress towards the formal operational stage may be accelerated
by a conscious effort to present at least four viewpoints in any
historical topic. In order to help pupils to realise how many factors
have to be balanced and compensated before any historical judgement is reached, situations such as the following could be devised:

(a) Two contemporary opinions on Peter the Great's life were
given to a class of fourteen-year-old, able pupils, after they had
learnt some facts about him: a sycophantic funeral oration by an
archbishop was contrasted with some antipathetic opinions. After
analysing the content of each opinion (the concrete level), the pupils
were asked to discuss in small groups whether they thought Peter
deserved to be called 'the Great' referring only to his public work.
The groups then reported their findings to the whole form.

(b) The same class helped to compose arguments for and against
Bolshevik ideas and events in Russia from 1917 to 1920. They then
wrote an imaginary argument between a White and Red Russian in
1920. Later in the term, they discussed the value and influence of
Communist ideas at the present day.

(c) A fifth-year O level class was given A. J. P. Taylor's views on
Bismarck's policies after they had learnt a more traditional interpretation of them. These were compared with the beliefs of Bismarck's
contemporaries about the aims of his plans.

Such work can be exciting and invigorating for both the pupils and
the teacher but it may be suitable only at the fifth-form level with
most children. If the pupils do not have the ability to reason near the
concrete or formal levels then they will either ignore or reject the
material; if they are at the transitional levels, however, such methods
might help them progress to the next stage of thinking.

Some of the more usual methods of teaching history will now
be discussed in light of this general approach to improving thinking
in history.

ORAL WORK
'Recent surveys of the methods of history teaching suggest that there

is too much classroom lecturing [and] note giving.'[40] These methods can, and no doubt do, conceal serious inadequacies in the thinking processes of children. Piaget recommends discussion, especially with one's peers, as the main educational method of improving thinking: 'When I say "active" I mean it in two senses. One is acting on material things. But the other means doing things in social collaboration, in a group effort. This leads to a critical frame of mind, where children must communicate with each other' (quoted by Sigel and Hooper[41]). Elsewhere Piaget[42] argues that we should 'try to create in the school a place where individual experimentation and reflection carried out in common come to each other's aid and balance one another'.

School or class debates in history would seem to offer the opportunity for 'contact with the judgements and evaluations of others'[43] but they can all too often simply consist of the more voluble and/or intelligent monopolising the arguments while most pupils allow their minds to rest. The IAAM[44] points out, moreover, that many teachers 'find debates alien to the true spirit of historical study, which calls for balanced assessments rather than whitewashing or denigration'. Class discussions could probably be educationally more valuable but are similarly prone to be controlled by a small number of children. Possibly the best way to allow discussions is to divide the class into small groups of four or five pupils. These can be formed spontaneously in any particular lesson or through sociograms.[45] The groups then discuss the issues involved. Children seem to enjoy this as one method of learning history but they need the preliminary information and necessary cognitive skills with which to build constructive arguments. Inhelder and Piaget do realise the limitations placed on discussion through the inadequacy of the pupils' reasoning powers. They remark that for discussion to be successful the children need the appropriate group structure. This implies that they probably need to be near the formal operational level of thought.

Evans[46] states that while 'most workers seem to agree that there is little difference in the amount learned by students under the two methods', children enjoy their work more under group methods. Hannam[47] also argues that group work means that children work more enthusiastically in a self-disciplined way. Whether such methods lead to an improvement in thinking skills still has to be proved.

WRITTEN WORK

When a class seems ready for such exercises, teachers could set written work which demands reflection and interpretation. These methods can be far more valuable in developing thinking skills than the usual copying of notes but they do require far more work by both the teacher and pupils. The following suggestions have been tried with some degree of success, but the pupils often have to be warned that they are historical exercises demanding the intelligent use of historical facts and not merely imaginative flights of fancy.

1   Making visits in time can help to provoke contrasts. Pupils can imagine, for example, that they are taking part in the burial of a relative in a long barrow, then explain why archaeologists know the facts they have used. A soldier or his wife can write to Rome describing life along Hadrian's Wall. Children often like to be a visitor or a guide to a medieval castle, village or town.

2   Pupils can also be asked to contrast features of their own life with those of a child in the past. A story about an eighteenth-century foster boy who lived in an open-field village and then went to work in London engaged the interest of many children of below average ability. They then contrasted their lives with his.

3   Dialogues can be re-created between people with different viewpoints. After learning about Leonardo da Vinci a primary school class was given an imaginary conversation between two Florentines:

Marcello; I've just been allowed into Leonardo's workshop and seen his painting of Giacondo's wife. It's the strangest painting I've ever seen: all dim greens and a peculiar rocky background.
Filippo: Hm – let's hope he finishes this painting. I'm getting tired of hearing how wonderful Leonardo is. Do you remember all the fuss when he went off to Milan and all the great things he was going to do?

The conversation continued on these lines, then the pupils were asked to discuss and write whether they agreed with Marcello or Filippo.

Under careful guidance the children can also be asked to write their own dialogues between people with different viewpoints, such as a group of villagers arguing over enclosures; George Stephenson and a landowner; a southerner and a northerner in the USA over slavery.

4   Obituaries can also make children think about the historical

character whom they are studying and his times. An intelligent first-year secondary class did a very successful one on Socrates.

5 A 'trial' in which prosecutor and defence put forward different arguments can be used with people like Cromwell, an eighteenth-century French aristocrat, Hess.

6 The titles of compositions should stimulate reflection; for example instead of 'Describe the life of a medieval villein' the title could be 'The life of a villein was not a happy one. Discuss.'

7 More difficult exercises which are possibly suitable only for older pupils are to ask them to find causal links and relationships. For example:

a. Explain what is missing:
'Peace, land and bread'——————Bolsheviks in power in Petro-
grad, November 1917

b. Which of the following alternatives is correct and why?
Watt's steam engine led to:

(*i*) factories being built on coal fields
(*ii*) fewer accidents in mines
(*iii*) better living conditions for working people in the nineteenth century.

DISCOVERY METHODS

'Projects' are often recommended as a means of solving some of the many problems involved in teaching history. It is claimed that children will show more interest and learn more through discovery methods than they will if they follow more conventional classroom methods. Bruner[48] argues, for example, that discovery methods have certain advantages over expository methods in that they lead to: (a) making information more readily viable in problem solving; (b) an intrinsic interest in the topic instead of the need for extrinsic rewards; (c) the learning of the techniques of discovery; (d) an improved memory of the material.

There are, however, many difficulties in using discovery methods. Among the most serious of these seems the lack of suitable books, especially for children of average and below average ability. Research work[49] indicates that these children are incapable of understanding many words which are the stock-in-trade of history writers and teachers. As is well known, children can also spend an inordinate amount of time on completing one sketch or a minute piece of writing. If the primary, perhaps only, aim is to interest children in history, then projects can no doubt be very worthwhile.[50] Whether they will develop thinking skills as well as more expository methods cannot be determined at present. Ausubel[51] states that 'It appears that the various enthusiasts of the discovery methods have been . . . generalising wildly from equivocal and even negative findings.' This comment underlines the need for a well-financed, national effort where different methods of teaching history are carried out in the actual classrooms of different types of schools.

Notes

1   B. Inhelder and J. Piaget, *The Growth of Logical Thinking from Childhood to Adolescence*, Routledge, 1958.

2   W. Kessen and C. Kuhlmann (eds), *Thought in the Young Child*, Monograph for the Society for Research in Child Development, 27, no. 2, 1960; B. Inhelder and J. M. Tanner (eds), *Discussions on Child Development*, *IV*, Tavistock, 1960.

3   *Op. cit.* but see also J. Shields, *The Gifted Child*, NFER, 1968.

4   Inhelder and Tanner, *op. cit.*, p. 126.

5   P. E. Vernon, *The Structure of Human Abilities*, Methuen, 1961, p. 170.

6   L. S. Vygotsky, *Thought and Language*, John Wiley, New York, 1962, p. 102.

7   J. Piaget, *Psychology of Intelligence*, Routledge, 1950, p. 32.

8   M. Stones, 'Factors Influencing the Capacity of Adolescents to Think in Abstract Terms in the Understanding of History', MEd thesis 1967, University of Manchester, unpublished.

9   E. A. Peel, *The Pupil's Thinking*, Oldbourne, 1960, p. 145.

10 R. Goldman, 'Some Aspects of the Development of Religious Thinking in Childhood and Adolescence', PhD thesis 1962, University of Birmingham, unpublished.

11 R. N. Hallam, 'An Investigation into Some Aspects of the Historical Thinking of Children and Adolescents', MEd thesis 1966, University of Leeds, unpublished; R. N. Hallam, 'Logical Thinking in History', *Educational Review*, vol. 19, 1967, 183–202.

12 R. N. Hallam, 1966, *op. cit.*, pp. 295–323.

13 Otis Gamma Test: Form D.

14 Inhelder and Piaget, *op. cit.*, p. 255.

15 R. N. Hallam, 1967, *op. cit.*, p. 200.

16 W. H. Burston and D. Thompson, *Studies in the Nature and Teaching of History*, ULP, 1967, p. 162.

17 M. M. Hughes, 'A Four Year Longitudinal Study of the Growth of Logical Thinking', MEd thesis 1965, University of Leeds, unpublished; K. Lovell, 'A Follow-up Study of Inhelder and Piaget's "The Growth of Logical Thinking"', *British Journal of Psychology*, 52, 1961, pp. 143–53.

18 G. W. Bassett, 'The Comprehension of Historical Narrative', PhD thesis 1940, University of London, unpublished.

19 J. Coltham, 'Junior School Children's Understanding of Historical Terms', PhD thesis 1960, University of Manchester, unpublished.

20 M. B. Booth, 'A Critical Analysis of the Secondary School History Curriculum', MA (Ed) thesis 1967 University of Southampton, unpublished.

21 K. Lovell and A. Slater, 'The Growth of the Concept of Time', *Journal of Child Psychology and Psychiatry*, I, 1960, pp. 179–90.

22 Quoted by G. Jahoda, 'Children's Concepts of Time and History', *Educational Review*, vol. 15, 1963, pp. 87–104.

23 M. Sturt and E. C. Oakden, 'The Development of the Knowledge of Time in Children', *British Journal of Psychology*, vol. 12, 1921, pp. 303–36.

24 G. Jahoda, *op. cit.*

25 F. Musgrove, 'Five Scales of Attitude to History', in *Studies in Education*, III, University of Hull Institute of Education, 1963.

26 G. Jahoda, *op. cit.*, p. 97.

27 Quoted in G. Jahoda, *op. cit.*, p. 97.

28 J. G. Wallace, *Concept Growth and the Education of the Child*, NFER, 1965, pp. 126–9.

29 M. E. Bryant, 'The History Syllabus Reconsidered', in *History in the Secondary School*, Historical Association, 1967.

30 E. M. Lewis, *Teaching History in Secondary Schools*, Evans, 1960.

31 J. Bareham (ed.), *Changing World History*, Holmes McDougall, Edinburgh, 1969.

32 R. Place, *Prehistoric Britain*, Longmans, 1959.

33 M. V. C. Jeffreys, *History in School*, Pitman, 1939.

34 M. M. Hughes, *op. cit.*, p. 109.

35 G. H. McLaughlin, 'Psycho-Logic', *British Journal of Educational Psychology*, 33, 1963, pp. 61–7.

36 McV. J. Hunt, *Intelligence and Experience*, Ronald Press, New York, 1961; M. Pines, *Revolution in Learning*, Allen Lane, 1969; I. E. Sigel and F. H. Hooper, *Logical Thinking in Children*, Holt, Rinehart & Winston, New York, 1968.

37 B. Inhelder and J. Piaget, *op. cit.*, p. 337.

38 M. Pines, *op. cit.*, p. 35.

39 I. E. Sigel and F. H. Hooper, *op. cit.*, p. 430.

40 C. L. Hannam, 'Project and Group Work', *Teaching History*, Historical Association, 1969, pp. 72–5.

41 *Op. cit.*, p. 431.

42 J. Piaget, *The Moral Judgement of the Child*, Routledge, 1932, pp. 411–412.

43 J. Piaget, 1932, *op. cit.*, p. 408.

44 Incorporated Association of Assistant Masters, *The Teaching of History*, CUP, 1952, p. 60.

45 K. M. Evans, *Sociometry and Education*, Routledge, 1962.

46 K. M. Evans, *op. cit.*, p. 74.

47 C. L. Hannam, *op. cit.*, p. 73.

48 J. S. Bruner, 'The Act of Discovery' in J. P. Dececco (ed.), *Human Learning in School*, Holt, Rinehart & Winston, New York, 1963.

49 J. Coltham, *op. cit.*; Schools Council, *The Place of the Personal Topic in History*, Examinations Bulletin no. 18, HMSO, 1968.

50 G. Preston, 'The Value of Local History', in *Teaching History*, 1969, pp. 87–91.

51 D. P. Ausubel, *Educational Psychology: A Cognitive View*, Holt, Rinehart & Winston, New York, 1968.

SHEILA FERGUSON

The Project Method

THE PERSONAL PROJECT AND THE CSE EXAMINATION

A great deal of interest in the project method of history teaching has developed over the last few years, especially since most of the Regional Examination Boards have included the Personal Project or Topic as an integral part of their Certificate of Secondary Education examinations in history. When the form and syllabus of the new CSE examinations was being hammered out by the teachers who control the examinations in each region, there was much discussion about the need to introduce other forms of assessment as well as the traditional examination paper. The alternative that seemed to have the most to offer was the Personal Project which gave the candidate the opportunity to submit work he had chosen to undertake himself as part evidence of his attainment in history.

As a result of the large amount of CSE project work now in progress in the schools, teachers are having to give much more thought to the organisation of this kind of work throughout their schools. At first some teachers were daunted by the complexity of supervising separate individual projects by large numbers of children but now that this part of the examination has been in progress for a few years it has become accepted as normal practice. Some anxieties still arise, however, on matters like the possibility of a 'black market' in old projects, the burden of five or six projects in different subjects and the difficulties of joint projects. Some teachers who were very enthusiastic at first about the inclusion of projects in the CSE examination are somewhat disenchanted when they are presented again with pedestrian examples on well-worn themes. The project is nevertheless very much part of the history-teaching scene not only at CSE level but also all through school life. It is not a method that 'teaches itself' and to achieve good results much guidance and organisation is needed.

THE DALTON PLAN AND AFTER

In the normal teaching situation the 'project method' means the provision of facilities under which the child can undertake a research assignment into a chosen topic and produce a 'book' or modest thesis, or a group of children can mount a joint presentation. This is not, of course, anything very new and many teachers have been organising work on these lines for a long time. Back in the 1920s the Dalton Plan epitomised the revolt against unenterprising 'chalk and talk' teaching. The Dalton scheme of personal work assignments aimed at developing individuality by directing the child in self-chosen occupations and study. Where the plan was adopted wholesale a restructuring of the school day, the integration of subjects and the abolition of the normal time-table were necessary. It had the serious weakness that it was difficult for the teacher to give adequate guidance to a class of pupils working at a whole range of subjects. Though producing some interesting results it was not an entirely practical system for most secondary schools. Much of its message was, however, suitable for adaptation in the primary school where it helped to influence the break-away from formal class teaching and the acceptance that children benefit from working individually.

The more recent manifestations of the project method in secondary schools have not normally involved the wholesale abandonment of subject divisions on the time-table nor the disappearance of specialist teaching. These projects play their part in the year's work and need not supplant the teaching of history chronologically, or by the 'line of development', 'patch' or 'thematic' approach and may either proceed simultaneously with the ordinary class lessons or may have part of a term reserved for concentrated work on individual or group projects. By continuing to study some general history with the whole class the teacher is able to encourage some sense of historical continuity and to indicate the way in which individual topics fit into their appropriate places. The teacher can act as a bridge or link, putting the individual young 'specialists' in touch with each other, indicating where their interests overlap and where they can help each other with material and ideas. Plenty of visual material in the classroom, especially time charts and diagrams, are invaluable here.

PERSONAL CHOICE
One of the reasons for the success of the project method is that it has the special psychological advantage of personal choice and commitment and it gives opportunity for each child to progress at his own pace. It encourages the inquiring mind and gives the child the moti-

vation to dig more deeply into a subject that he has chosen for himself. A child usually works with more enthusiasm at a topic of his own choice than on a course over which he has no influence or control. Once a child has had his imagination stirred the interest aroused may be a lasting one. Identification with one's own subject is particularly valuable with less able children. I have known many quite backward children who have devoted themselves with such enthusiasm to their projects that they have quite lost their sense of academic inferiority and have felt themselves to be authorities on their subjects.

Often the child who has found it difficult to keep up with the class in traditional academic work reveals unsuspected talent and interests when he is able to work at his own pace on his chosen subject. When he can write and draw at his own speed, the quality of his work may improve immeasurably and he may be willing to give up more of his spare time, to continue with his work, than he would ever do on normal homework. Some 'slower' children who have struggled for years to get down notes, or write something up in limited periods of class time, have come to accept it as inevitable that their spelling and handwriting are poor. But when they are allowed to take their time there is frequently a marked improvement in performance and, in consequence, a rise in morale. On the other hand the academically able children do not suffer as they can forge ahead at the pace that suits them best and are not bored by waiting for the slowest to catch up or by unnecessary repetition.

THE TEACHER'S ROLE

Some teachers may have thought that projects were a useful fill-in at the end of term when it is difficult to get the class to concentrate on normal lessons, or that they might be the solution to behaviour problems with a class that has been uncooperative so far. But these hopes are likely to be disappointed, for a class engaged on projects is very demanding and unrestful.

Far from giving the teacher the chance to put his feet up, project work tends to be more exhausting than normal class teaching. A class at work on individual or group projects is noisier and more fluid than one where all the children are working on the same subject. The teacher has to be able to maintain 'order in disorder' and to allow movement around the room for the exchange of ideas, information and materials and at the same time to make sure that the talk is purposeful. The children have to be trained to exercise self-discipline so that the noise of the class at work is not a hindrance to those who are trying to concentrate on something complicated. The ideal is an atmosphere of freedom and cheerful concentration but it is not always easy to achieve.

The teacher must move around the class offering help and advice on materials, presentation and illustrations. He must try to remember all the children's subjects and to keep his eyes open for useful sources of information. He should train the children to look ahead at television and radio programmes which may be helpful and he should be able to recommend books and suitable films, plays, exhibitions, museums, art galleries and houses to visit.

The teacher's role is positive and many-sided. He must stimulate and try to instil enthusiasm when the response is half-hearted; he must advise on the practicable limits of a proposed study, help in planning its 'shape' and suggest additional lines to explore; he must criticise, constructively of course, providing ideas for further research or for reorganisation of the material gathered. He should be a mine of useful ideas on which the pupil can draw, though by no means omniscient and allowing the pupil to be the 'authority' on his subject. Teachers can add a new dimension of interest by using their general knowledge to suggest further avenues of exploration. I recently saw a project on the history of the London docks prepared by a docker's son, with photographs taken by the boy and including his father's union card, with an explanation about the demarcation between the stevedores' union and the Transport and General Workers' Union. It was a good piece of work but had nothing on the Dockers' Strike of 1889 and nothing on Ernie Bevin or the National Dock Labour Board. It seemed a pity that the boy's teacher had missed the opportunity to direct him to such interesting research possibilities.

TRAINING IN HISTORICAL RESEARCH

The project method of teaching history is, in fact, training in historical research and, if well done, is more valuable than making children memorise large numbers of facts to regurgitate at examinations. 'The pupil ceases to be a mere receptacle into which the master pours information like water into a glass,' wrote G. P. Gooch, 'and joyfully recreates for himself the life, colour and movement of the past.' A successful piece of research can arouse the historical imagination of the pupil so that discoveries made in this way have more impact and last longer than ill-digested information learnt by heart and discarded when the examination is over.

The Schools Council has identified the aims of the project method as 'a sense of time and of process of development' and the skill of 'the development of judgement in collecting, examining and correlating facts'. In educational terms they grouped these principles under five headings: (a) *cognitive skills*, or the ability to understand concepts and causal relationships, to evaluate evidence and draw valid conclusions, to develop a sense of time and imaginative insights and judgement; (b) *motivational factors*, or interest and enthusiasm for the subject, curiosity, persistence and personal satisfaction; (c) *moral insights*, or consciousness of bias and prejudice and the ability to be aware of historical judgements and to have opinions of right and wrong actions; (d) *knowledge of subject-matter*, or the ability to retain some of the information acquired and to present it as an organised piece of work; and (e) *practical skills*, or the ability to write or talk about the subject clearly, to use reference material and maps and diagrams.

This method has the advantage of developing self-reliance in children and encouraging them to work on their own initiative. Training in historical research shows them how and where to find the information they require and ways of assembling and organising the material they have acquired. The planning of their time, decisions about what is relevant and what irrelevant, what to put in and what to leave out and the completion of the task in a given time will have involved persistence and self-discipline.

But training in the methods of historical research is quite a sophisticated activity, especially if the pupils are not accustomed to this kind of work. It is not enough for the teacher to announce to a class that they are now going to do a project on say Elizabethan England, provide some books and stationery and leave them to go their own sweet ways. Guidance, advice, and encouragement as well as practical instruction in technique are essential.

It is, of course, preferable if training in the techniques of research has been given throughout a child's school life. Many primary schools do excellent and usually exciting group projects and some get children to produce individual topic or 'centre of interest' folders on whatever subject appeals to them. When my son was at a primary school he did a study of medieval warfare, mostly in the form of drawings but including a great amount of detailed technical information on siege weapons, the construction of castles, crenellation, machicolation and so on.

In the secondary school it is useful if part of at least one term each year in the lower part of the school is spent on topic work. In the first year the children might start with simple assignments, like Roman Britain or the Vikings, using two or three books of reference and working under suggested headings. The work could be mounted for wall display with contributions in writing and drawing and possibly models.

Projects in the lower forms of the secondary school are valuable as a bridge between the informal and permissive methods of learning now usual in the primary school and the more formal academic approach of the secondary school. The change of schools can be an alarming experience and many children find it hard to adapt themselves to the new ways. In the primary school there was probably freedom to move about the classroom or from room to room in search of information, there was the opportunity for personal choice and to work at the child's individual pace. By providing periods of project work with an atmosphere more like that of the primary school the teacher may help in the settling-down process. By the third and fourth years pupils often prefer to do personal folders rather than mounted displays. They may tackle biographies of great figures of the past, the voyages of discovery or social life in the century they are currently studying. They should by this time be familiar with the layout of a library and be confident about finding the books they need. They should also know how to use more than one source and be able to select useful material and summarise it in their own words.

CHOICE OF SUBJECT

The first problem to be solved when launching a class on project work is to get each child to choose his subject. If the topic is to be submitted for the CSE examination it is especially important that each pupil's subject is one in which interest can be maintained over several months. Many children rush in too impetuously while others find it hard to come to a decision. At this stage the teacher must be as stimulating as possible, so that some of his enthusiasm for particular topics can be passed on to the pupils. It is not a good idea to read out a list of possible subjects but rather to draw out suggestions from the class, though the teacher may like to get the ball rolling by mentioning some examples that make good project material. It is very useful at this point if the class can go and browse in the school or public library in search of topics of interest.

If the response of the children is apathetic the teacher should try to discover any personal interests, hobbies or convictions that can be exploited. Interests in the theatre, cinema, music, ballet, cars, sport, politics, religions or voluntary organisations could provide rewarding subjects. A child's intended future career such as nursing, the police, the army or the Post Office could give rise to many subjects. Sometimes family interests or connections provide valuable stimuli. The granddaughter of a suffragette, the son of a fireman, the child of a miner or an active trade unionist or the child of an immigrant may be encouraged by interest at home in their research and perhaps help in providing unusual material and illustrations. Occasionally an original historical document comes to light as a grandparent produces writing or photographs from the past. First- and second-generation immigrants from Ireland, the West Indies, Cyprus, India or Pakistan often get a deep satisfaction from a study of their native land and many write to relatives for help with material and illustrations.

Skills in other school subjects may guide the choice of topic. Those good at drawing will enjoy such studies as fashion, architecture or furniture which involve many illustrations. The girl who enjoys domestic science will get a lot out of a study of the food, kitchens and domestic appliances or home life through the ages; the boy keen on science will understand technicalties when considering the lives of great scientists or the development of inventions. Enthusiasm for sport could be directed towards a history of leisure pursuits.

Some children who are not very interested in any subject that goes at all far into the past may well be attracted by a topic that is reasonably up to date. They might enjoy a study of the history of space travel, of the United Nations, of the USSR since the Revolution, or the recent history of Africa or China. A dramatic recent event might stir the imagination of a pupil to look into the background giving rise to the particular news item: for example, the assassination of President Kennedy might lead to research on assassination as a political weapon, or on American presidents; the demonstrations against the Springboks might be followed up by an investigation on apartheid in South Africa; the death of a statesman or national figure might give rise to work on his life and times. A film currently on release may inspire interest. *Exodus* led one pupil of mine to do an excellent project on the history of the persecution of the Jews, while *A Man for All Seasons* encouraged more than one to choose to study the life of Sir Thomas More.

It is worth persevering to get a subject which really appeals to the child rather than allowing him to embark apathetically on to 'anything which will do'. It is a depressing experience if many children choose to do the same well-worn topics such as great lives, transport, or costume, as it usually indicates that they have made their choice out of indifference or because it seems a soft option. It is also, I find, infinitely better for there to be a wide choice of subjects in the class. This adds to the interest all round and makes the problem of finding suitable books a bit easier.

THE TECHNIQUE OF RESEARCH

After the subjects have been chosen it is very important that the children should be given some guidance on the methods of research. Many think that all that is needed is to get themselves a book on the subject and then diligently copy out large chunks. The teacher must disabuse them of this idea but not frighten them by making it sound too complicated. He should explain that the job of the researcher is to collect and collate material from several sources and then to write a continuous narrative incorporating the most interesting information acquired. It is difficult to master the skill of assembling information from a variety of sources into a coherent piece of writing. It is an advantage if children have been trained throughout their history course to answer questions or write essays using two or more text and reference books. It should be explained that they will need to take notes from several books and not rush into writing a final version too quickly.

One very valuable lesson soon learned by the project worker is that different books give a different story of the same event and sometimes contradict each other. They must learn to compare different accounts and may perhaps even come to recognise the bias or prejudice shown by some writers. It is really encouraging if a child gets to the point where he writes 'Some historians say . . . so and so . . ., others believe . . . this and that . . ., but on the whole I think that . . .'

Many teachers get alarmed about plagiarism and argue that copying from other people's books is a worthless exercise. Much reputable non-fiction, however, is a 'scissors and paste' operation and the amount of original research is comparatively small. But the children should be taught never to copy unthinkingly, never to use words which sound pompous or artificial to them, or to use words or expressions they don't understand. They should never accept complicated phrases which sound stilted or unnatural but should try to translate the information into the sort of words they use themselves. It is easy to give the child an example of this. Would you really say 'affectations which lent an appearance of bucolic simplicity'? Surely you would rather say something like 'a fashion for wealthy ladies of dressing up in simple country styles'. It can be explained, however, that if the child finds certain passages not in his own idiom particularly colourful or expressive, he can use the actual words in quotation marks and give an indication of the source.

The importance of keeping careful records of all sources of information cannot be stressed too often. They should keep a list of all the books they have consulted and also notes on visits (with dates), films, etc., and a collection of cuttings or postcards. There is always the child who wants to return to the 'fat red book' or the 'one with a Tudor house on the front', and who cannot identify it in the library. At the end of the work a complete bibliography of books consulted must be given and this may be accompanied by comments on the usefulness or interest of the books listed.

After the work has been in progress for some time the teacher should get each child to make a rough plan of the 'shape' of his project, either in the form of headings or chapters. Most children want to rush in and write an introduction first but I usually advise them to write the introduction last of all as one can only tell the reader what he is going to find in the work when it is complete. That is the purpose of an introduction. At this point the pupil should have some idea of the scope of his project – how far back he wants to go and how up to date he intends to come. The teacher should advise on whether the plan is too ambitious or too modest and whether an over-large subject should be limited in certain ways or a too narrow subject should be extended. I regard this stage of skeleton plans as a vital one in project work. Schemes, of course, can always be amended and adapted but a good clear plan of work at an early stage seems to be a valuable discipline. It helps to prevent the aimless type of 'rag-bag' project which has no form and little point. It also makes it much easier to organise the work as it progresses. It means that the child does not necessarily have to do the work in chronological order but, as he finds he has enough material on one section, he can write it up. For instance a researcher on trade unions might have ample material on the 'New Model' Trade Unions but little or nothing on the Combination Acts. It makes it much easier to do the topics on loose-leaf paper so that there is no need to begin at the beginning and write straight through – even when a section seems finished an extra, useful snippet can then be slipped in at the appropriate place. Page numbering, contents sheets or indexes should be left to the very last.

HELP IN GATHERING AND PRESENTING THE MATERIAL

Once the subjects have been chosen children need time and as much help as possible while they get on with their assignments. Most children have a squirrel instinct and enjoy collecting postcards, pictures and cuttings with which to illustrate their work. The teacher should, therefore, accumulate weekend colour supplements, magazines, old radio and television pamphlets, guide books etc. which may come in handy. Where possible visits to museums, public buildings and 'stately homes' in the neighbourhood should be organised and children should be advised of places to visit themselves at weekends or during the holidays.

It is, of course, essential to get the pupils to use their public library. However good the History Room and school library may be, it is difficult to have enough material for whole classes of children engaged in project work. Many children allow their membership of a public library to lapse after leaving primary school. They should be strongly urged to rejoin. The teacher should tell them that the best source of material for them is the children's library. This often startles them as they think the children's library contains only story books for little children. Once they have seen the excellent and varied non-fiction sections of most children's branches they change their minds. They should also be recommended to ask librarians for help if they cannot see what they want and be advised that even if nothing is available immediately books can be obtained from other libraries on payment of the cost of a stamped postcard.

Publishers have become very aware of the market for well-illustrated, attractively presented books for project work. There are a number of useful series such as Longmans' 'Then and There' series, Methuen's 'Outline' series, Batsford's 'Past-into-Present', the ESA 'Information' books, the Hamish Hamilton 'Look at . . .'

series, the ULP 'Discovering the . . .' series and Faber's 'World Outlook' study series.

It is also a good idea to encourage children to read historical novels set in the periods they are studying. Contemporary novels such as Defoe, Dickens, Mrs Gaskell and Charles Kingsley are valuable source material but many children find them hard going. There are, however, many excellent modern writers of historical fiction for children whose books provide a useful atmosphere and background. Reviews and criticisms of any relevant books read and plays or films seen should be included in projects.

SOURCE MATERIAL

Most teachers will wish to encourage the use of contemporary documents and other direct source material wherever possible. Provided that they are helped to interpret 'difficult' writing and/or words, children are impressed by seeing what the 'real thing' looked like and by studying the authentic records of the past. Recently a great deal of source material in a form which children can understand has become available. Local museums have begun to provide documentary evidence and photographs as background material to their exhibits. Record Offices, such as the Essex Record Office which have published some attractively illustrated pamphlets, are keen to provide selections of documents, maps etc. suitable for teachers or for use by the children themselves. Mr F. G. Emmison of the Essex Record Office has also written some excellent guides to local history and archive work – *How to Read Local Archives* and *Guide to Illustrative Material for Use in Teaching History* (Historical Association), *Archives and Local History* (Methuen) and *Some Types of Commonfield parish* (National Council of Social Service). Teachers' associations have done valuable work in preparing units of work based on local archives, such as *Coals from Newcastle*, produced by the Newcastle Institute of Education. The Greater London Council Record Office and Library, for instance, has a collection of documents on manorial records, archives of charities, societies and schools, parish registers, information on building and local government, the business records of a wide range of companies, records of the School Board and bodies like the Metropolitan Board of Works and the Metropolitan Asylums Board. Much of this kind of archive material could not be handled unaided by children but the Records Offices have done a lot of work on making selections of records on particular subjects and providing explanatory guides. They are often willing to provide xerox copies of documents and photographs. A very comprehensive account on Archives in School was given by Dr J. Fines, now at Bishop Otter College, Chichester, in *History*, vol. LIII, no. 179, October 1968. Three review articles by Miss M. E. Bryant of the Institute of Education, London University, which will provide up-to-date information on source material are to be published in *Teaching History*, April and November 1970 and May 1971.

There is also, of course, commercially produced documentary material, especially the invaluable Jackdaw series. Books of extracts such as the *They Saw It Happen*, *They Too Were There* series and *Human Documents of the Industrial Revolution* and *Human Documents of the Victorian Golden Age* by E. Roysten Pike provide quotable evidence on many topics.

Many children get great satisfaction from 'writing off' for help on their project from some outside organisation. There must now be a flood of requests of this kind, and in fact the British Trades Alphabet has published a journal of educational projects in which manufacturers and public bodies who wish to interest children in their organisations advertise and indicate that they have project material available. Apart from this journal, which is primarily an advertising medium, most government departments, trade unions, borough councils, public organisations and individual firms are prepared to be very cooperative if asked to supply material.

CONCLUSION

Finally I would like to state again that the project method seems to me to have a great deal to offer to the history teacher and his pupils. With slow-learning pupils exploration is likely to be more successful than exposition and even with the brightest children discovery for themselves may be more attractive and therefore produce better results than formal learning methods. Projects are essentially child-centred, with the individual child exercising personal choice and having as a consequence the motivation to do a good job. But to avoid superficiality, lack of system and of intellectual discipline, projects should proceed side-by-side with ordinary class teaching. The teacher can then integrate the collection of projects into a system of knowledge and can try to inculcate some sense of historical perspective.

The Steering Committee of the Schools Council set up to investigate the value of the Personal Project in the CSE history examination concluded that while it presents challenges to teachers it has many advantages. For the pupils 'there are the chances of following their own interests . . . and, in the process, deriving the satisfaction of producing worth-while pieces of work, facing the difficulties of presenting a polished piece of sustained writing and using initiative and originality in production – as well as demonstrating self-discipline in compilation and completion to a deadline'.

WILLIAM LAMONT

The Uses and Abuses of Examinations

History does not repeat itself; examination papers in history do.
The first London Matriculation History paper was set on 5 November 1838. The questions have the smack of familiarity:

> What was the effect of the Wars of the Roses on the Royal prerogative? What were the actual limits of the Royal authority under the most nearly absolute of the English sovereigns?

> Mention the leading facts in the history of the negotiation for the Spanish match under James I, and point out in what manner the issue tended to weaken the power of the Crown.

> What were the engines and resources used by Charles I to carry on the government without Parliaments? Relate the events which led to the calling of the Long Parliament.

Ever since that paper Charles I has been using his engines and resources. Questions have changed remarkably little since 1838. We would not now expect our pupils to answer twelve questions of that nature within three hours. But, at both Ordinary and Advanced level standard, we would still expect our pupils, confronted with an unseen paper, to be able to write within three hours a number of long essays which reveal a capacity to retain a formidable amount of factual information. This is not to say that the assumption that this is the only, or best, way of assessing historical skills has gone without challenge between 1838 and 1970; only that the challenge has not been markedly successful.

The prospects for a successful challenge have never been brighter than now. Yet on at least two occasions in the past – between 1927 and 1928 and between 1965 and 1967 – the prospects seemed equally bright. The successful way in which the conventional examination papers rode this challenge should itself repel an easy optimism. But it should not induce a contrary despair, for the argument put forward in this essay will be that the conventional examination papers were able to beat off the critics because the critics never attacked them at their most vulnerable point. This may become clearer by a closer look at the critics.

1927 was a year for heart-searching among history teachers. There was a good reason why it should be. Ten years after the first School Certificate examination was a time for stocktaking. The pages of *History* during the next couple of years[1] reflect a lively concern about the effects of external examinations on the teaching of history. D. C. Somervell pointed out that there were times when even the most commonplace history teacher struck sparks from his pupils: these rarely came when he was preparing them for external examinations. Miss Davis disliked heartily the 'air of omniscience' which her Bexhill pupils assumed in answering questions and argued that the 'potted answers', which the papers had forced upon them, limited their horizons. O. G. Welch pleaded for shorter periods of study: 'unless history be studied in detail the imagination cannot be stimulated by the action and interaction of human personalities'. More radical still, F. T. Happold – in an essay entitled 'A New Type of Question in History Papers' – argued in favour of the pupils bringing their critical faculties to bear upon carefully selected extracts from original sources. He appended a specimen question which called upon pupils to comment upon extracts from different contemporary views of Napoleon. C. H. K. Marten, reviewing some of these criticisms, began to wonder whether there was a case for saving the subject by abandoning the examining of it.

He need not have worried. Napoleon was powerless against the engines and resources of Charles I. The conventional examination papers were soon revealed to have powerful friends. And even their ostensible enemies were found to be, at the very least, ambivalent towards them. Marten might concede the justice of some of the claims but he remarked comfortably that 'grind is not necessarily a bad thing'. Somervell was revealed to be more concerned, in the final analysis, about 'examiners trying out-of-the-way subjects, or putting questions in an unexpected and "tricky" way' than about the wretched effects of external examinations upon good teaching: he asked the examiner not to be afraid 'to set questions on the old subjects or even in the old ways'. A. J. Williams' revealing critique of Happold's paper was that 'a capable pupil, with little knowledge of history, could gain high marks on intelligence alone . . . it would not prove the possession of a body of historical knowledge'. Sixty teachers who met at Oxford in 1930 echoed Williams' resolve to keep intelligence and history apart: they expressed their approval of the conventional examination papers. Happold lost his temper with them, and an interesting controversy dribbled away in recriminations and counter-recriminations. Interest in reforming the teaching of history continued to be expressed in the pages of *History*, but interest had decisively shifted from examinations to 'line of development' syllabuses and, later still, to the teaching of more contemporary history.[2]

In successive years, between 1965 and 1967, there appeared: the third edition of the Incorporated Association of Assistant Masters' *The Teaching of History in Secondary Schools*; Professor Barraclough's Presidential Address to the Historical Association, *History and the Common Man*; a collection of essays, *Studies in the Nature and Teaching of History*, edited by Mr Burston and Mr Thompson. All three challenged conventional assumptions about history teaching in schools, but all three reflected the post-Happold shift in interest from examinations to syllabus construction. The essayists in Mr Burston and Mr Thompson's symposium accepted Mr Jeffreys' diagnosis – that history teaching in schools suffers from incoherence, even though they rejected his 'line of development' cure. Professor Barraclough gave a twist to the term 'contemporary history' undreamed of by Mr Henderson and Mr Thomson when they had argued for its importance twenty-five years earlier. They were, however, still talking about the same sort of thing. And the authors of *The Teaching of History* hailed the new CSE examination for the 'variety of syllabus' which it promised, rather than for the variety of questioning which it was to achieve.

Of these three works, only *The Teaching of History* addressed itself directly to examinations. It is a good book, but its section on examinations is weak. It knows the enemy of good history teaching: an over-emphasis on the acquisition of factual information. Its opening chapter shows the lengths to which this went in Victorian textbooks. Above all in Ince: the doyen of stodge. His *Outlines of English History* sold nearly a quarter of a million copies. Schoolchildren, brought up on Ince, knew that George II's son died 'from the blow of a cricket ball' – what else? – and learned by heart great portions of his reign, such as:

> Death – This monarch died suddenly, from a rupture in the heart. On the morning of his death he walked in Kensington Gardens, but on his return, being alone, he was heard to fall upon the floor; an attempt was made to bleed him, but without effect, for the vital spark was extinct. He was buried at Westminster.

The quaint language provokes a smile. Perhaps too easy a smile: Ince induces complacency. Whatever direction the teaching of history has taken since the time of Ince, it can hardly have been for the worse. And so the effect of producing this, and a number of other quaint specimens of Victoriana in the opening chapter, *is* to induce complacency; especially when we move on, in later chapters, to a description of the more adventurous classroom techniques – many derived from successful primary school practice – in the teaching of history today. Ince is dead.

'Long live Ince!' comes back a derisive echo. The authors of *The Teaching of History* have only told us half of the story. They tell us the way in which primary school teachers and secondary school teachers (of junior forms, at least) have succeeded – with project work, dramatisations, imaginative essays, use of source material and the like – in transforming the subject into something Ince would not now recognise. But the other half of the story remains as it was – dictated notes in the classroom from the rugger coach; weekly date tests; reading around the class; GCE Model Answers; history coming bottom of the poll for interest and enjoyment in a Schools Council survey of 9,677 early leavers. Mary Price is right then to scold *The Teaching of History* for its smugness in claiming that the complaint that school history is dull is 'happily less heard in these days'. Fourteen-year-old Judith brings out both halves of the story admirably:

> Four years ago in the primary school we crouched spellbound as the snake's prey before the glittering eyes of the Roman gladiator. . . . Now I am labouring my way through a grey mechanical tangle of drudgery or 'British Social and Economic History 1700–' . . . a jarring flood of facts, machines, names and dates. I now know by heart a long list of inventions in the 18th century textile industry: John Kay, Flying Shuttle, 1733 . . . spinning machine with rollers, 1738 – it didn't work anyway . . .[3]

If Judith can now only look forward to 'eighty minutes of the toneless drone of the master's voice and the pendulum swing of his leg over the desk' this may not be unrelated to the examination that Judith will soon be taking in history. It is true that Judith's history teacher may drone because he is one: dictated notes are the last refuge of the scoundrel. But, again, he may drone because he is conscientious. External examinations require the coverage, and retention, of a vast amount of material. The history teacher feels an obligation to his pupils, to their parents, to his headmaster, to make sure that they pass their examination. In the present context of history examining, dictated notes are the most efficient method of securing this end. There is a third possibility. If we are honest, most of us have appalling discipline problems in our beginnings as history teachers. The strain upon the young student is often insupportable. He begins with high ideals, has his project wrecked by 4Z, and discovers the merits of dictated notes. In other words the subject *becomes* the disciplinary weapon: dictated notes are the guarantee of a quiet, if unexciting, life. And for his cowardice under fire he will be rewarded with glittering O level successes.

The authors of *The Teaching of History* are not on the side of dictated notes. Against Ince, they argue that the long-term consequences of what the history teacher does 'will not be the facts that linger but the attitudes of mind that are formed'. But they seriously underrate the effect of examinations, which themselves give highest priority to 'the facts that linger', upon the teaching of the subject in the schools. We are back in Oxford in 1930 when the authors argue that 'the majority of our correspondents do not feel themselves cramped by the external examination. Indeed, most say that the examination acts as a stimulus upon the pupils.' The summit of their radicalism is the concession that external examining bodies are not perfect; that there are, occasionally, obscure questions set; that teachers should make constructive criticisms through official channels. They conclude this section with this splendid piece of forelock-tugging obsequiousness: 'To state more than this in the Memorandum would be presumptuous and irrelevant.'

If this section were typical of the book as a whole it would be misguided to waste time on it. But it must be emphasised again that this is, in other respects, a decent and humane report; only on examinations is there this fatal stop in the mind. It is typical of the authors' confusion that they can reproduce the pages of Ince as an example of the horrors which we have left behind, but can also reproduce the first London Matriculation Paper without seeing it as a horror which we have *not* left behind. The most disturbing feature of current examination papers is the extent to which they would not have disturbed Ince.

And yet Ince's practice flowed from his theory. That theory was outlined in his preface to his *Outlines of English History*:

The importance of having the outlines of every study accurately defined, and the leading points and bearings correctly acquired before the *minutiae* are entered into, will be readily conceded; and also that if the groundwork be clearly traced in early life it will scarcely ever be obliterated; but that subsequent reading and even conversation, will continue to supply materials for the completion of the sketch.

And that theory was perfectly acceptable to the university historians of Ince's day. A disservice to Ince is done by wrenching him out of the context of the historical thought of his time. Ince in the schools was the natural complement of Lord Acton and the first *Cambridge Modern History*. With the establishment of the School of Modern History at Oxford in 1872 and the Historical Tripos at Cambridge in 1874 the first graduates who went out to teach transmitted the assumptions of history that underlay the teaching of their subject at the university. The correlation between school and university teaching was marked not only by the formal university awarding of the examination but also by the tireless encouragement given to the schools in setting up examinations by university teachers like A. L. Smith of Balliol.

What went wrong was that professional historians began to lose that ruddy Actonian optimism about the merits of accumulating factual information. E. H. Carr, in his *What is History?*, has entertainingly summarised, in his first chapter, the distance that modern historians have travelled from their Victorian predecessors: most notably in their recognition of the contingency of historical evidence; in their emphasis on the structural role of the historical imagination; in their repudiation – heeding here Marc Bloch's eloquent warning – of assembling facts before thinking what they may add up to. That reappraisal had begun much earlier. But it stopped short at the university; it did not extend to the schools. The fatal dichotomy was beginning. The more willing university historians became to emphasise the contingencies, the hesitancies, the gropings of their craft, the more authoritarian classroom teaching of the subject became. It would be wrong to speak of a *trahison des clercs*. For one thing, not all university historians had turned their backs on Acton. For another, those who had, felt some diffidence about dictating their beliefs to the schools. Even so, the gap between university and school was becoming too wide to be ignored. Inevitably it was in the late twenties – in the general ferment of ideas about examinations –

that a conference on 'The Correlation of School and University Teaching' was held. Three eminent scholars – Woodward, Feiling and Miss Clarke – faced an audience of schoolteachers in 1929. This interesting division was recorded:

> In general the discussion never wandered very far away from weighing the relative merits of imparting exact historical knowledge in more or less formidable doses and the training in critical method and a scholarly mental outlook. The University teachers emphasised the desirability of the latter, and this was criticised by almost all the school representatives.[4]

The teachers remained loyal to Acton; in A. J. Williams' words they valued highest 'the possession of a body of historical knowledge'. Mrs Frances Lawrence has recently produced an interesting research study, showing how this concept haunted school textbooks, handbooks for teachers, examiners' reports and the like throughout the twenties and thirties.[5] Long after the Actonian ideal of one universal history book had faded, the ideal of one universal school textbook persisted:[6] palely reflected in such offerings as Warner and Marten's *The Groundwork of British History* and *The House of History* with its different 'Storeys'. But it was less easy to retain Ince's optimism that 'if the groundwork be clearly traced in early life, it will scarcely ever be obliterated'. This was wryly recognised by His Majesty's Inspectors in their *Report on the Teaching of History* in 1927 when they argued defensively for the value of having 'a few rocks to cling on in a sea of ignorance'.

We are now at the heart of the mystery of the resilience of the conventional examination papers: they might be recognised empirically as of doubtful value (as in this 1927 report by HMIs and also in examiners' reports[7] throughout this period) but the philosophy behind them was not attacked. Fleetingly F. T. Happold seemed to have this insight in the course of his polemics with the teachers from the Oxford course. They had condemned his suggestion that pupils bring textbooks into the examination. They declared that this was 'contrary to the true purpose of an examination, which is to test what a candidate knows, not what he can find out'. It suddenly struck Happold that he had been arguing for experiment when he should have been arguing for reform – reform of the ideals and methods of teachers of history:

Is our history teaching to be reduced to filling our pupils with a mass of facts which on a certain day they must 'know'? Might we not be better employed in teaching them to 'find out' – to search out references quickly and accurately, to co-ordinate the results, and to set them down in clear and vivid form?

This was the premise of history teaching which might have been challenged: that our aim was to fill our pupils with a mass of facts. Instead Happold's defeat switched the course of attack (and ensured the survival of conventional examinations): reform was now envisaged as filling our pupils with 'better' facts – facts more relevant to a 'line of development' approach (Jeffreys) or to the world in which the pupils were living (Henderson, Thomson). Indeed, Jeffreys pointed out that dates and factual information could be learned just as effectively under his reformed syllabus as under the chronological one.

Nor was this premise challenged by the three works published between 1965 and 1967, however timely and telling their criticisms were in other respects. In *The Teaching of History* there is no chapter, 'Why Have We Been Teaching History?', as there is in the otherwise inferior Ministry of Education pamphlet, *Teaching History*. Jeers at Ince are no substitute for a reasoned critique of the philosophical assumptions behind Ince's excesses. This is especially true when we find, in its absence, many of the Ince assumptions creeping in by the back door. The writers' (admittedly lukewarm) defence of lecturing to sixth-formers is that it will offer 'an introduction to university methods'. Their section upon source materials in the classroom is mainly devoted to emphasising their limitations. They say that 'it would be dishonest to pretend that pupils can use documents in the way in which a research historian does'. This is almost the only time in the book that they concern themselves with the question of whether the activities of the historian can be a model for the activities of the history pupil; and then to deny it. If there is a use of source material in the classroom it is 'as illustration – illustration of historical facts': the concept which, more than any other factor, has damned the Jackdaw series to remaining an elegant irrelevancy. Professor Barraclough also wants to fill us with better facts: pupils can learn from Cook, Borah and Simpson what *really* happened when the Spaniards conquered America. Most of the contributors to the volume edited by Mr Burston and Mr Thompson also want the pupils to be filled with better facts: not more ornamental (Jackdaws), or more relevant (Barraclough), but more

logical. The key word here is 'colligation': the logical grouping of
material in such a way that it becomes coherent and intelligible to
the pupil. The essayists break new ground by their insistence that
the behaviour of the historian is relevant to the behaviour of the
history teacher. This is a real advance, and Mr Thompson warns
against forgetting the role of the pupils – 'to ignore the limitations
and claims of those you are teaching will almost certainly mean, in
fact, that you are not teaching at all'. This is, however, a constraint,
setting the necessary context within which the history teacher may
simulate the historian's craft. But what of the more radical concept –
brusquely rejected by *The Teaching of History* – that the history
pupil may simulate the historian's craft?

This has seemed a less preposterous idea since Jerome Bruner's
pioneering researches begat the 'new' mathematics and the 'new'
physics. Bruner argued that the fallacy enshrined in traditional
curricula was the assumption that children should master, in imperfect form, the *conclusions* of the specialists in the subject. Bruner's
quarry, on the other hand, was the *mode of inquiry* of the specialist.
If once we grasped the structure of the subject, any topic could be
taught to any child at any age. The pupil, working from raw data,
would himself become the scholar: sifting evidence, weighing
probabilities, drawing conclusions. The idea – seductively simple
when stated in this way – requires very close collaboration between
specialists in the subject and practitioners in the field to produce
carefully structured material. Work has begun in the United States
along these lines for history, and details are to be found in Edwin
Fenton's *Teaching the New Social Studies in Secondary Schools: An
Inductive Approach* (Holt, Rinehart & Winston, 1966). It is far too
early yet to make sweeping claims for the 'new' history, but Bruner's
researches have already been invaluable in reopening questions that
seemed to have been buried with Happold's honourable failure in
the late 1920s.

For if there has not been the same systematic attempt in England
as in the United States to test Bruner's hypotheses for our subject,
there have been at least four encouraging developments which owe
something to that decisive shift from content to mode of inquiry
which Bruner made respectable.

First, there has been a rethinking about curriculum reform. The
fusion of history with other subjects, under whatever fancy label,
'Integrated Studies', 'Social Studies', 'Humanities Programme'; the

case for 'World History', 'Contemporary History', 'Line of Development': all have hitherto been advocated, and opposed, on grounds of
content. Inasmuch as they have been advocated on grounds of
content, history specialists who opposed such schemes are now to be
seen as no prejudiced backwoodsmen: on the contrary, they show a
healthy rejection of the use of history as a milch-cow for other
specialisms or of the fallacy that a change of content will itself be
sufficient to involve the pupil. On the other hand, inasmuch as they
have been opposed on grounds of content, these now seem less
relevant: the historians, emancipated from the 'traditional belief
that there is a body of content for each separate subject which every
young school leaver should know',[8] can judge these alternative
reforms coolly on their merits; their criteria will be how far they give
weight to the *mode of inquiry* of the historians.[9] Mr Carpenter advocated the 'patch' syllabus, precisely because it 'engendered a spirit
of inquiry': his own preference for the term 'era' may have been, as
he argued in the preface to his book,[10] merely because the term
'patch' was 'inelegant', but it may also reveal that he had not
succeeded entirely in freeing himself from assumptions about the
value of content. Certainly Mr Welch who had argued in 1927 for
shorter periods, in order that the pupils' imagination could be more
easily kindled, also believed that the periods should hold as 'dramatic
unities'. And emphasis on 'era' and 'dramatic unities' still suggests a
virtue in *period* (albeit shorter ones) rather than *problem*. This was
what Franklin Patterson found when he tried to apply Bruner's
findings to a 'patch' of Roman history. Concern to test the mode of
inquiry of his pupils led him from a narrative source kit to a problem
source kit: from his original Caesar unit to one which centred upon
the problem of power in Republican Rome.[11]

Indeed, the second encouraging development in England is the
move from the ornamental Jackdaw source kits – the 'illustration
of historical facts' – to the problem-solving kits produced by the
University of Newcastle, on the Bruner model of a collaboration
between professional historian and teacher.[12]

A third source of hope is the attention which is now being paid to
the capacity of young children for historical thinking: crucial in an
argument which pivots on the ability of the pupil to imitate the
mode of inquiry of the historian. Rejected out of hand by *The
Teaching of History*; seen by Mr Thompson, in the volume which he
co-edited with Mr Burston, more in the spirit of a negative restraint

(what the history teacher can reasonably expect to get away with in *his* task to imitate the mode of inquiry of the historian); this concern is given a quite new dimension in the researches of Brown, Booth and Hallam.[13]

All these developments are linked with a fourth encouraging development which has reinforced, and been reinforced by, each of the other three. This is the Certificate of Secondary Examination, which began with no lofty academic ambitions. Rather it seemed to begin with the pre-Bruner assumption that children could only be expected to master, in imperfect forms, the *conclusions* of specialists. The less academic child could only be expected to master, in even more imperfect form, the conclusions which his more academic, O level, peer could already master. Hence O level questions were set at this level but with links already provided to make his narrative essay easier to construct. But the very fact that teachers felt less under an obligation to impart a body of information, and were concerned to create something which had meaning for the child, led them into directions undreamed of by O and A level examiners. Hence the paradox: in reacting against the 'academic' aridities of the conventional examination papers many of the CSE papers moved closer to the academic criteria of the professional historian. CSE candidates are increasingly being asked to reflect upon, and draw inferences from, raw material in the shape of graphs, cartoons, statistics, literary sources and the like. They bear an uncanny family resemblance to questions reproduced in Fenton's volume as examples of ways in which the 'new' history can be assessed. And it is significant that when the Schools Council brought out its interim report recently on the Personal Topic it could note with pleasure that it was contributing to the secondary school 'something of the enthusiasm that this sort of activity engenders in the primary school'. The Council turned for its essential justification of this work, on the lines of Fenton and Bruner, to a consideration of how far such activities properly stretch historical skills (the understanding of concepts, the detection of bias, the development of imaginative insights are among those isolated).[14]

None of these developments is original. We have seen that shorter syllabuses, use of original sources, inter-disciplinary programmes, had their champions in the past. But although critics then made legitimate attacks upon individual points, they never succeeded in challenging the basic premise behind the 'old' history, although

Happold came near to it, that the purpose of history teaching was to impart information. There is an analogy here with the resilience of the witch-craze in sixteenth- and seventeenth-century Europe. Professor Trevor-Roper has pointed out that even when men 'revolted against the cruelty of torture, against the implausibility of confessions, against the identification of witches' they did not revolt against 'the central doctrine of the kingdom of Satan and its war on humanity by means of demons and witches'. Conventional examination papers in history now face their sternest challenge, because not only Ince, *but the philosophy which sustained Ince*, is being repudiated. We are a long way from the millennium, but we are beginning to inch our way forward from 1838.

Notes

1 The comments that follow come from: C. H. K. Marten, 'The First School Examination and the Teaching of History', *History*, 1928, pp. 17–29; F. T. Happold, 'A New Type of Question in History Papers', *History*, 1928, pp. 126–30; a communication from Oliver G. Welch, *History*, 1927, pp. 241–3; and one from A. J. Williams, *History*, 1931, pp. 135–7; F. T. Happold, 'The Case for Experiment in Examinations', *History*, 1931, pp. 35–7.

2 M. V. C. Jeffreys, 'The Subject Matter of History in Schools', *History*, 1935, pp. 233–42; 'The Teaching of History by Means of Lines of Development', *History*, 1936, pp. 230–8; G. B. Henderson, 'A Plea for the Study of Contemporary History', *History*, 1941, pp. 51–5; D. Thomson, 'The Historian's Contribution to Contemporary Thought', *History*, 1942, pp. 156–61.

3 Mary Price, 'History in Danger', *History*, 1968, pp. 342–7; E. Blishen (ed.), *The School that I'd Like*, Penguin, 1969, pp. 66–7.

4 G. Talbot Griffith, 'The Correlation of School and University Teaching: A Discussion', *History*, 1929, pp. 33–42.

5 Frances Lawrence, 'Forms of Bias in History Writing for Schools', University of Sussex MA thesis, 1967, unpublished.

6 The IAAM *Memorandum on Teaching of History*, CUP, 1925, saw the main function of a textbook as a 'mine of facts'. One published 'in many parts' may present 'a serious drawback' since the pupil needs 'a complete outline which he can take with him through his school

career having the more advanced parts provided as he goes up the school. This complete book he should be expected to know thoroughly.'

7 For example HMSO, 1931, *School Certificate Examination Report* was sharply critical of pupils' techniques but accepted that the pupils *should* leave school with a 'permanent knowledge of the bare framework of history'.

8 *Society and the Young School Leaver*, Schools Council Working Paper no. 11, p. 3.

9 See the Schools Council paper: *Humanities for the Young School Leaver: An Approach Through History*, Evans/Methuen Educational Publications, 1969. I am testing the history element in a Humanities Programme which Thomas Bennett Comprehensive School, Crawley, is presenting for CSE and GCE O level in the summer of 1971. In our tripartite discussions Mr P. Mitchell (as Head of the Humanities Programme), Mr J. Townsend (as Head of the History Department) and myself (as external assessor) have been concerned to isolate the historian's mode of inquiry within the general Humanities Programme.

10 P. Carpenter, *History Teaching: The Era Approach*, CUP, 1964.

11 Franklin V. Patterson, *Man and Politics*, Social Studies Curriculum Programme, Occasional Paper IV, Educational Services Incorporated, 1965.

12 For example *Coals from Newcastle*, Newcastle-upon-Tyne Archive Teaching Units, 1, ed. J. C. Tyson *et al.*

13 L. M. Brown, 'An enquiry into the attitudes and understandings involved in the study of history . . .', University of London PhD thesis, 1959, unpublished; M. Booth, 'A Critical Analysis of the Secondary School History Curriculum', University of Southampton MA (Ed) thesis, 1967, unpublished; R. N. Hallam, 'Logical Thinking in History', *Educational Review*, 19, 3, 1967.

14 *The Certificate of Secondary Education: The Place of the Personal Topic-History*, Schools Council Examinations Bulletin no. 18, 1968, p. 5.

PETER BAMFORD

Original Sources in the Classroom

In a short article, one can do little more than suggest a few possible lines of thought to teachers of history, in the hope that they may recognise in them some worthwhile ideas which may be easily adapted to the particular circumstances of their own schools and environments. What follows has no claim to be regarded as an exhaustive list of possible original sources, nor have I attempted to cover all the possible uses of each. It has, rather, been my concern to suggest some simple ways in which readily available sources may easily be employed by a hard-pressed teacher of children of average ability.

I start with three propositions: first, that it is necessary and desirable to spice more orthodox history teaching with work specifically designed to enable one's pupils to appreciate something of the nature of history and of the historian's craft, his tools and methods; second, that this can successfully be done even with the less able children; and third, that the term 'original sources' should be interpreted more widely than may be usual.

Before children can embark upon such work as I shall outline, it is necessary to introduce them to certain techniques. Essentially, these are the techniques of the detective who, confronted with an amount of unorganised evidence, imposes some order upon it and uses it to tell him as much as possible. One could begin by recounting to the class the story of Sherlock Holmes and the hat, telling how, by intelligent deduction from the most meagre evidence, the detective was able to draw a large number of important, if conjectural, conclusions. Sherlock Holmes' methods, if not his raw material and purpose, are those of the historian.

From such an introduction, one could proceed to a similar exercise for the class. For instance:

A wallet is found, containing the following objects:

A recent photograph of a young lady
A recent newspaper cutting of a wedding
A membership card of an exclusive golf club
Two one-pound notes

A number of printed cards, with the same name and address on
   them
An Oxford class list (explain) of 1939
An airmail letter from Turkey
A DFC ribbon

Write as much as you can reasonably conjecture about the owner of
the wallet.

Given this exercise, a child of fourteen wrote:

> He is most probably of the upper class. These are the reasons
> pointing to this assessment: (a) He belongs to an exclusive golf
> club. (b) He carries printed cards. (c) He has been awarded the
> DFC. (d) He went to Oxford. He most probably has a cheque
> book, because a person in his position would be more wealthy
> than the amount in his wallet suggests. Perhaps he is careful with
> his money, and never carries more than he immediately needs.

This account, it hardly needs pointing out, can of course be
criticised on grounds both of commission and of omission. But its
author has perceived the purpose of the exercise – he has drawn
tentative, organised conclusions from the evidence, and has achieved
a nice balance between opinion and supporting evidence. In a
further lesson on this theme, his work could be analysed, to make
these points, and some useful research could be undertaken to test
the validity of the argument that the wallet's owner is 'of the upper
class'. Each of the four pieces of evidence quoted in that connection
could be followed up, to see whether there is any strong connection
between it and 'the upper class'. At this stage, one could also put
quite a different interpretation upon the evidence, based on the
assumption that the wallet's contents, which suggest an age of about
fifty-two for the owner, are in fact mementoes of the owner's father,
and that the owner is a young man of about twenty-six. Such an
exercise would be a salutary demonstration of the fact that the same
evidence can lead to very different conclusions.

So much by way of introduction. From such exercises, one can
proceed to more genuinely historical work, using much the same
techniques but this time on actual historical sources. I shall confine
myself to a selection of sources which are readily available and easily
reproduced; time, difficulty of access and the inherent difficulties of
sources contained therein may well preclude more ambitious or
sophisticated work based on official Record Offices. (It should be

noted in passing, though, that many Record Offices are most cooperative, and that a little time spent with a photo-copier can enable one to build up an impressive mini Record Office of one's own.)

Let us first consider the use of historical sites. Why be content merely with a visit, the value of which so often is more social than historical? Take, for instance, a local church (chosen because almost any area of Britain will contain an historically fruitful church). A visit could be organised and planned to elicit a mass of information, which could then be assembled and used back in the classroom. For instance:

(a) The list of incumbents, usually posted in the porch. This often reflects the history of religious changes (e.g. the frequency of change in the period *c.* 1530–1714), and may well reflect something of the nature of the benefice if the same family name recurs significantly. The pupils' work-sheet could instruct them: (*i*) to count and record the number of incumbents in the periods 1300–1500; 1500–1700; and 1700–1900; (*ii*) to note if the same name recurs at all frequently and, if so, to note the relevant details. Back at school, the class could then be helped to research into and discover possible explanations.

(b) The graveyard. Look for, and record, such evidence as repetition of names, which may indicate continuity of settlement; or make a graph of the incidence of death over a given period, to discover, and later perhaps explain, significant fluctuations (e.g. the Plague).

(c) Building materials and styles. Record these, and later use them as possible indices of dates and changes to the church.

(d) Plaques and memorial tablets. Record the details of these, to see if any general conclusions may be inferred from them.

(e) Relate the church to its immediate community. Draw a map of the village or area, marking each building according to its age and use. What conclusions may be suggested from a comparison of that evidence with the evidence drawn from (a) to (d) above?

From a mass of data which could be forthcoming from such a directed visit as this, one could develop along all sorts of lines back in the classroom. Occasionally, one may be particularly fortunate. For instance, on one such project, in which I had the generous and long-suffering cooperation of the rector, I had one group looking through eighteenth-century parish records in the vestry. Much of the material was incomprehensible to them, but they did come across the original accounts for the building of the church tower, part of which is reproduced below:

John Swetland and Timothy Swetland Bill for work in repairing
Minstead Church

		£	s	d
August 27th 1774				
Philip Etherdge	2½ days	0	5	0
Thomas Hayter	2½ days	0	3	9
Sept. 3rd				
Philip Etherdge	3¾ days	0	7	6
John Compton	2½ days	0	5	0
Thomas Hayter	3¾ days	0	5	7½
Stephen Early	3 days	0	6	0
Thomas Belbin	2 days	0	4	0
¾ 100 12 nails		0	0	9
¼ 100 20 nails		0	0	5
Sept. 10th				
Thomas Belbin	3 days	0	6	0
Stephen Early	4 days	0	8	0
400 12 nails		0	4	0
John Compton	3¾ days	0	7	6
James Belbin Jun.	2 days	0	3	6
Sept. 17th				
John Compton	6 days	0	12	0
James Belbin Jun.	6 days	0	10	6
Thomas Hayter	6 days	0	9	0
750 tiles and carridge		0	17	6
Mortar, lime and hair		0	10	6
37 feet of ¾ inch Deal at 2		0	6	2
4 feet 2 inch of Oak Plank at 5		0	1	8
100 of 8 nails		0	0	8
¼ 100 20 nails		0	0	5
½ 1000 4 nails		0	1	6
Thomas Belbin 1 day lyning stairs in the tower		0	2	0
		£6	18	11½

Quite apart from the value of the boys' eagerness at handling and 'discovering' the authentic stuff of which history is made, this achievement added significantly to the records which could later be extensively used back in the classroom. This particular item could be used as the basis for some interesting conclusions on, say, wage rates, cost of materials etc. It so happened that the father of one of the children in this group was the foreman on a building site, and with his cooperation we were able to draw some interesting comparisons with modern prices, costs and materials. Also, research in the graveyard of this church enabled us to draw tentative conclusions about the number of the workmen listed who came from the immediate vicinity.

From such work as has been outlined in this section, one can easily build up 'kits' of raw source material for use with successive classes. Essentially, one would be compiling something similar to Jonathan Cape's 'Jackdaws' – an excellent concept, but I have found them to be of very limited value with children of only average ability, since the nature of the material, and more particularly the level of the text, is generally too difficult.

Written sources constitute the largest single body of material available to the teacher for the sort of work under consideration. Investment in one or more volumes of Eyre & Spottiswoode's *English Historical Documents* – and Hutchinson Educational's *Portraits and Documents* series (ed. J. S. Millward) – would be wise. Within the daunting covers, there is a mine of fascinating and valuable material which may be used with profit by less able children, although much of the material is of course inappropriate to them. Such material may well need editing, and of course the number of such books that a school can afford will be extremely limited. Here is a case for the typewriter and duplicator. In one hour, one could select, edit and duplicate a foolscap sheet of original source material on which to base a number of lessons or individual work-sheets. 'What can you infer about eighteenth-century travel from this letter?' 'What does this extract from *Humphry Clinker* tell us about eighteenth-century Bath?' 'What does that speech tell us about the conditions of the Army in the Crimean War?' And so on.

Another written source is the newspaper. There was a dramatic growth of the provincial press in the eighteenth century, and back copies of newspapers are often available either from the newspaper offices or on microfilm in the town library. Such material can be used to great profit. Set a child the job of studying and analysing such a newspaper, its editorial, news and advertisements, and he may derive an amazing amount from it. But here as elsewhere one must be careful to urge on him the importance of analysing the contents, drawing inferences from them, stating opinions and supporting evidence, rather than allowing him merely to copy or summarise the contents. Collecting information can be useful, as with the church visit, but generally only if it is collected with a purpose, so that it is later used to good effect.

A boy studying an issue of *The Cambrian* dated 8 May 1819 wrote

> In the days of this paper, it must have been a hard time, judging by the contents of the court cases. Many families seemed short of food, clothes and money. One man had hitch-hiked or walked from Wales to London looking for food. On his return he was caught stealing a chicken and was also charged with stealing other goods. In the court he said that he had never stolen before but he was so hard pressed for food that he had to.

Here we have evidence quoted to support a general conclusion about life in those times, and this could form an excellent and imaginative introduction to more orthodox textbook work on conditions at that time, and might prompt the author to research into contemporary penalties for such thefts. Such a boy will derive much more insight from work done this way than from a treatment of the subject based solely upon the more generalised textbook. Once motivated he can be brought willingly to the textbook, which he will then regard as serving a more definite purpose.

Another boy wrote of his issue of the same newspaper dated 24 April 1819

> The births, deaths and marriages show some more facts. There were 13 deaths, 2 births and 2 marriages. This could mean two things. One, the mortality rate was higher than the birth-rate, or people felt more about deaths than they did of births. . . . Although the paper was made up of only one sheet of paper, it cost sevenpence. This was a great deal then and papers are much thicker and cheaper now than they were 150 years ago. Communications could have been one cause of the high cost, but the most likely would be the cost of setting the type. It all had to be done by hand, back to front. It must have taken hours for one man to do just one column. All the type is set correctly and without a single mistake.

There is evidence in the passages quoted of thoughtful observation and consideration of possible explanations for what has been observed – qualities which our work should surely strive to inculcate.

Pictorial sources can also be extensively used for deductive exercises of the type described.

BRASS RUBBINGS

These can be successfully used for simple deductive exercises such as that based on the wallet contents. The chosen rubbings, for example, can be used as the basis for drawing certain inferences abount infant mortality, women's death in childbirth, and even the honour accorded to husband and father (note the direction of the wives' and children's eyes, hands and feet). Such conclusions can be elicited from a class, if their careful attention is drawn to detail, and if they have been taught to observe as well as merely to look. Readers who are ignorant of monumental brasses and brass rubbing will find *Brass Rubbing* by Malcolm Norris (Studio Vista, 1965) an invaluable aid. It explains the very simple and inexpensive methods involved, contains interesting material on brasses, and lists the more significant ones by counties.

THE BAYEUX TAPESTRY

Reproductions of parts of the Bayeux Tapestry are easily available. One can acquire picture postcards of various scenes and no self-respecting book on the Norman Conquest is without several illustrations from the Tapestry.

A boy given a 'strip' of the Tapestry to study and write about included the following observations and conclusions in his work:

> This tapestry tells us basically about the Battle of Hastings. But at the same time it has a mine of information about the way of life in those times. . . .
> The departure scenes from France depict men carrying goatskins of wine to the ships. If wine was taken to battle it must have been the staple drink of the time. It also would have a low alcohol content, or the soldiers would get drunk and so useless in battle. (Perhaps they were given it to give them courage.) . . .
> The masts [of the boats] can be taken in and out. This means that the boats must have been precision made in some places at least. This in turn means that at that time there were skilled carpenters. . . .
> All of the trees are in flower or leaf in the tapestry. This would mean that the tapestry was made in the summer months. (Or could it mean that the events took place then?)

A word in conclusion. I have deliberately moved at random about the various periods of English history, and I of course appreciate that most history teachers work within a fairly strict chronological framework (the merits and demerits of which practice fall outside my present terms of reference). But the ideas contained above are for the most part easily adaptable to a particular period of history, and it is my belief that the inclusion, in more orthodox work, of a regular element of such activity as has been suggested would be of benefit. The burden of organisation and preparation is not great, and the benefits to the pupils' work on the period are considerable. They can achieve a deeper understanding of some of their history, and a new dimension may have been added to their studies by their being made to do the job of real historians for a change, instead of – as is all too often the case – their being the unwilling recipients of *n*th-hand material which is already dead before it enters their experience.

Further Reading

I append a selection of titles of books and other sources, additional to those referred to in the chapter, which contain original material of a type which is useful to the sort of work I have suggested. It should be noted that this is merely a selection compiled largely on the basis of personal experience, and has no claim to be a complete list. Many publishers have, in recent years, taken an interest in books of the nature of those listed, and reference should be made to their catalogues for further guidance.

Historical Sites
Almost any church, country house, etc., would lend itself to the work suggested in the chapter. The Imperial War Museum has a vast collection not only of weapons but also of relevant posters, etc. (reproductions of many of which can be bought from the Museum), and it also has an unrivalled library of film material, selections from which are willingly shown to visitors in the Museum's cinema. You will need to write for information and make detailed arrangements well in advance.

Mainly Pictorial Sources
The pamphlets which the BBC produce to accompany their schools broadcasts often contain a large number of authentic contemporary illustrations. Since these pamphlets are so easily available in bulk, one can

use them to build up a picture library on any given topic, or sets of identical pictures for work with a whole class. Purnell's *History of the Twentieth Century*, in Sunday colour-supplement form, and comprising 128 sections, also contains a vast amount of pictorial source material. Each of the thirty volumes in Cassell's *Caravel* series (stretching from *The Pharaohs of Egypt* to *Russia in Revolution*) contains a large number of illustrations taken from original sources.

Mainly Written Sources
The booklets in Longmans' well-known *Then and There* series contain a large amount of original material, and the six volumes of Allen & Unwin's *Picture Source Books of Social History* (ed. Harrison and Wells), in addition to their pictorial sources, contain also extracts from contemporary written sources, designed to expand the subject considered in each picture. Similar in concept are the three sets of *History Class Pictures*, published by Macmillan and arranged and edited by George Lay. The pictures themselves are not all authentic and are of variable quality, but each set of sixty has a companion volume which, in addition to suggesting questions to be asked on each picture, also contains much useful background source material.

Basil Blackwell has published a number of series based on contemporary records, both written and pictorial. The volumes entitled *They Saw it Happen* contain eyewitness accounts and descriptions of scenes and events in English and European history. Two books edited by Grant Uden and entitled *They Looked Like This* comprise authentic word-portraits of men and women in English and European history. Finally, the three volumes under the title *How They Lived* contain contemporary records of social history.

Old newspapers are, of course, legion, and I would particularly recommend the use of your local newspaper, if it is of sufficiently early foundation. Application should be made, in the first instance, to the head office. Among national publications, of sufficient vintage and of particular interest are *Punch* and the *Illustrated London News*. The nature of each is such as to make it a fascinating source for hours of interesting research, and one can learn a great deal from an intelligent study of cartoons – until recently, surprisingly little used in history textbooks, and a source that has yet to have its full potential realised.

Finally, there are some publications which are 'forthcoming' at the time of writing, and would seem to merit close consideration. Blackwell are to publish a volume edited by G. Cawte and called *We Were There* – a source book for younger children but dealing with modern events. (Most source books on modern history, such as Edward Arnold's excellent *Archive* series – general editors C. P. Hill and G. H. Fell – and R. W. Breach's *Documents and Descriptions: The World Since 1914*, published by OUP, seem designed for older and more able children.) Blackie are publishing a series called *Topics in Modern History* (general editor – I. D. Astley), whose books include much written and pictorial source material. Dent are bringing out two books edited by N. Niemeyer and called *Stories from History*. They cover early and medieval history, and are compilations of long extracts from original sources. By the time this is published, Wayland will have published two series which seem very promising, one entitled *English Life* and the other, *Documentary History Series*. The wide variety of sources used would seem to justify careful consideration of these.

Three other 'forthcoming' books concern the teaching of history and seem most appropriate to the subject of this chapter. Blond Educational are publishing two teachers' handbooks, one edited by J. Fines and called simply *History*, the other edited by T. Corfe and called *History in the Field*. Both are concerned with sources and their use, and the latter would seem an invaluable guide to work based on historical sites. Oliver & Boyd are to publish a series called *Discovering History* (ed. J. Salt and F. Purnell), designed for children of average and below average ability, and involving deductive exercises, imaginative work and the development of an appreciation of historical evidence and method.

COLIN C. BAYNE-JARDINE

A Practical Approach

There is evidence that secondary school history teachers are responding to the challenge that is being made to the traditional patterns of subject teaching.[1] They are beginning to combat the despair of George, Mr Albee's embittered college teacher, who cries: 'I'm very mistrustful. Do you believe . . . do you believe that people learn nothing from history? Not that there is nothing to learn, mind you, but that people learn nothing.'[2] Yet a constructive response is not made easily. Much history teaching in English secondary schools still reflects the certainty of the nineteenth century. British history is treated chronologically with a fairly liberal sprinkling of modern European history.[3] This traditional approach does represent some sort of security in a rapidly changing world. History has become institutionalised and examined in such a way that many history teachers have become prisoners of the past. However, the changing organisation of secondary schools has forced rapid developments, and history teachers in large comprehensive schools have had to grasp the nettle of how to make their subject relevant and vital to today's children. I plan to highlight three problem areas and to suggest tentative ways forward in each area.

First, the history teachers in many comprehensive schools are asked to justify the teaching of their subject during the first two years of a child's life in a secondary school. In order to give one teacher plenty of contact time with a particular group of children, many schools have adopted a coordinated programme, crossing subject barriers, for the eleven and twelve year old children. Longmans have now produced textbooks for just such a programme in their series, *The Developing World*.[4] At Henbury School we use a team of teachers drawn from the history, geography, and religious education departments. We have developed a coordinated programme and a series of lead lessons and structured follow-up work. This programme has proved successful but it has demanded that the historians, as well as teachers of other subject disciplines, should be clear in their own minds as to what they wish to introduce in this area of the school. We have concentrated on asking for a basic training in the historian's mode of inquiry and for encouragement of the children's awareness of the past. The programme begins by looking out from the school and asking questions about the immediate environment. The first section, called 'a study of our community', deals with the physical setting, the history of the buildings, and the life of the people in Henbury. The important dimension of past experience is the business of the historian and he can bring a knowledge of methods of inquiry into the past to such a coordinated programme.

Secondly, the historian must be clear as to how he can develop children's self-awareness through a study of their past during their third year in secondary school. For many children this year may be the only time during their life that they make a formal study of history. It is essential that history teachers work out satisfactory criteria for choosing the syllabus for this area in the school. Bruner argues that 'any subject can be taught effectively in some intellectually honest form to any child at any stage of development'.[5] The history teacher has to consider this challenge and choose his syllabus with an awareness of stages of mental growth and of individual patterns of learning. He must also consider the special interests of the teachers available, the resources of the environment, and the immediate interests of the pupils. Building upon a careful analysis of such factors, he can develop a syllabus which harnesses the great resources of the past to the task of developing the individual's self-awareness. This process is dynamic and should undergo constant revision and questioning. Later in the school it is now possible to escape the restrictions of the examination system, as we have found at Henbury, by developing a CSE Mode Three syllabus of our own.

Finally, such an approach to the teaching of history in secondary schools has certain clear practical implications in the classroom. Historians use difficult language and abstract concepts; secondary school children do not all have a grasp of a linear time sequence; and much historical material is difficult to use and understand.

> When students set about learning 'history', they are trying to learn facts outside the context of problems. Thus the facts of history fail to achieve the status of data. For many students the facts remain lifeless and courses in history seem pointless.[6]

Children are not uniform in their levels of thinking so that no blanket programme could begin to cover the problems raised by individual differences and by individual responses. When we attempt to develop the individual's self-awareness through a knowledge and understanding of the past, general exposition to a class must be kept to a minimum. Of course the vivid imaginative reconstruction of the past and exciting exposition are key elements in history teaching. Nevertheless history teachers too often become deaf to any voice but their own. The pupils should be encouraged to verbalise their learning and develop a greater understanding of language by involvement. As far as possible the individual should be encouraged to work along his own line of interest within the subject.

Accepting that this approach makes sense, many history teachers make extensive use of the project method. The danger here is that the individual learner finds the material difficult to handle and so resorts to copying out large sections from books or spends many hours drawing maps and illustrations. Furthermore history lessons can become a mere repetition of projects and the exercise becomes as pointless as a hamster turning a wheel in a cage. There must be an 'increase in directive teaching aimed at producing eventual self-direction'.[7] Probably the best way to achieve this is by opening up a topic by an impact lesson and then helping the class to work on their own by giving them as much resource material as possible and a work-sheet or card. R. F. Mackenzie[8] describes the way in which imaginative use can be made of material from the past when he outlines how a programme could be developed from one old book – *The Story of the Forth*, published in 1913. He points out that the story of the lowland 'moss lairds' is 'an epitome of the story of human beings colonising the earth and compelling it to serve their purposes'. In such a way the history of the area round a Fife coal town could be used as a resource for lively inquiry.

The impact lesson can take many forms. Most history teachers can tell a good story and even if they cannot sing they can make use of records. Short extracts from films are effective. The flogging scene from *Billy Budd* makes an excellent introduction to a study of Nelson's navy. The scene on the Odessa steps makes a fine introduction to the study of the Russian Revolution and raises interesting questions about the validity of film evidence. From an impact lesson of this sort the teacher must go on to produce work-sheets. This requires a great deal of careful thought for it is not merely a matter of writing down a series of questions based upon a handy text.

The teacher should start by making a situational analysis. He must find out what resources are available and sort through them so that he can give helpful guidance. Secondly he must assess the general ability of the group with whom he is working. If the pupils find the written word hard to handle most of the material presented to them might be visual. A picture of a bison and another of a Cheyenne warrior can provide the starters for an exciting study of the American West for children who find history textbooks meaningless. Finally, the teacher must try to assess what things will interest the group and link them in with his own enthusiasms. When he has a particular interest in a subject he will very often be able to bring it alive by adopting an unusual approach. Once he has a clear idea of the situation before him, the teacher must consider how best to encourage the group of children to handle material from the past, organise it, and develop some understanding of it. Then there must be some form of evaluation built in to the process. This last point is complex, as many CSE boards have found when they come to assess Mode Three Examinations. Nevertheless it is vitally important that there is some attempt to check what has been done. This process is not a simple one and to be successful it requires a great deal of preparation and constant revision. Last year's notes will not do for next year's classes and work-sheets require constant revision in the light of changed situations.

Perhaps it may help if I end with an example of the sort of approach which could well be developed further. A group of thirteen-year-olds in a comprehensive school drawn from the top band of a nine-form entry are to study the American War of Independence. Copies of *The American Revolution 1775–83* by Clorinda Clarke in the Longmans *Then and There* series are available. In addition, apart from that book a wall display has been pinned up in the classroom. This contains material from a Jackdaw wallet and some material collected by the history department over the years. The impact lesson is based upon a film: *The American Revolution*. This can be had by the school for two units from EFVA. After this introduction the class are issued with the books and the work-sheet.

WORKSHEET ON AMERICAN WAR OF INDEPENDENCE
Source book: *The American Revolution 1775–83* by Clorinda Clarke

1   *Essential work*
    (a) Draw a map of the thirteen colonies.
    (b) Mark in the following places: Lexington, New York, Boston,

Saratoga, Yorktown. Write down the reasons why these places became important during the American Revolution.

(c) Write down a list of grievances that the colonies had against Britain.

(d) Who were the Loyalists and what happened to them?

2 *Choose two of the following topics for further follow-up*

(a) What was General Burgoyne's plan? Why did it not work? (See page 40)

(b) Imagine you are a soldier in Washington's army wintering in Morristown 1779–80. Write a letter home describing the hardships. (See pages 70–1)

(c) Write a newspaper account of the Boston Tea Party for an American paper and then write a contrasting account for a British newspaper.

(d) Write a short essay showing which side you would have supported and give your reasons.

(e) Outline the part played by the navy and show why it was so important.

(f) Write a poem about or draw a picture of any event in the American Revolution which you feel is particularly exciting.

3 *Check your knowledge*

(a) What were Minute Men?

(b) Why did Congress choose Washington to command their army?

(c) Who were the Green Mountain Boys?

(d) Who wrote *Common Sense*?

(e) Who was the main author of the Declaration of Independence?

(f) Why do Americans celebrate 4th July?

(g) What was the first American flag? How does the present flag differ?

(h) What vital part did France play in the war?

After the work-sheet had been used for a number of lessons the topic could be developed by some informed class discussion based upon the showing of slides.

'History is not what you thought. It is what you can remember. All other history defeats itself.'[9] Those of us who have been brought up on school syllabuses based on the grand sweep of history all too often find that what we can remember is the off-beat or the amusing. I would argue that there is a sound justification for teaching history in secondary schools, but teachers will have to stop trying to force facts that they consider important into children's heads. They must first establish a mode of inquiry in collaboration with their pupils. Then they must turn their attention to producing as great a variety as possible of historical material for a series of topics to be studied in depth. These topics will often range over the whole of recorded time. They will become more complex and include more variables as the children grow older.

Historians have realised that if history is to win back the place it has so nearly forfeited in schools it must do so 'by going over to a central concern with the central human problems'.[10] I have attempted to show how this might be achieved by an altered approach to the teaching of history in secondary schools. History must cease to be a nasty medicine which has to be swallowed and become a pleasant tonic which, when sampled, will build up the individual.

Notes

1   M. B. Booth, *History Betrayed?*, Longmans, 1969.

2   E. Albee, *Who's Afraid of Virginia Woolf?*, Cape, 1965, p. 29. See also J. H. Plumb, *Crisis in the Humanities*, Pelican, 1964.

3   V. Rogers, *The Social Studies in English Education*, Heinemann Educational, 1968, p. 53.

4   R. Pitcher (ed.), *The Developing World*, Longmans, 1969. History one, 'Man Makes His Way' coordinated with Geography one: 'Man Alone'; Religion one: 'From Fear to Faith'; Science one: 'The Science of Man'.

5   J. S. Bruner, *The Process of Education*, Harvard UP, 1960, p. 33.

6   M. P. Hunt and L. E. Metcalf, *Teaching High School Social Studies*, Harper, 1955, p. 353.

7   D. Holly, 'Self-directed Learning in the Comprehensive School', *Forum*, vol. II, no. 2, Spring 1969.

8   R. F. Mackenzie, *The Sins of the Children*, Collins, 1967, pp. 108–17.

9   W. Sellar and R. Yeatman, *1066 and All That*, Methuen, 1930.

10 M. I. Finley, 'Unfreezing the Classics', *The Times Literary Supplement*, 7 April 1966.

G. R. ELTON

What Sort of History should we Teach?

In the current debate about history in the schools, we hear rather more about the manner than the matter – about the various ways in which the study of history can be made exciting, useful or 'relevant' than about the particular bits of history it is advisable to convey to school children. And even when the contents of syllabuses are under discussion, attention concentrates on the attraction of 'new areas', or on this or that bit of the past, while hardly anyone seems to think that there may be issues of principle involved. I should like to suggest that what is wrong with the teaching of history at school level has little to do with method or with narrowness (though both these problems arise as by-products of the real difficulty) but a great deal with the fact that the whole concept of historical study in the schools is distorted by being assimilated to a concept proper to quite another compartment of historical studies, namely that rightly prevalent at the universities.

Mainly because what I see before me is the end-product of school courses, I will essentially confine myself to the work of the sixth form where a possibility of choice exists; below that level it is hard to prescribe, or even contemplate, the contents of an historical syllabus which must be determined by a sort of desperate desire to give some interest in the past to children by nature interested in the present and the future only. The well-known fact that 'serious' history requires some maturity weighs inescapably upon those who have to teach the altogether immature; and all that I would wish to say about those earlier years may be summed up in one phrase – concern and amusement. There are some children whose inclination is fixed upon the past: they pose no problems. The rest – the great majority – should be excited by stories and descriptions distinguished from other similar tales by being about real people; to try to give them more – to try them with the history of economies, or constitutions, or ideas – is utterly mistaken. That sort of history need not be at the Alfred and the Cakes level, but it would do well to confine itself to stories of war, exploration, great men, and especially progress in science. The teacher of the under-fifteens should not be worried if he cannot instil any notable sense of the past or any grasp of differences, or if he finds himself always driven to the sort of progress-mongering which to the true historian is abomination (the linear development of man's habits and circumstances): in that way, he will be able to persuade his charges that history – seemingly the way in which things have come to the condition in which now they are – has point and could repay further attention, and if he achieves so much he has done all that is necessary and more than is commonly encountered. Pre-sixth-form history has failed only if the child does not in the least want to go on with history in the sixth form, and any conscientious attempt to demonstrate what 'history is really about' is likely to produce precisely this result.

What, then, determines the sort of history that is taught at school at that level which becomes recognisable as 'real history'? At present there are three main criteria of decision: examination syllabuses, available books, and the teachers' own training. It is obvious that the demands of A level and university-entrance examinations do most to shape the courses taught; and the unhappy fact is that these task-masters impose a peculiarly rigid structure on the work. English and European history, mainly political (with some poorly understood economic history thrown in) – these ancient stand-bys remain dominant. There appears to have been a shift recently from the sixteenth and seventeenth centuries to the nineteenth and twentieth; or at any rate, the old class distinctions between independent schools leaning towards the earlier period and maintained schools showing their contemporary relevance by leaning towards the later appears to have dissolved as part of the general proletarisation of our society. Nowadays everybody wants to be progressive, which in this context means confine himself to the last two hundred years.

This unmoving rule of the old conventional historical themes is reinforced by the fact that books are readily available for them, and by the even more powerful fact that teachers were themselves brought up on them. At first sight, these criteria thus look entirely pragmatic – the accidental consequences of availability, haphazard organisation, and refusal to re-think. But this is not true, for the present situation embodies a very real principle, though unfortunately a mistaken principle. Examination syllabuses are in the last resort designed by universities; books are written by members of the teaching profession at various levels; teachers of history are trained in universities. What is taught in sixth forms rests in very large measure upon the kind of history which universities – dons – think the right kind and is therefore fundamentally academic, a less-developed specimen of the type with which the student finds himself confronted when he comes to university. This type itself is only a less-developed specimen of the sort of history that working historians study and write (history as the product of advanced research). The whole structure of historical teaching from the sixth form onwards assumes (tacitly, of course) that the only end of teaching history is to produce scholars. And this assumption, it seems to me, is shared by most schoolteachers of history because they are themselves products of a system designed in this image, and because the most exciting moments of their lives as historians were those in which they found themselves involved in the scholar's existence. They wish to bring back the latest news from the frontiers of knowledge, the latest debates (often very far from finished) of the pioneers out in their untamed wilderness, the latest new tool grasped by those pioneers in their often desperate attempts to reduce the wilderness to comprehensible order. The ideal boy in their scheme of things is the potential or actual researcher. Hence the popularity of all those projects, those local investigations, those studies of original materials, those individual enterprises (which too often they are not) in libraries, muniment rooms, and churches. Interest in history is to be maintained by making the schoolboy as much as possible like the only real thing, the research scholar; and since he must necessarily be confined to the relatively straightforward questions and the distinctly proximate problems, the prevalence of standard forms of history (English in the main, and conventionally interested in traditional issues) is further reinforced. The only variation in this inexorable progress towards the higher levels of academic history is introduced by the elements of indoctrination which are – or perhaps have been – strong among those teaching and learning history at school: the virtues and glories of England, as taught before 1914, were no more one-sidedly biased than the vices and shames of England as taught between the wars (and nowadays?).

Now let me emphasise that the principles underlying this kind of historical teaching are respectable and deserve to be treated seriously, whether they are conscious or not. With most teachers that I have met they remain unconscious, being simply the way in which they were interested in history and the manner in which that interest was exploited during their own training at a university.

Few people seem to consider that, at least at sixth-form level, any other form of involvement in history can exist. Yet two things should surely call these convictions in doubt.

In the first place, the method is most obviously useful for those who least need to be kept at work on history. Studying historical problems in the manner of a budding researcher attracts the budding researcher; but he will, in any case, seek out such chances himself. We are all familiar with the youthful antiquary who finds his way to his local record office; and very admirable he, no doubt, is. But he is also far from typical. Moreover, an interest in this manner of studying history can be very limiting, and one of the most striking things about even good students of history in their early days at the university is their inability to think at all largely, to see things in perspective, their ignorance of so much history and their lack of any articulated cultural background. It cannot be right that at eighteen a man should have seen some manorial documents but have no idea of the way in which the agrarian population of Europe colonised the Continent; or that he should be familiar with some nineteenth-century diplomatic documents but have no conception of the struc-ture of the nineteenth-century state system.

And secondly, too often this method, even where it is successful with the individual, is manifestly premature. If there is any particu-lar purpose in studying history at a university, it seems improbable that it can usefully be anticipated at school. And indeed, that is what experience suggests. Nowadays a good many undergraduates have read a lot of highly specialised history before ever they come up; some have done at school the sort of work that one ordinarily expects from them in their first university year; few, however, can be said to be at all well-equipped along those lines despite the amount of work done. The results are very unfortunate. Students quickly decide that the university is only going to put them through what they are already familiar with, a point they rightly resent; and by the time that they discover the contrary – inasmuch as they commonly need to start from scratch again to meet the real demands of the university – the damage is done. Premature involvement in aca-demic history also produces a closed mind and a fixed set of atti-tudes. In sum, the standard approach to teaching history in the sixth form turns out too many prematurely aged minds, supposedly competent in the academic study of history but in actual fact unable to shed acquired knowledge and unwilling to think again. And the universities are in consequence being asked to provide the necessary loosening by ranging courses of study, by bringing in new and superficially practised themes, by throwing loose philosophies and dubious historiographical titbits before the student. As the schools have more and more turned to a form – sometimes a parody – of academic history, the universities are supposed to remedy the defects of the method by abandoning academic methods and standards. At the very least, this can hardly be right or sensible.

Thus, school courses of history dominated by the ultimate academic principles involved in the most highly developed forms of historical studies must be thought ill-advised, however honourable. This is not, however, to throw the schools back on producing some inferior kind of history, so that the universities may have a free run. (Indeed, in practice the present liking for academic history quite often produces just this state of affairs, in which school teaching becomes preparatory to something else only, and thus in itself inferior.) On the contrary, what is urgently required is the discovery of an alternative principle by which the study of history at school can be justified and therefore animated, and one, moreover, which is more appropriate to a group of students many of whom are not specialising in history. One must ask once again just why children and adolescents should be asked to concern themselves with history.

To this question there are, notoriously, many answers, most of them (to my mind) not very satisfactory. The simple fact that some like studying history is not quite enough for them, and of no virtue at all to the many who do not like history and yet should be introduced to it. It is true that, at a proper academic level, history provides an exceptional training in analytical thought, tempered by reasoned reflection and an understanding of the possible, which makes it superior as a school for the man of business and affairs to either the natural or the social sciences. But we have already ruled out academic history, and since the special contribution of historical study to that sort of human mind depends to a large extent on the student having at least some experience of life and the possible, the schoolboy is unlikely to reap these benefits. Accumulation of knowledge about the past deserves rather more respect than would conventionally be accorded to it – training a memory is a worthy enterprise – but by itself it cannot constitute a principle on which to erect a course of study.

It seems to me that there is one particular way in which history can contribute to the process of education: one way in which it creates something universally useful, and moreover a way open to it alone. If the study of history requires maturity, then, by that same token, it can, rightly regarded, help to advance maturity. And by maturity I here mean the achievement of a balanced, receptive mind, flexible and open to new ideas but at the same time capable of assessing them against the traditional, aware of mankind in its variety and uncertainty, capable of appreciating the consequences of action, responsible to itself and to others. The sort of maturity in question is perhaps most easily defined by its opposite. Increasingly today one hears university teachers complain of the extraordinary naïvety of their charges on arrival. They have much less understanding of the world and much less ability to cope with it than they used to have. This fact expresses itself in various ways – in the thoughtlessness of passionate ideals, the recklessness of self-centred preoccupations, the striking youth (= childlikeness) of so many beliefs, attitudes and reactions. Whatever may be true of physical maturing, it does look as though the whole process of mental and emotional growing-up has lately been slowed down a good deal. These are not the fulminations of a bigoted reactionary, but the apprehensions, born of experience, of one who fears the consequences not for himself but for these children themselves. Above all, and notwithstanding all those much praised involvements with others (usually physically remote), too many products of the schools in our day proclaim their immaturity by their exceptional concern with themselves alone.

How, then, can the study of history help to remedy this kind of naïvety and promote a better kind of maturity? The intellectual faults in the situation may be pinned down: excessive concentration on one line of thought, absence of understanding for other points of view, belief in simple solutions, lack of balance of mind, absence of an imaginative understanding (empathy), intolerance, an overriding concern with the present. These are, in fact, the characteristic weaknesses especially of the bright mind in late adolescence, traditionally subjected to that training of the human being that we call education, but today rendered more serious by the unthinking adulation so often bestowed on them. And they are exceptionally amenable to historical study, properly treated. History can tackle the two underlying errors better than any other form of study. The errors are, one, the false assurance of rightness produced by an insufficient range of experiences, and two, the mistaken ascription of universality to one's own preoccupations and needs. History can deal with the first by creating doubt, showing the inadequacies of any single or simple explanation, bringing out the conflicts among historians and the continuing processes of research. It can attend to the second by instilling a real awareness of the range of human experiences through time. Its own preoccupation with 'real' people of great variety is as good a specific for self-centredness as formal study can provide. But to do all this, the course must be designed: not any old bit of history will achieve the desired end. And it should be apparent that, if the task before one is to break down self-centredness and lack of wide understanding, the chief characteristics demanded of the aspects of history studied must be that they should incorporate a sweeping range and actively stimulate the imagination – even though they must also control the imagination with touches of the discipline provided by the investigation of precise problems.

If this is so, it follows that the conventional sixth-form courses at the moment are peculiarly ill-designed. They are at their worst when they concentrate on recent times, and the fact that the period most commonly studied is now, increasingly, the last two hundred years is really most disturbing. It is an illusion that knowledge of this period enables a young man or woman to understand their own present better; and it would, I think, remain an illusion even though such things as the history of the British Empire, or the Russian Empire, were taught in the best imaginable fashion possible, rather than as forms of mild indoctrination. Quite apart from the valid argument that no one can understand the 1970s unless he takes in rather more than two hundred years, I very much doubt the general conviction that studying the past provides a better understanding of the present; and I think I am supported by experience – the experience of historians' pronouncements on their own time. However, this may be a matter of opinion; what is not, is the fact that studying the history of societies very like our own, and mainly with an eye to explaining our own, is the worst conceivable way in which to liberate the mind from a preoccupation with the present day, and from an inner conviction that the standards, values and attitudes of the present are the only standards, values and attitudes possible to man. If recent times are to be taught at school – and there are reasons for doing so, even if they are no better than that the ignorance of the taught demands this – they must, at any rate, be accompanied by attention to very different ages and types of human organisation. It is right that all history courses should include some part of the history of the student's own country, because he will be better able to acquire some grasp of the techniques required for understanding the past if he starts from relatively familiar ground. But, at school at least, over-concentration on one's own country is quite wrong because what the student should learn about is the differences which make his own country particular, and this he cannot do except by creating standards of comparison. Differences in both space and time: these are the things that begin to teach an historical attitude, and with it the (as I have suggested) necessary and desirable elements of true maturity which historical understanding can create.

Therefore, it is very important that sixth-form students should be introduced to the quite serious study of societies and places so very different from their own that a very real effort of the imagination is required for them to see the point. Rather than taking a long stretch of European history, I should like to see studies – superficial, of course, and rightly so – of Han China or the Incas, of the Middle Kingdom of Ancient Egypt or Rome's conquest of the known world. In fact, ancient history has much more value at this point than any number of parliamentary reform acts or analyses of the growth of great corporations – indeed, far more value than a study of Thomas Cromwell's administrative reforms or of storms over the gentry. To me, the incipient undergraduate who has not some awe in face of the magnitude of the past, some vision of ages not his own, some ability to sink himself in minds and circumstances so very different from those with which he has been equipped by the accident of birth, has not even begun to be ready for the study of academic history; and what is more, he is a long way from being a valuable human being. Certainly, I should wish to accompany the study of such large and distant things with a good look at things more confined and familiar: I should hope to train the reasoning power on closely defined problems, even while feeding the imagination on the vast themes. I should be least concerned with instilling precise, detailed and very full knowledge, though I should encourage any student who wishes to do so to commit as much to memory as he may. In actual fact, since the study of vast themes is not possible without the acquisition of a reasonably established outline, memory and the zest for facts would readily be satisfied by it. But my main concern would be to introduce children to the *range* of man's historical experience, to the untold variety of concerns and beliefs and reactions, to – if the term be permitted – the sheer romance (a romance controlled by the intelligent asking of questions) of history.

I know that much of this may sound absurd, especially coming from an academic historian fairly notorious for his dislike of romanticised history. And I must stress that when I speak of romance I mean the illumination of the envisaging mind, not the feeding of idle curiosity. But I have grown ever more convinced that at best school teaching in history can really hope to do only two things: to maintain a passionate interest in the past, and to create a willingness to think about the past as real – as real as the present and as fully entitled to its own existence. Given those achievements (and they are very great) the schools would instil a genuine ability to study history and at the same time create the real foundations of intellectual and emotional maturity. Can they wish to do more? By all means, continue to practise that other, milder stimulus to the imagination, the study of the locality or the look at original materials. But let it be set in and against an emphasis on range, on the immensity of time, and on the relative insignificance of the present moment.

That these are counsels of some sort of perfection I do not deny – whether or not it is a perfection which others may agree with me to be eminently desirable. If we are to teach about Aztecs and medieval popes, about the fall of the Roman Empire and the growth of historical science, and if we are to do these and other things with conviction and success, we need books and teachers capable of such work. There are some, though surely not enough. We need to adjust our attitudes at the universities, believing that the training we can best provide consists of strictly academic history but aware that we must enable the teachers we produce to enlarge their own imaginative understanding of much greater ranges of history. Above all, we need totally to revise our examinations. I am willing to suppose that what I have here suggested raises some very thorny practical problems. But I do think that these problems should be studied. After all, the solutions I have tried to prescribe are those pressed on the universities when the inadequacy of courses and the dissatisfactions of undergraduates are mentioned. Common sense, some understanding of the manner in which minds progress, and some knowledge of people surely suggest that to concentrate on academic history at school and enlarge into speculative and imaginative history with insufficient academic foundations at the university is an absurd reversal of the true need. Let the schools feed the imagination, enlarge mental capacity, and lay the foundations of universal sympathy; we shall soon enough, at the university, attend to the search for truth and the promotion of precise analytical thought.

Naturally, I am most obviously concerned with those sixth-formers that go on to read history at the university, but it should be stressed that the suggestions I have put forward seem even more suitable to that larger number that do not. For those whose formal study of history ends at eighteen the need to produce vision and excitement, rather than mere precision and boredom, is vastly greater still; and since they will have no further obvious chance of correcting their present-centred attitudes they must even more urgently be led to range through space and time, and to be made to think history fascinating. Historical studies should never be just fun, but they should always be a pleasure.

Notes on Contributors

Notes on Contributors

Martin Ballard is Director of the Educational Publishers' Council. He is the author of a number of educational books on history. He taught history for six years in Brislington Comprehensive School, Bristol, and in 1968 was Schoolmaster Fellow of Clare College, Cambridge.

Peter Bamford is Head of History at Richard Taunton Sixth Form College, Southampton. He was for two years a Lecturer in History at King Alfred's College of Education, Winchester.

Colin C. Bayne-Jardine is school-based tutor at Bristol University and teaches at Henbury Comprehensive School.

Marcus Cunliffe is Professor of American Studies, University of Sussex. His various books on American history include *American Presidents and the Presidency*.

C. D. Darlington is Professor in Botany at the University of Oxford and the author of *The Evolution of Man and Society*.

Robert Douch is the author of *Local History and the Teacher*. He is Senior Lecturer in Education at the University of Southampton School of Education.

G. R. Elton is Professor of English Constitutional History at the University of Cambridge. He is the author of works on sixteenth-century history (including *England under the Tudors*) and on the problems of historical study (including *The Practice of History*).

Sheila Ferguson is Head of the History Department at Peckham Girls' School, and author of *Projects in History*.

Roy Hallam is Head of the Upper School, George Ward School, Melksham, and the author of *Logical Thinking in History*.

Charles Hannam is Lecturer in Education at the University of Bristol School of Education.

Derek Heater is Head of the History Department, Brighton College of Education. He is the author of various books (including *Political Ideas in the Modern World*) and of numerous articles on the teaching of contemporary affairs. He is editor of *The Teaching of Politics*.

Dwight W. Hoover is Professor of History at Ball State University, Indiana. He is the author of *Understanding Negro History, Henry James, Sr, and the Religion of Community*, and co-author of *The 21st Century: Directions in Social Change*.

William Lamont is Reader in History and Education at the University of Sussex. He is the author of *Marginal Prynne* and *Godly Rule*, and a number of articles on seventeenth-century history. He has taught at St Paul's School, Hackney Downs Grammar School and Aberdeen College of Education.

William H. McNeill is Professor of History at the University of Chicago, and author of *The Rise of the West: a History of the Human Community*, among other books.

Peter Mathias is Chichele Professor of Economic History at the University of Oxford, and a Fellow of All Souls College. He is the author of *The Brewing Industry in England, 1700–1830, English Trade Tokens, Retailing Revolution* and *The First Industrial Nation*.

Arnold Toynbee is Emeritus Director of Studies at the Royal Institute of International Affairs and Research Professor of International History at the University of London. He is the author, among other books, of *A Study of History*.

D. C. Watt is Reader in International History at the London School of Economics, and Secretary of the Association of Contemporary Historians.

E. A. Wrigley is a member of the Cambridge Group for the History of Population and Social Structure, Fellow and Senior Bursar of Peterhouse, and Lecturer in Geography in the University of Cambridge. He is the author of *Industrial Growth and Population Change* and *Population and History*, and the editor of *An Introduction to English Historical Demography*.